Ambivalent Embrace

AMBIVALENT EMBRACE

Jewish Upward Mobility in Postwar America

Rachel Kranson

◆ ◆ ◆

THE UNIVERSITY OF NORTH CAROLINA PRESS

Chapel Hill

*This book was published with the assistance of the
Anniversary Fund of the University of North Carolina Press.*

© 2017 The University of North Carolina Press

Manufactured in the United States of America

The University of North Carolina Press has been a member
of the Green Press Initiative since 2003.

A version of chapter 6 was first published in *Journal of Jewish Identities* 8, no. 2
(2015): 59–84. Reprinted with permission by Johns Hopkins University Press.
Parts of chapter 3 were first published in *Rites of Passage: How Todays Jews Celebrate,
Commemorate, and Commiserate* (West Lafayette: Purdue University Press, 2010), 9–23.

Cover illustration: "L'Shana Tova" (Happy New Year) postcard from the collection
of Dr. Haim Grossman. Used by permission of Dr. Haim Grossman.

LIBRARY OF CONGRESS CATALOGING-IN-PUBLICATION DATA
Names: Kranson, Rachel, author.
Title: Ambivalent embrace : Jewish upward mobility in postwar
America / Rachel Kranson.
Description: Chapel Hill : The University of North Carolina Press, [2017] |
Includes bibliographical references and index.
Identifiers: LCCN 2017019368 | ISBN 9781469635422 (cloth : alk. paper) |
ISBN 9781469635439 (pbk : alk. paper) | ISBN 9781469635446 (ebook)
Subjects: LCSH: Jews—United States—Social conditions. | Jews—United States—
Attitudes. | Wealth—Religious aspects—Judaism. | Wealth—Moral and ethical
aspects. | Wealth—Psychological aspects. | Jews—United States—Identity.
Classification: LCC E184.36.S65 K73 2017 | DDC 305.892/4073—dc23
LC record available at https://lccn.loc.gov/2017019368

For Jamie, Sasha, and Ezra

Contents

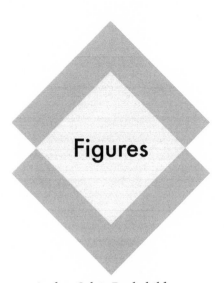

Figures

Acknowledgments

I have been living with this project for longer than I care to admit. Counterbalancing the solitary hours I spent in front of my computer, however, were the many personal and professional relationships that developed and deepened as I worked on this book. I am honored to finally be able to thank the institutions, colleagues, family members, and friends who offered me practical help with my scholarship and the emotional support I needed to move forward with my research and writing.

In the initial phases of my research, fellowships from the Graduate School of Arts and Sciences at New York University and New York University's department of history sponsored my work. Additional grants from the Immigration and Ethnic History Society, the Memorial Foundation for Jewish Culture, the American Jewish Archives, the Feinstein Center at Temple University, and the History of Women and Gender group at New York University allowed me to continue developing the project. Summer funding and a research leave from the University of Pittsburgh's Dietrich School of Arts and Sciences offered me the time and resources I needed to transform the manuscript into a book, while the Richard D. and Mary Jane Edwards Endowed Publication Fund supported the final aspects of production.

I am indebted to the archivists and librarians who ensured that I could access all the materials I needed. These include Susan Woodland, Boni Joi Koelliker, Tanya Elder, and many other archivists and librarians at the Center for Jewish History in New York City who have been generous with their time and expertise; Kevin Proffit, Dana Herman, and the rest of the team at the American Jewish Archives who were so hospitable during my weeks in Cincinnati and have continued to offer me assistance in the years since; Amanda (Miryem-Khaye)

Seigel at the Dorot Jewish Division of the New York Public Library; and the staff at the Tamiment Library at New York University. Susan Weidman Schneider and Naomi Danis at *Lilith Magazine* not only were able to find articles I needed on a moment's notice but have long been mentors and dear friends. My thanks also to Allan Litwack, executive director of Temple Solel in Highland Park, Illinois, who allowed me to sift through the treasure trove of documents located in the Temple basement, and to Karen Kohn, who offered home hospitality as I did so. I am grateful to Adam Soclof and the managers of nostol.co.il for tracking down the cover image for this volume and to Haim Grossman for permission to use it. And finally, I thank Laurie Cohen of the University of Pittsburgh's Hillman Library, who makes Jewish studies research at Pitt possible by maintaining the Jewish studies collection and securing access to the relevant databases.

My editor, Elaine Maisner, and the entire team at the University of North Carolina Press expertly shepherded this project from manuscript to book. I am thankful for their professionalism, their keen editorial sensibility, and their hard work in contributing to a final product that we can all be proud of.

Of all the people who contributed to this book, I owe my deepest debt of gratitude to Hasia Diner, who nurtured my passion for scholarship and supported this project from its inception. She is a brilliant scholar, an exemplary mentor, a fierce advocate, a generous and exacting critic, and a model of integrity. Above all, she has inspired me with her expansive vision for what the field of American Jewish history has the potential to accomplish. I can only hope that this volume—whatever its flaws—does justice to that vision and to her unwavering faith in my work.

I am also grateful to the scholars who have read through substantial sections and even full drafts of this project, generously contributing their comments and critiques at significant junctures in the writing process. I humbly thank Marion Kaplan, Linda Gordon, Lila Corwin Berman, Andrew Needham, Melissa Klapper, Alexander Orbach, Riv-Ellen Prell, Kirsten Fermaglich, and Michael Alexander for offering my work a careful read. Along with Hasia Diner they comprised what I consider to be a dream team of interlocutors, and this book is much improved for their efforts.

My thanks also to colleagues and mentors who offered encouragement, shared references, wrote letters of support, invited me to panels and workshops, let me peek at unpublished drafts of their own scholarship, and asked crucial questions at conference presentations, seminars, coffeehouses, restaurants, and online chats: Rebecca Alpert, Joyce Antler, Adriana Brodsky, Jessica Cooperman, Daniella Doron, Jodi Eichler-Levine, Gill Frank, Joshua Furman, Jennifer Glaser, Karla Goldman, Rachel Gordan, Shiri Goren, Ronnie

Grinberg, Bea Gurwitz, Sarah Imhoff, Brett Kaplan, Emily Katz, Barbara Kirshenblatt-Gimblett, Shira Klein, Rebecca Kobrin, David Koffman, Shira Kohn, Josh Lambert, Ann Lapidus Lerner, Laura Levitt, Keren McGinity, Samira Mehta, Deirdre Moloney, Bethany Moreton, Hannah Pressman, Shari Rabin, Lara Rabinovitch, Michael Rom, Jonathan Sarna, Shuly Rubin Schwartz, Bryant Simon, Michael Staub, and David Weinfeld.

I have benefited from excellent feedback from colleagues at the Association for Jewish Studies conference, the annual meeting of the Organization of American Historians, the biennial scholar's conference of the American Jewish Historical Society, the Berkshires Conference of Women Historians, the conference on Jewish Attitudes toward Wealth and Poverty at Brown University, the Klutznick-Harris Symposium in Jewish Studies at Creighton University, the History of Women and Gender Colloquium at New York University, the Religious Studies Colloquium Series at the University of Pittsburgh and from invited presentations at Yale University's Modern Jewish history Colloquium, Temple University's Workshop Series on Food, Consumption, and Jewish Life, and the Jewish Studies program at Michigan State University. Thanks also to colleagues from the University of Michigan's Frankel Center for Advanced Judaic Studies, who read drafts and offered advice as I completed the final stages of this project and began the initial steps of a new one: Deborah Dash Moore, Beth Wenger, Dorothy Kim, Benjamin Baader, Max Strassfeld, Marjorie Lehman, Anita Norich, Verena Kasper-Marienberg, Evyatar Marienberg, Shachar Pinsker, Christine Achinger, Suzy Dessel, and Ricki Bilboim, z'l.

I also count myself tremendously fortunate to have become a member of the Religious Studies department of the University of Pittsburgh and to have been so warmly welcomed by the Jewish Studies and Gender, Sexuality, and Women's Studies programs. I could not have asked for a more collegial or supportive environment in which to do my work. Many thanks to Linda Penkower, Adam Shear, Paula Kane, Clark Chilson, Tony Edwards, Jeanette Jouili, Ben Gordon, Milica Hayden, Rebecca Denova, Brock Bahler, Maureen Henderson, Kristen Tobey, Todd Reeser, Frayda Cohen, Lina Insana, Irina Livezeanu, Irina Reyn, and Laura Gotkowitz. Talented students like Avigail Oren, Emily Stewart, David Givens, Alex Malanych, Emily Bailey, and Susie Meister give me hope for the future of my fields of study. I am also grateful for the incredible team of Jewish studies scholars, educators and archivists located at other institutions in Pittsburgh: Michal Friedman, David Schlitt, Lauren Bairnsfather, Rachel Herman, Melissa Hiller, Annie Gitlitz, Susan Melnick, David Grinnell, Kathryn Spitz-Cohan, Danielle Kranjec, and Martha Berg, who also prepared the index for this volume.

Dear friends made the years I spent on this project rich and enjoyable. My deepest thanks to Amy Greenstein, Irrit Dweck, Anne Hinton, Stephanie Harad, Jeronimo Romero, Andrew Greene, Aliza Hochstein Froman, and all of my friends who have remained close even though I no longer live close by. Thanks also to new friends who have turned Pittsburgh into a home—happily too many to mention by name, but I am grateful for all of them.

I also remember my friend Leah Hait Goldman, who passed away while I was working on this project. So much of my thinking about Jews and class came out of conversations I had with her, well before I began my career as a historian.

I have been blessed with a close, loving, and thoroughly bizarre family that has always supported me and made me weep with laughter while doing so. I am profoundly grateful to my parents, Annette and Jerry Kranson, and my siblings and their families: Donny, Karen, Lauren, and Lily Kranson, Sarah Rosenbaum-Kranson, Jordan Warner, and Andy Shugerman. I have been just as blessed with in-laws who belie all of the negative stereotypes associated with in-laws: Esther Forrest-Berkowitz, Ira Berkowitz, and Larry, Mike, Daria, Dylan and Callie Forrest. Bubbie Annette and Nana Esther deserve special thanks for providing weekly childcare as I wrote the initial drafts of this project, though all of the grandparents, Tanties, and Tontos have pitched in over the years. Thanks also to Hallsi Killian and Bonnie Banner for taking such excellent care of the Kranson-Forrest kids when their parents were at work.

Finally, I get to thank the loves of my life. From our very first conversation I knew how lucky I was to have met Jamie Forrest, however nothing could have prepared me for the sweetness of building our lives together. Our children, Sasha and Ezra, have brought me immeasurable joy. Being part of the Kranson-Forrest household has made everything not only possible but worthwhile. I dedicate this book, and so much more, to the three of you.

Ambivalent Embrace

Introduction

In a 1954 article for *Commentary* magazine, Sylvia Rothchild, writing under the pseudonym Evelyn Rossman, expressed her dissatisfaction with synagogue services in postwar America. "If the service reminded me of the little *shul* [synagogue] my father went to, I was sad because I remembered how shabby and poor it was," she complained. "If I found a wealthy Conservative or Reform temple I sat there like a stranger thinking how insincere and hypocritical it all was. Weren't all good Jews supposed to be poor?"[1]

Sylvia Rothchild herself represented one of the many American Jews who, by the postwar period, had left behind economically unstable childhoods and entered the swelling ranks of America's middle class. Born on January 4, 1923, to Yiddish-speaking immigrants from Romania, she grew up in the densely Jewish neighborhood of Williamsburg, Brooklyn. Before the birth of her first child in 1948, she and her husband, chemist Seymour Rothchild, moved to a spacious, single-family home in Sharon, Massachusetts, an affluent suburb of Boston. There, she witnessed the establishment of her adopted town's synagogues and religious schools, all funded by the growing group of upwardly mobile Jews who chose to live in leafy, suburban Sharon instead of the urban enclaves in which they had been raised.

By 1951, Rothchild started publishing essays and short stories in American Jewish periodicals such as *Commentary*, *Hadassah*, and *Moment*, and her first novel, *Sunshine and Salt*, appeared in 1964. Uneasiness about her new life among the middle class surfaced as a prominent theme throughout her work. While she acknowledged the appeal of the space, greenery, and quiet she had never known growing up in the city, she also suffered an acute sense of loss

Author Sylvia Rothchild.
Used with permission from Howard Gotlieb Archival
Research Center, Boston University Archives.

over the vibrant intellectualism and sincere religiosity that she believed her new, well-heeled neighbors lacked.[2]

Rothchild was far from alone in her critical assessment of the new, Jewish, middle class. As Rothchild pondered the possibility that poverty might be a necessary component of being a "good Jew," she joined a chorus of American Jewish commentators who expressed misgivings over the consequences of Jewish upward mobility in the two decades following World War II.[3]

Ambivalent Embrace traces these concerns over Jewish upward mobility, challenging the notion that American Jews welcomed their postwar economic rise without reservation or hesitation. On the contrary, the subjects of this study continued to identify with the Jewish history of poverty, even as their fortunes grew. Because they understood economic and social marginality as something integral to the Jewish experience, they could not wholeheartedly celebrate American Jews' ascent into the middle class. Jewish anxieties over upward mobility, I argue, emerged out of this dissonance between the financial and social successes of midcentury American Jews and their deeply felt histories of exclusion and want.[4]

Despite widespread worries over the effects of upward mobility, Jewish life seemed to thrive in the economic boom following the Second World War. Newly prosperous American Jews used their growing resources to transform Jewish culture and practice, creating new modes of ritual and socialization that harmonized with their middle-class standing. They exhibited their devotion to Judaism and Jewish communal life by constructing a spate of up-to-date, modern synagogues. And the unprecedented numbers of Jewish children being educated in religious schools and summer camps spoke of their ongoing commitment to a vibrant American Jewish culture.[5]

Postwar American Jews also dared to build their new cultural and religious infrastructure on the suburban fringe of America's cities, where Jews generally did not constitute the majority of residents. Their willingness to invest in communities with a Christian majority demonstrated the new social acceptance that they had achieved along with their financial gains. While most of these suburban Jews would continue to socialize primarily with coreligionists, and "gentlemen's agreements" still restricted their residence in some of the toniest developments, they nonetheless felt confident enough to branch out of ethnic enclaves. Their acceptance as racial whites, coupled with their rising finances, offered them a relatively smooth entry into areas that were once Protestant strongholds.[6]

While newfound affluence and acceptance seemed to offer American Jews security and opportunities for innovation, it also tested the ways in which they constructed their Jewish identities and conceived of their differences from other Americans. After all, much of American Jewish life before the postwar years had been shaped by exclusion and economic instability. The distinctive political leanings of American Jews, their religious practices, and their attitudes toward gender had all been forged in an atmosphere of social and economic uncertainty. The rapid upward mobility of the postwar years threatened to undermine Jewish distinctiveness in all of these areas. These transformations led to the idea, expressed most forcefully by the religious, intellectual, and cultural leadership of American Jewry, that the ostensible blessing of prosperity presented a dire threat to the integrity and viability of American Jewish culture. The words of Rabbi Harold Saperstein, the spiritual leader of Temple Emanu-El in Lynbrook, New York, encapsulated the mindset of many of his contemporaries when he declared that "the great test of Jewish life in our time is whether it can survive in the affluent society."[7]

As postwar American Jews adapted to lives of prosperity, their leaders came to suspect that an authentic Jewish life could thrive only in an environment of scarcity. The history of Jewish poverty loomed large in their writings, and idealized images of economically insecure Jews living richly satisfying Jewish lives provided the measure against which middle-class Jews invariably fell short. For many of those American Jews who had grown up in densely Jewish, urban neighborhoods, the affluent, suburban Jewish communities of the postwar years seemed to pale in comparison to the politically charged, Yiddish-speaking enclaves of their childhoods, which they often recalled through a rosy, nostalgic lens. They looked even less like the impoverished Eastern European *shtetlach* that, in the imagination of the thousands of American Jews who wept at the 1964 Broadway production of *Fiddler on the Roof*, served as an idealized setting for a profound and genuine Jewish religiosity. Finally, taking their cues from popular novels such as Leon Uris's *Exodus*, many midcentury American Jews had also come to imagine a nascent state of Israel populated by heroic idealists who eschewed financial gain in order to pursue the dream of Jewish autonomy. In contrast to these romanticized sites of Jewish vitality, some American Jews, and particularly the Jewish leadership, began to view middle-class, Jewish life in postwar America as tragically complacent, superficial, and incapable of nurturing future generations of committed Jews.[8]

The Jewish rise into the middle class also destabilized worldviews fostered by histories of poverty and exclusion. Jewish activists who had formerly taken their status as oppressed outsiders for granted now had to forge political identities that better reflected their privileges. Religious leaders struggled to engage constituents who, they suspected, joined synagogues largely to increase their social standing in middle-class suburbs that linked respectability with religious affiliation. Additionally, the gender ideologies adopted by Jews as they entered the American middle class often seemed limiting to those who had been raised in a working-class milieu that upheld more expansive conceptions of appropriate masculinity and femininity. As upward mobility forced American Jews to reimagine their political affiliations, religious expressions, and gender ideologies, Jewish leaders questioned whether an authentic Jewish culture could emerge out of this process of transformation and negotiation.

Those postwar Jews who worried about the authenticity of the Jewish middle class unwittingly participated in a discourse with a history that dated back to eighteenth-century romanticism. Romantic nationalists such as German philosopher Johann Gottfried von Herder, for instance, presumed that each nation possessed its own unique, timeless genius and inimitable ways of functioning in the world. They feared, however, that nation-states would lose their cultural authenticity as their cities became more cosmopolitan, modern, and affluent, and their people began to borrow the customs and habits of other nations. Unsurprisingly, therefore, Herder viewed the diversity, complexity, and wealth of modern life as evidence of cultural degradation and loss. At the same time, he idealized the lives of the isolated, poor, and rural "volk" who, to his mind, continued to uphold their pure and authentic national traditions and to protect them from alien influences.[9]

Herder's understanding of cultural authenticity resonated well into the twentieth century. Indeed, the assumption among my postwar American Jewish subjects that a genuine Jewish life could be found only in isolated and impoverished Jewish communities, and their concern that increased acculturation and financial resources would somehow dilute or degrade Jewish civilization, hearkens back quite directly to romantic notions of cultural authenticity and the corrupting nature of a diverse and wealthy modern world.[10]

Recent thinkers have deconstructed the notion of authenticity, refusing to view it as an objective entity that can be found, traced, lost, or corrupted. Rather, they understand authenticity as a set of collective expectations regarding how people ought to behave, how events ought to transpire, and how rituals ought to be performed. Scholars like Dean MacCannell, Eric Hobsbawm, and Benedict Anderson have traced the ways in which various institutions, from nation-states to tourist attractions, invented and manufactured the images and customs that have come to feel authentic to those who encounter them. They argue that events, rituals, and behaviors feel authentic when they are able to live up to people's preconceived notions of how they ought to happen, and not because they tap into an essential, and unchanging, cultural truth.[11]

Though I, too, am deeply suspicious of the notion of authenticity, I nonetheless take postwar Jews' yearning for it quite seriously. The customs and values that my subjects sought to protect may well have been collective fictions about the essential nature of Jewish identity. Still, they felt absolutely real, meaningful, and important to those who upheld them. Their desire for a genuine Jewish life shows how highly they valued their distinctive heritage, however they understood it, and uncovers their distrust of any influence, even one as appealing as upward mobility, that seemed to threaten it. Moreover, their laments over the loss of Jewish culture during a moment of rapid economic change were in themselves productive, forcing them to conceive of new, albeit ambivalent, ways of expressing their Jewish difference in a middle-class environment. How American Jewish leaders articulated their longing for authenticity, then, can reveal much about their hopes, fears, and concerns as they moved up the economic ladder.

Popular, ugly stereotypes of Jews as preternaturally good with money heightened the stakes of these anxieties surrounding Jewish upward mobility. Denigrating Jews as exceptionally money-hungry, a convention that dated back to medieval European antipathy against Jewish moneylenders, emerged as a common anti-Jewish trope in the American context as well. While American antisemitism in all its forms dropped markedly during the postwar years, negative portrayals of Jewish greed continued to circulate, and to sting. Both implicitly and explicitly, those American Jews who expressed ambivalence over their newfound affluence engaged with the long-standing tendency to depict Jews as acquisitive and grasping. Certainly, critiquing the foibles of the Jewish middle class served as a means by which Jewish leaders sought to police the behavior of their constituents so as not to aggravate antisemitic assumptions of Jewish avarice. But more importantly, as they romanticized the history of Jewish poverty, these leaders also pushed back against stereotypes of Jewish greed by denying the existence of materialism in an authentic Jewish culture.[12]

The Jewish leaders who composed these critiques of affluence responded not only to the antisemitic tropes that circulated in the United States during the postwar years but also to the calamitous history of European antisemitism. While the preservation of an authentic Jewish culture in its encounter with a prosperous American society had long been a concern for American Jewish leaders, the genocide of European Jews during the Second World War intensified this impulse. After the vibrant Jewish communities of Europe had been annihilated in the Holocaust, they came to believe that the enormous responsibility of sustaining Jewish life and providing leadership for the rest of the Jewish world rested on their shoulders. Historian and Jewish educator Israel Goldberg, writing under the pen name Rufus Learsi, declared in his 1954 history of American Jewry that the Jewish population of America had become "the most influential and also the largest in the world. The war made it a dominant factor in the destiny of the Jewish people as a whole." Many of the leaders who condemned the habits of middle-class Jews considered it an unthinkable tragedy that, even after the destruction of Jewish life in Europe, the privileged Jews who lived in the United States seemed ready to give up crucial elements of their heritage in exchange for the comforts of affluence. While upward mobility may have provided American Jews with opportunities for innovation and transformation, knowledge of the destruction of Jewish life in Europe fostered a particularly strong desire for cultural preservation. In the years after World War II, the transformative power of economic gain came into stark conflict with the impossible desire to uphold the Jewish world that had existed before the Holocaust.[13]

To many of the subjects of this postwar study, thinking of Europe as the doomed wellspring of authentic Jewish culture hinged on family histories of migration. *Ambivalent Embrace* traces the descendants of the 2.5 million Jews who, like the parents of Sylvia Rothchild, had immigrated to America from Eastern Europe between 1870 and 1924, stopping only once the Johnson-Reed Act reduced the flow of Jewish migrants to a trickle. These impoverished Jewish immigrants made their homes in urban slums throughout the United States, with most settling in New York City. They eked out a living on the margins of the American economy, through factory work, taking extra boarders into their already cramped quarters, or engaging in small-scale retail and wholesale trade. These turn-of-the-century Jewish immigrants far outnumbered the approximately 200,000 Jews from Central Europe—commonly, but mistakenly, referred to as "German" Jews, since Germany did not become a state until 1871—who had come to America in the middle of the nineteenth century. While many of these Jews from Central Europe had already climbed into the middle class by the turn of the twentieth century, the influx of struggling, new Jewish immigrants ensured that most of America's Jews remained mired in poverty.

As early as the economic boom of the 1920s, the financial situation of American Jews started to improve. Jewish laborers in the garment industry benefited from the strong unions they helped to create, and small,

Jewish-owned businesses flourished. Higher incomes enabled them to move from their original immigrant slums to more desirable urban neighborhoods, which struck them as quite fine with their wide, clean streets and solid housing stock. The gracious avenues of these new, densely Jewish enclaves, where residents chatted easily in both Yiddish and English and enjoyed pickles and pastrami in their local delicatessens, made them feel, in the words of historian Deborah Dash Moore, "at home in America."[14]

While the depression of the 1930s slowed their economic growth, American Jews nonetheless moved gradually toward greater financial stability in the first half of the twentieth century. Despite continued discrimination against Jews in many fields of professional employment and the quotas that restricted Jewish students from attending prestigious educational institutions, their increasing resources allowed them to improve their standard of living and provide the next generation with educational opportunities and commercial contacts.[15]

In fact, quite a few Jewish writers and filmmakers were already expressing their concerns over Jewish upward mobility in the early years of the twentieth century. From films like *The Jazz Singer* (1927) to books like Abraham Cahan's *The Rise of David Levinsky* (1917), Anzia Yezierska's *Salome of the Tenements* (1923), Samuel Ornitz's *Haunch, Paunch and Jowl* (1923), and Jerome Weidman's *I Can Get It for You Wholesale* (1937), popular narratives depicted protagonists who abandoned the poor Jewish masses, often losing—at the very least—their moral compass in the quest for upward mobility.[16]

By the postwar years, however, it seemed to many Jewish leaders that there were no longer any poor Jewish masses left to abandon, at least not in the United States. The financial mobility of America's Jews spiked, dwarfing the relatively modest economic successes of the early twentieth century and affecting much larger swathes of the American Jewish population. In the decades after World War II, Jewish clergy, writers, and intellectuals no longer worried about the exceptional Jews who "made it"; instead, they fretted over the integrity and viability of the entire American Jewish community.[17]

Born in America, and raised amid the uncertainty of the depression, the subjects of this study entered adulthood in the flush 1950s, where they prospered during a decade of economic growth that had transformed the lives of many Americans, especially those of European extraction. Like the other descendants of the approximately 12 million Southern and Eastern European immigrants who entered the United States between 1870 and 1924, these postwar Jews also benefited from the home loans and educational grants offered predominantly to white-skinned, male veterans of World War II through the Servicemen's Readjustment Act of 1944. These government programs, combined with the investments made by their own families earlier in the century, gave American Jewish men a secure base from which to participate in a flourishing economy.[18]

American Jews experienced a particularly rapid rate of upward mobility during the postwar decades, often outpacing Americans of other ethnic backgrounds. A survey of male college graduates in 1947, for instance, revealed that more Jews than non-Jews went on to become professionals, proprietors, managers, and officials, though fewer of their parents had enjoyed these high-status, lucrative occupations. And, after conducting studies in 1953 and 1955, the National Opinion Research Center found that salaries of American Jews had eclipsed those of other religious groups. During those years, Jewish households enjoyed a median family income of $5,954, while the average income of a Roman Catholic household fell at $4,340 and Protestant households at $3,933.[19]

These quantitative measures of the income and occupations of Jewish men underlay, but cannot transparently explain, the middle-class identity claimed by so many American Jews during these years. After all, class identity is a notoriously slippery category that can hardly be dictated solely by a person's income, or, as Marx would have had it, by a person's relationship to the means of production. Labor historian Daniel Walkowitz's apt example of early twentieth-century, female social workers largely understood to be "middle class," but who nonetheless earned salaries similar to, or lower than, contemporaneous male factory employees of the "working class," offers a sense of some of the complexities involved in class identification. In the context of postwar America, middle-class identity operated most often as an articulation of how people perceived themselves or others in relation to what they viewed as an American "mainstream" defined not only in terms of income and occupation but also by such factors as gender norms, race, religion, consumer patterns, education, and geography. Indeed, it was not only the growing income of Jewish men that enabled American Jews to be so widely classified as "middle class" but also such factors as their racial identification, the decision of most married Jewish women to refrain from wage work, the new and widespread acknowledgment of Judaism as a legitimate American religion along with Protestantism and Catholicism, Jews' relatively high rates of educational attainment, and their suburban migration.[20]

While certainly constituted by categories such as gender and race, postwar Americans generally understood the concept of class differently in that they assumed that a person's class status was malleable, while they considered a person's gender and racial identity to be essential and permanent. The powerful, long-standing myth of the American Dream, defined by Jennifer Hochschild as "the promise that all Americans have a reasonable chance to achieve success . . . through their own efforts," depended on the assumption that every American, regardless of background or creed, could raise their class status through determination and hard work. That this ideology ignored the very real obstacles that made it more difficult for some Americans to achieve prosperity than others, and in fact served to blame poor Americans, rather than an inequitable economic system, for their poverty, did little to diminish the significance of this myth in the eyes of many Americans throughout the twentieth century and beyond.[21]

The notion that American Jews could move up the economic ladder— and, moreover, that this mobility served as a prerequisite to their becoming fully American—became a source of tension for my subjects. They were uncertain that a genuine Jewish life, in any of its various political, religious, or cultural iterations, could be reconciled with this process of upward mobility. At the same time, however, they could not realistically expect Jews to forgo their opportunity to embrace the American Dream.

As my subjects expressed their concerns over the economic rise of American Jews, they simultaneously participated in a widespread American discussion regarding the supposed perils of upward mobility. Midcentury prosperity led to a deluge of best-selling sociological studies and journalistic treatises that bemoaned the effects of wealth on the "American national character." Works like David Riesman's *The Lonely Crowd* (1950) and William H. Whyte's *The Organization Man* (1957) argued that material abundance effectively destroyed the ethos of individualism that had once constituted the backbone of America's greatness, and they portrayed the growth of middle-class suburbs as the physical manifestation of a conformist culture. In *The Affluent Society* (1958), John Kenneth Galbraith condemned the accumulation of private wealth that, he felt, had led to the impoverishment of America's public infrastructure. And in *The Feminine Mystique* (1963), Betty Friedan leveled a forceful invective against a wealthy American society that had imprisoned its women into suburban homes she characterized as "comfortable concentration camps," rendering them incapable of self-fulfillment. For these journalists and social scientists, growing prosperity had trapped Americans within the confines of a culturally bland and morally complacent middle class.[22]

Some of these writers, specifically David Riesman and Betty Friedan, came from Jewish backgrounds.[23] While their Jewish heritage may have had a formative impact on their thinking and writing, and likely played a role in their tendency to link suburban conformity with their fears of totalitarianism, their work displayed little overt acknowledgment of the distinct concerns of upwardly mobile Jews. Friedan and Riesman, no less than Whyte and Galbraith, spoke for and about all middle-class, white Americans and did not directly contribute to the particularly Jewish conversation examined in this study. Rather, their discussions of postwar wealth provided a general framework of ideas that the members of many ethnic and religious subcultures would adapt to their specific circumstances.[24]

Christian leaders, for instance, participated in this postwar critique of affluence and related it to their particular theological and communal concerns. In 1961 religious sociologist Peter Berger's *The Noise of Solemn Assemblies* accused American churches of sanctifying middle-class conformity and complacency, values that he believed to be at odds with true, Christian faith. Gibson Winter, then a professor of ethics and society at the University of Chicago's Divinity School, penned *The Suburban Captivity of the Churches* in 1962. In this work, Winter accused suburban Protestant churches of retreating from their religious responsibility to ease urban poverty and suggested the idea of a "metropolitan church" that would simultaneously serve the suburban affluent and the urban poor. Catholics joined these Protestant thinkers in decrying the effects of postwar affluence in books like Andrew M. Greeley's *The Church and the Suburbs*, which pondered the adjustments that American Catholicism would have to make as it transitioned away from being "the Church of the working class" and engaged a more prosperous constituency.[25]

Sociologist E. Franklin Frazier also contributed to this wider conversation regarding the dangers of postwar wealth and considered the specific impact that it had on African Americans. Published in 1957, Frazier's *Black Bourgeoisie* condemned the behavior and the priorities of the new, black middle class. He charged that affluent black Americans spent both time and resources emulating the extravagant lifestyles of white Americans instead of providing leadership to the impoverished masses of the African American community.[26]

Like their intellectual counterparts who spoke on behalf of Catholic, Protestant, and black Americans, many American Jewish leaders absorbed the critiques of affluence that filtered through American society in the postwar years and built on those ideas as they created a distinctly Jewish conversation. Although critics like Riesman, Whyte, and Galbraith professed to speak on behalf of all white, middle-class Americans—a position that most American Jews, by the postwar era, had come to claim—the leaders of American Jewry insisted that upward mobility posed unique dangers to the survival of Jewish life in America. Their discussions referenced Jewish cultural symbols and interpreted the events of Jewish history to evince a specifically Jewish ambivalence toward postwar prosperity.

The Jewish leaders who expressed ambivalence over Jewish upward mobility inhabited an array of positions within the American Jewish world. Some, like Sylvia Rothchild, expressed their concerns in the pages of magazines and novels. Most of the fiction and nonfiction writers profiled in this study found their readership within the Jewish community. Others, like Philip Roth and Herman Wouk, found much broader audiences, although they generally understood themselves, and were understood by others, to be writing from a distinctly Jewish perspective. Jewish intellectuals, academics, and scholars also participated in this conversation, publishing their views in the Jewish press, academic journals, and full-length books. Finally, American rabbis composed many of the critiques of affluence that circulated during the postwar years and voiced their trepidation from their pulpits, in the press, and in congregational newsletters.

While the religious and intellectual leadership of postwar American Jewry had the most to say about the threat of Jewish affluence, the leaders who lamented Jewish upward mobility did not necessarily hold radically different views from the laypeople who hired them as rabbis, listened to their sermons, read their novels, and discussed their essays. Indeed, in certain ways, it is difficult to distinguish between the "leadership" and the "laity" of American Jews during the postwar years. Generally, both groups, though from economically modest upbringings, came to enjoy middle-class incomes after the Second World War. The same rabbis who lambasted opulent suburban synagogues often spearheaded the building drives that made their construction possible; and the writers who condemned Jewish life in the suburbs, such as Sylvia Rothchild, often lived there themselves. Rather than disgruntled elites lashing out at an ignorant public, the leaders who complained about Jewish upward mobility were very much a part of the communities they disparaged, and their writings contained a good measure of self-critique.

Moreover, the leaders who lamented Jewish upward mobility also depended on newly affluent American Jews for their status and income. The laity voted to hire the rabbis who spoke out against the perils of wealth, and these rabbis collected middle-class salaries provided by their well-off constituents. Jewish intellectuals secured speaking engagements at synagogues and Jewish community centers, and the Jewish authors who savaged the Jewish middle class often depended on these same people to purchase their books.

This situation reveals, at the very least, a Jewish laity willing to support the leaders who questioned the benefits of upward mobility. While this does not necessarily mean that people defined here as "leadership" and "laity" agreed with one another about the dangers of their economic rise, it points to a wide community of Jews who legitimated concerns over affluence through their institutional and financial backing.

Relying primarily on the writings of the leadership excludes many voices from this project. Not one denomination of American Judaism ordained women as rabbis during these years, effectively eliminating the opinions of women from one of the main sources of evidence on which this study relies. Furthermore, women proved far less likely than men to be hired as academics or accepted as intellectuals in the postwar era, further restricting their capacity to publicly express their views on upward mobility. While I pay close attention to the ways that all of my subjects understood gender and its effects, this study nonetheless makes a concerted effort to include sources written by women, and not only in the sections specifically devoted to issues of gender and gender roles.

Geographic scope also limits this research. As it would have been impossible to read every single sermon and community newsletter produced in the twenty-year period that bounds the core of this study, I decided to restrict my local sources to those produced in the largest metropolitan areas that experienced rapid suburbanization in the postwar years. Therefore, in addition to going through the national Jewish press, I concentrated my local research on records that came out of Jewish communities in the New York, Boston, Philadelphia, and Chicago areas. So, while the conclusions of this study applied broadly to many American Jews during the postwar years, these issues may not have played out in quite the same way in places outside my areas of focus, such as small towns, small cities, or the South. They may also have been appreciably different in the sunbelt cities of Los Angeles and Miami, areas that did not have major Jewish communities until the postwar years and, therefore, were not destabilized by suburbanization to the same extent as the older urban centers were.

Additionally, not all midcentury American Jews fit neatly into my historical narrative. Some Jews did not undergo a process of marked economic change in the decades after World War II. Elderly Jews who lacked younger family members to propel them into the middle class did not necessarily experience upward mobility in the postwar era. Neither did many of the single, divorced, or widowed Jewish women who did not have male partners to reap the high salaries offered predominantly to men during these years.

Furthermore, while most postwar American Jews could trace their origins to the 2.5 million Jews from Eastern Europe who migrated between 1870 and 1924, not every Jewish family shared this background. This study does not reflect on the histories of American Jews whose families migrated to the United States earlier in the nineteenth century and had achieved middle-class status well before the postwar era, nor does it register the distinct concerns of Sephardic and Mizrachi Jews and their responses to financial success. Finally, though they too saw upward mobility during the flush postwar years, my research does not separate out the experiences of Jews who immigrated to the United States just before or after World War II, such as the refugees from Hitler's Germany, Holocaust survivors, the growing numbers of ultra-orthodox Jews, and later Jewish immigrants from Hungary, Poland, Cuba, and the Middle East. I look forward to future research that will include more of the diverse histories that made up American Jewry in the years after 1945.

Finally, not all American Jews joined the chorus of ambivalence over their postwar financial success, and at times Jewish leaders applauded the Jewish move into the American middle class. In fact, public celebrations of Jewish contributions to America often painted a triumphant picture of upward mobility that contrasted sharply with the critiques of affluence that circulated primarily, although not entirely, among Jews themselves. For example, the 1954 Tercentennial celebration of Jewish settlement in America, which American Jews commemorated with a series of dinners, concerts, museum exhibits, and scholarly publications, extolled the achievements and integration of American Jews. In highlighting Jews' successful "participation in every circle and corner of American life," wrote Tercentenary chairman Ralph E. Samuel, the celebration offered evidence of "how a so-called minority group can thrive in a climate of freedom and democracy."[27]

The 1954 Tercentennial provides only one example within a long history, dating back at least to the nineteenth century, of how American Jews publicly claimed a space for themselves as Americans and as Jews, stressing as they did so the fundamental complementarity of Jewish and American cultures. Indeed, several American Jewish scholars have studied the ways that American Jews, more or less successfully, proclaimed to the non-Jewish public that they were both fully American and also fully Jewish, and that these two identities enhanced one another.[28]

This project uncovers the flipside to these declarations of mutual compatibility between American and Jewish values. When postwar American Jewish leaders articulated their fears over upward mobility in missives that were most often, though not always, directed at Jews themselves rather than at the wider

American society, they created a tense, ambivalent discourse that questioned the success of the Jewish encounter with America. During the postwar period, these troubled conversations circulated contemporaneously with upbeat messages of a triumphant American-Jewish synthesis, revealing the many, sometimes conflicted, ways in which Jews understood their American experience.

Relatively little of the work in American Jewish history has concentrated on the ways in which American Jews have expressed doubt or reservations about the American Dream of upward mobility. Most of the literature has focused on how American Jews effectively adjusted to American abundance, and, indeed, this approach has served scholars well. Some of the most groundbreaking studies of Jews in postwar America have showcased American Jews' ability to build thriving institutions in their new, affluent communities, and this study builds on their insights.[29]

While this approach to American Jewish history has been productive in many respects, focusing solely on the positive aspects of the Jewish adaptation to the American middle class often masks concerns that have long plagued American Jews. Within much of the historical literature on twentieth-century Jewish life, American Jews seem to be able to reinvent themselves as consuming Americans, and then middle-class Americans, without significant debate or discussion. If upward mobility has long been a catalyst for creativity and innovation within American Jewish communities, it has also spurred impassioned arguments over how to protect the integrity of Jewish life from its influence. Downplaying these concerns obscures some crucial reservations that Jews have had over their encounter with America and the value of the American Dream.

While most historians have focused on American Jews' constructive encounter with prosperity, not all scholars have had such a positive spin on the history of Jewish life in the years after World War II. Indeed, some have echoed the rhetoric of the postwar critics who condemned middle-class American Jewish culture as inauthentic and compromised. In his study of American Jews after World War II, for instance, historian Edward S. Shapiro posited an "inverse relationship between social mobility and Jewish identity," mirroring postwar-era arguments that Jews had become cultural and economic insiders at the cost of their commitment to Jewishness. Others bemoaned the purported moral decline of American Jews as they entered the middle class and accepted white-skin privilege, or lamented the breakdown of ethnic patterns of identification as Jews left urban neighborhoods.[30]

This project attempts a fresh approach to the study of Jewish upward mobility and the ways that Jews responded to their economic rise. My intention is neither to celebrate Jewish financial success nor to echo the critics of the era who condemned postwar Jewish culture as shallow, inauthentic, or destined for decline. I think we can learn more about American Jews by taking a step back, examining the language and images through which they voiced their anxieties over upward mobility, and teasing out the concerns that underlay their unease. The result, I hope, will be a work of history that adopts neither a tone of triumph nor one of lamentation, but instead uncovers the doubts, desires, and aspirations of postwar Jews as they embraced, however ambivalently, the American Dream.

After all, as pessimistic as these Jewish critiques of upward mobility might seem, they nonetheless represented a significant way in which American Jews adjusted to postwar American realities. My subjects keenly felt the tension of identifying with a Jewish history of poverty and oppression as they moved into the privileged middle class. In response, they did not advise American Jews to cease striving for financial growth, nor did they reject their own economic security. Rather, decrying their affluent communities as inauthentic and compromised enabled them to retain their sense of being different from the American mainstream, even as they continued to engage in the process of upward mobility. In ways both subtle and direct, these critiques became their way of insisting that, while American Jews might have been *in* the middle class, they were most certainly not *of* it.[31]

ONE

Materially Poor, Spiritually Rich

Poverty in the Postwar Jewish Imagination

On February 12, 1961, Dr. Judah Pilch of the American Association of Jewish Education took the podium at the Stephen Wise Congress House in New York City to discuss the culture of the *shtetlach*, those "little towns" of Eastern Europe that had once been home to the ancestors of most American Jews. During his presentation, Pilch portrayed the shtetl as a place of extraordinary "cohesion," "warmth," and "spiritual bliss." It fostered these idyllic qualities, he claimed, because of the "precarious state of life" and "complete isolation" suffered by the Jews who lived there. For Pilch, the poverty and oppression that Jews experienced in Eastern Europe led directly to the heightened faith and joy that characterized the shtetl, making life "bearable" for them in spite of their misery.

Pilch believed that the remarkable virtues of the shtetl continued to animate the lives of the Jewish migrants who left Eastern Europe, but only so long as they remained poor and ostracized from the wider population. The Jews who bore "privations and hardships" in the immigrant slums of New York City at the turn of the century, he contended, retained a "spiritual kinship" with their Eastern European forebears. Similarly, he maintained that the *halutzim*, the Jewish pioneers who left "their comfortable homes and pleasures" to live in the economically insecure and war-torn state of Israel, nurtured the ideals of the shtetl.

But if, for Pilch, the Jewish inhabitants of the Lower East Side and Israel succeeded in preserving the meaningful and authentic Jewish life of the shtetl because of their shared poverty and isolation, the middle-class, well-integrated Jews of postwar America most assuredly did not. "In an atmosphere of 'all is well,'" Pilch lamented, "there can be little Jewish creativity."

Only through suffering and dissatisfaction, he concluded, could there be any hope of "re-introducing those *shtetl* values . . . which may re-Judaize the de-Judaized Jews."[1]

Judah Pilch's presentation illustrated a common mode of romantic invention, intertwined with self-critique, that threaded through the conversations of American Jews during the postwar years. As the fortunes and social status of American Jews grew, the symbolic power of the shtetl, the immigrant slum, and the struggling, new state of Israel gained in importance. Jewish writers, educators, and clergy depicted these communities as deeply authentic Jewish spaces, uncorrupted by the influence and the comforts of the non-Jewish world. Isolated rather than integrated, impoverished rather than affluent, they seemed to represent the opposite of midcentury American Jewish life.[2]

As American Jewish leaders looked to the shtetl, the Lower East Side, and the nascent state of Israel from a position of relative privilege and economic security, the deprivations suffered by their ancestors and current coreligionists became transformed into sources of pleasure, strength, and Jewish authenticity. In the imagination of postwar Jews, poverty and isolation had become integral components of a genuine and deeply satisfying Jewish identity.

Such romantic renderings provided a crucial set of images through which American Jewish leaders expressed their concerns over Jewish upward mobility. Even as they benefited from the opportunities and comforts that their new status afforded them, they still maintained a complicated relationship with their new and relatively privileged status. For far too long, experiences of exclusion and want had been part and parcel of their Jewish self-image. The relative acceptance and abundance of the postwar years, therefore, seemed to threaten the very essence of their Jewish difference. By idealizing isolated and impoverished Jewish communities, they preserved their sense of a Jewish identity intertwined with exclusion and suffering without compromising their recent social and economic gains.

We begin our discussion with romantic depictions of the Jewish shtetl, the rural market villages of Eastern Europe. Postwar American rabbis and scholars were not the first Jews to look back to these villages as the wellspring of authentic Jewish culture. Yiddish writers such as Isaac Leib Peretz had been romanticizing the shtetl since the late nineteenth century, when the villages began their slow decline in the face of the uneven industrialization and urbanization of Eastern Europe.

The tendency to idealize the shtetl reached new levels of poignancy, however, after the Holocaust wreaked its abrupt and complete destruction of Jewish life as it had existed in Eastern Europe. In fact, the word shtetl did not enter common English parlance until 1949, when the *YIVO Annual of Jewish Social Science* translated and published Abraham Ain's 1944 study of the Belorussian town of Swislocz. The translator's decision to retain the Yiddish word *shtetl* instead of translating it into English offered American Jews a new vocabulary through which to commemorate the destroyed culture of Eastern European Jews.[3]

Indeed, during this period, some scholars even acknowledged the trend among postwar Jews to wax poetic over the virtues of the shtetl and to gloss over the many problems that had existed there. Discussions of the shtetl have "invariably been tinged with romanticism and nostalgia," insisted historian Abraham G. Duker, president of the College of Jewish Studies in Chicago. Similarly, Irving Howe and Eliezer Greenberg admitted in their introduction to *A Treasury of Yiddish Stories* that postwar Jews conveniently forgot that shtetl society had often been "ignorant, provincial, superstitious, and corrupt. . . . [But] once this world had been destroyed in the gas chambers," they continued, "the romantic impulse became irresistible; [the shtetl] acquired a new and almost holy authenticity."[4]

Despite these warnings, postwar American Jews continued to compose idealized depictions of the shtetl, and this discourse became one of many ways that they commemorated the genocide of European Jewry. Contrary to the pervasive myth that midcentury American Jews did not dwell upon the trauma of the Holocaust out of fear that it might distinguish them from their non-Jewish neighbors and threaten their ascent into the middle class, recent scholarship has demonstrated that postwar Jews actively memorialized the Holocaust during these years. They incorporated commemorative rituals into their holiday celebrations, consumed books and films featuring Holocaust themes, planned events in remembrance of the Warsaw Ghetto Uprising, and consecrated special areas of their synagogues in which they displayed sacred objects salvaged from the destroyed Jewish communities of Europe.[5]

Postwar Jews also used their growing financial resources to provide aid to those who survived the Holocaust. As early as 1939, American Jews had created the United Jewish Appeal for Refugees and Overseas Needs, a fund-raising organization aimed to support those Jews who were suffering oppression in Europe. In 1945 the United Jewish Appeal collected $45 million for the survivors of the Holocaust. A year later, when the UJA set a fundraising target of $100 million to address the pressing physical and emotional needs of the survivors, American Jews exceeded this goal, donating a full $131 million to the remnants of European Jewry. The remarkable success of American Jews' philanthropic drives during these years proves that postwar Jews actively grappled with the Holocaust. Their sense of the disparity between their own rising fortunes and the dejected state of the beleaguered Jews of Europe—from whom they were separated only by an ocean and the lucky decisions of immigrant grandparents—contributed to the romantic lens through which they viewed the Jewish life that had once thrived in the shtetl.[6]

The renderings of shtetl life that circulated among postwar American Jews depicted Jewish poverty as the handmaiden of deep spirituality, intellectualism, and generosity. They tended to emphasize three themes: first, that the inhabitants of the shtetl achieved a spiritual greatness that provided them with a refuge from poverty and persecution; second, that in an environment of scarcity, they learned to value the life of the mind over the accumulation of wealth; and, third, that they were extraordinarily charitable and community minded and made great personal sacrifices in order to provide succor to the poor. Jewish writers, scholars and rabbis cited these shtetl values as rebukes to their audience of postwar American Jews who, they imagined, lived their lives according to decidedly inferior standards.

One of the most influential works to portray the shtetl as a space that prioritized deep religious feeling over material wealth was Abraham Joshua Heschel's 1949 elegy *The Earth Is the Lord's: The Inner World of the Jew in Eastern Europe.* Heschel himself was born to a traditional Jewish family in Poland before benefiting from a wide-ranging education that included traditional yeshiva study, liberal Jewish ordination, and a doctorate in Semitics and philosophy from the University of Berlin. Efforts by Reform movement leaders to rescue Jewish scholars from the Holocaust enabled Heschel to escape from Poland months before the Nazi takeover. After moving to the United States in 1940 and taking on faculty positions at the Hebrew Union College and then at the Jewish Theological Seminary, Heschel ended up becoming a prominent Jewish theologian, philosopher, public intellectual, and activist. His roots in Europe, and his many loved ones who perished there, haunted his career.

The Earth Is the Lord's was Heschel's attempt to commemorate the destroyed world of his youth, which he painted as being the ideal Jewish life not in spite of, but because of, its destitution. The lyrical volume told the story of the impoverished Jews of Eastern Europe, "whose children knew only the taste of 'potatoes on Sunday, potatoes on Monday, potatoes on Tuesday,'" yet still "sat . . . like intellectual magnates . . . " to study the Torah and its commentaries.[7] Heschel lovingly described parents "ready to sell the pillow from under their heads" in order to enable their sons to study religious texts, and townspeople who happily "shared their scanty food" to support young men who studied the Torah.[8] He recounted the tale of the poor Hasidim of Seraph who, when given the opportunity to directly entreat God for sustenance, became so immersed in their prayers that they entirely forgot to ask for an end to their poverty. For Heschel, the physical deprivations of Eastern European Jews compelled them to develop a religious life so fulfilling as to make their physical suffering irrelevant.[9]

Heschel also presented the Jews of the shtetl as completely isolated from their non-Jewish neighbors. As he understood it, this segregation may have been the result of deep-seated hatred, ignorance, and oppression, but it nonetheless produced the shtetl's Jewish authenticity. Since shtetl Jews "borrowed from other cultures neither substance nor form," he insisted, their Jewish life "grew out of its own ancient roots and developed in an indigenous environment." Echoing romantic, nationalist notions of cultural purity, Heschel imagined the shtetl as the place where the Jewish people, untainted by outside influences, "came into its own."[10]

As Heschel romanticized both the poverty and the isolation of shtetl Jews, he simultaneously critiqued the spiritual lives of integrated, middle-class, American Jews. After all, if the history of the shtetl represented "the golden period . . . in the history of the Jewish soul," as Heschel insisted in *The Earth Is the Lord's*, then the souls of American Jews, not subject to the impoverishment and oppression that shaped their forebears, must have been deficient in comparison. To wit, in one of the closing paragraphs of the volume, Heschel beseeched the affluent, postwar Jews of America to cherish "the incomparable beauty" of their "old, poor homes."[11]

Heschel's tribute to the shtetl linked thematically with photographer Roman Vishniac's iconic portraits of impoverished, pious, Eastern European Jews taken in the months preceding World War II. Indeed, Heschel's "The Inner World of the Polish Jew," an essay that would later evolve into *The Earth Is the Lord's*, served as an introduction to *Polish Jews: A Pictoral Record* (1947), Vishniac's first published volume of pre-Holocaust photographs. The images in this collection, which featured traditionally clad old men and young boys poring over religious texts, perfectly matched Heschel's idealized vision of the otherworldly spirit of destitute shtetl Jews. The thirty-one images printed in this book portrayed, in the words of the preface to *Polish Jews*, "one great portrait of a life abjectly poor in its material condition, and in its spiritual condition, exaltedly religious."[12]

Vishniac carefully curated and captioned his images to create this idealized portrait of the religious poverty and cultural isolation of Eastern European Jewry. Although Vishniac would later deny it, the Joint Distribution

Committee had sponsored his travels to Eastern Europe and commissioned him to document only the most pious and most impoverished segments of the Jewish population. However, as art historian Maya Benton discovered upon studying Vishniac's unpublished archive of photographs, Vishniac had, indeed, captured images of some of the cosmopolitan and well-off Jews who also dwelled in the cities and towns of Poland alongside their indigent and traditional coreligionists. But Vishniac never published the images that did not correspond to the vision of piety and poverty that both he and Heschel advanced. Photographs of women wearing their hair in fashionable bobs, of bakeries filled with flaky pastries and of shops selling glowing oranges from Palestine languished in his personal archive as his images of poor and devout Eastern European Jews became enshrined in the public mind as the official visual record of pre-Holocaust Jewry.[13]

Much of the postwar scholarship on Eastern European Jewry echoed Heschel and Vishniac in portraying the shtetl as culturally isolated, materially poor, and spiritually rich. The decades after World War II produced an extensive trove of academic work focusing on the shtetl, the original funding for which came from a somewhat unlikely source. In 1946 anthropologists Ruth Benedict and Margaret Mead secured a grant from the Office of Naval Research to conduct ethnographic projects that sought to understand why certain cultures might end up becoming belligerent toward the United States. Their methodology consisted of interviewing exiles from Europe who had moved to America, and many of these informants turned out to be Jewish refugees. While Benedict and Mead had not initially set out to study Jews, the insights of their many Jewish interlocutors made them curious about Jewish life in Europe. With new backing from the American Jewish Committee's Department of Scientific Research, they formed a "Jewish research group" to start studying the recently destroyed culture of Eastern European Jewry.[14]

The best-known product of this "Jewish research group" was *Life Is with People*, the popular 1952 ethnography of the shtetl authored by Mark Zborowski and Elizabeth Herzog. Additionally, other researchers within the working group, such as sociologists Natalie Joffe and Celia Stopnicka Rosenthal and anthropologist Ruth Landes, published articles on the topic in prominent social-science journals such as *Social Forces*, the *American Journal of Sociology*, and *Psychiatry*. Some members of the group, like Zborowski and Stopnicka Rosenthal, had been born in Eastern Europe and brought their own memories to bear on this project. Though these researchers used the tools of the academy to conduct their research, their scholarship generally produced a romantic, elegiac picture of the shtetl that mirrored the literary and photographic portrayals constructed by Heschel and Vishniac.[15]

These scholars described the shtetl as a place where Jews treasured the study of Torah over the accumulation of wealth, a tendency that they saw as essential to an authentically Jewish value system. "Historically, traditionally, ideally, learning has been . . . regarded as the primary value and wealth as subsidiary or complementary," wrote Zborowski and Herzog in *Life Is with People*. If sometimes shtetl Jews failed to prioritize learning over wealth, they continued, this was due to "economic pressures and outside influences," factors they imagined were alien to the indigenous Jewish life that thrived in the shtetl setting. Natalie Joffe elaborated on this idea in *Social Forces*, insisting that "the greatest claim to status in the *shtetl*" was "the possession of learning . . . although the rich man was respected, the well-learned man was admired, loved, and held up as an example to children." Similarly, Celia Stopnicka Rosenthal claimed that shtetl dwellers who used their money "only to satisfy . . . physical needs" were considered to be "lacking in Jewishness" and "referred to as pigs." But someone who was learned in Torah "was never 'common' or a 'pig' . . . it was unimaginable that a man of learning could behave improperly."[16]

According to these researchers, the Jews of the shtetl never prized money for its own sake but only because it enabled people to perform good deeds. "There can be no study, no donations, no 'social justice,' no zestful celebration of Sabbath and the holidays, no proper rearing of children and setting them up to produce families of their own, unless one can meet the cost," wrote Zborowski and Herzog. Valuing wealth for its own sake, the ethnographers insisted, would have been considered an "anti-Jewish" attitude that contradicted "the community's basic beliefs about human relations." According to Stopnicka Rosenthal, shtetl Jews saw wealth as "a source of prestige only in so far as it enabled a man to contribute to the welfare of the community."[17]

As the scholars of the Jewish Research Group created this idealized conception of shtetl Jews' relationship to wealth, they intimated that American Jews had adopted a very different approach. After all, there would have been no need to memorialize the economic attitudes of the shtetl if postwar Jews had continued to uphold them. Implicitly, they argued that the shtetl's approach to money, which the ethnographers painted as the only authentically Jewish attitude toward wealth, had been destroyed in the Holocaust along with the shtetl itself.

In addition to the elegies and ethnographies composed by postwar Jewish scholars, American Jews also attended theatrical performances that sentimentalized the shtetl as both a locus of Jewish authenticity and the antithesis of their own spiritual impoverishment. Certainly the best-known example of a romanticized shtetl hit the Broadway stage in 1964, when the chorus of *Fiddler on the Roof* wondered if the Sabbath would ever "be so sweet" as in their "underfed, overworked" shtetl of Anatevka, and the influence of this popular musical has been well documented.[18]

While none matched the overwhelming fanfare accorded to *The Fiddler on the Roof*, other postwar performances featuring the shtetl took place as early as 1945. That year, *The Eternal Light* broadcast "The World of Sholom Aleichem," a radio play based on Maurice Samuel's 1943 book of the same name, which presented an idealized snapshot of the shtetl to the American public. The Conservative movement's Jewish Theological Seminary introduced *The Eternal Light* radio program in 1944, in partnership with the NBC radio network. The half-hour weekly radio show consisted of radio plays dramatizing aspects of Jewish life, history, or culture, with the dual goals of promoting Judaism in a positive light to the non-Jewish public and providing inspiration for Jews themselves. During the 1940s and 1950s, millions of listeners tuned in to the program.[19]

The broadcast introduced listeners to "Kasrielevky," the shtetl in which the famed Yiddish humorist Sholem Aleichem situated many of his stories. Sholem Aleichem, according to the script, wrote "with a humorous, exuberant lyricism of the life of the poor," taking for his subjects those Jews of Russia who "lived a life that was walled-in, shut off." But in this program, too, the poverty and isolation of the Jews of Kasrielevky led to the development of a superlative and deeply spiritual culture. There, the narrator insisted, religion proved "inseparable" from daily life and "a little learning" was the "first thing" that inhabitants "looked for in a man."

As with many of the other postwar renderings of the shtetl, *The Eternal Light*'s "The World of Sholom Aleichem" also compared American Jewish life unfavorably to the one lived by the indigent inhabitants of Kasrielevky. "The worlds of Sholom Aleichem are gone," lamented the narrator at the close of the program, "Now in America it is different. . . . And all of the surviving Kasrielevkites . . . remember now and again with a nostalgic pang the far-off magic of those sacred hours . . . for which even progress and freedom have found no substitute." The radio show left listeners with a clear message: that Eastern European Jews lost their otherworldly authenticity when they became affluent, integrated, American Jews.[20]

The first major staged performance of the shtetl dates back to 1953, eleven years before the production of *Fiddler on the Roof*. That year, Arnold Perl's *The World of Sholom Aleichem*, also based on Samuel's 1943 text, played at

Broadway's Barbizon Plaza Theater. While the entire play focused on the lives of impoverished, deeply spiritual, and idealistic shtetl Jews, the second act commented most directly on Jewish poverty with the tale of Bontshe Schweig, a story originally written by Yiddish author Isaac Leib Peretz in 1894. Bontshe Schweig was a poor man who had faced abuse his whole life, yet did not allow these experiences to embitter him or cause him to behave with anything but kindness toward his fellow human beings. When Bontshe finally died and entered Heaven, the angels tried to reward his goodness by offering him anything he desired. But Bontshe's final request was as modest as the life he lived: "Could I perhaps have, every day, please—a hot roll with fresh butter?"[21]

While the playwright only indirectly compared the lives of affluent American Jews to the penniless and saintly characters of *The World of Sholom Aleichem*, contemporary observers made the contrasts explicit. Journalist Alfred Segal, who reviewed the play for the Philadelphia-based *Jewish Exponent*, felt that Bontshe's simple wants and basic goodness contrasted sharply with the materialism of midcentury American Jews. The gentle innocence of Bontshe Schweig, he believed, shamed the acquisitive Jews who viewed his story in the theater. Using the image of a Jewish woman to stand in for the entire community's conspicuous consumption, he asked, "Could that lady in mink still be wanting a Cadillac after meeting Bonche who asked for no more than hot rolls and cream when he had all of heaven to choose from?"[22]

Most reviewers of *The World of Sholom Aleichem* praised the play, accepting it, as did the *New York Times*'s Brooks Atkinson, as a literal depiction of the "experience, hopes and dreams of a homogeneous group of fervent people who lived the spiritual life of their forefathers and the daily life of indigent villagers in an alien land." However *Commentary*'s Midge Decter argued that the play flattened the complexity and dynamism of shtetl life when it portrayed its poor inhabitants as folk heroes rather than conflicted, and often impious, human beings. According to Decter, *The World of Sholom Aleichem* rendered the shtetl as a "Never-Never-Land American Jews like to think they came from, quaint, not quite respectable, but abounding with a special sweetness." It also portrayed the inhabitants of the shtetl, Decter pointed out, as "poor," "pure and simple," and "close to their God." While Decter readily admitted that the Jews of the shtetl were, indeed, quite poor, she refused to accept the widespread notion that their poverty made them both innocent and devout. What if the poor Jews of Eastern Europe "weren't pure and simple?" Decter contended. "What if they were about the most God-forsaken, mixed-up, complicated people that ever lived?"[23]

For Decter, idealizing the poverty of the shtetl not only distorted Jewish history but also presented a political threat. Decter, then a liberal-leaning critic of the left, would develop by the 1970s into a fervent antifeminist and advocate of neoconservativism. She was deeply suspicious of the motivations of playwright Arnold Perl, who had been blacklisted from the film industry for his Communist ties, as well as those of the left-leaning actors, such as Howard Da Silva, who had been cast in the play. As Decter saw it, romanticizing the poverty of the "folk" too often served as a partisan strategy aimed at evoking sympathy for the "reprehensible politics" of the radical left. A segment of *The World of Sholom Aleichem* entitled "High School," in which revolutionary students passionately called upon their peers to strike, convinced Decter that Perl had indeed put Sholem Aleichem's work "to ideological use."[24]

Despite Decter's skepticism, the romantic vision of shtetl Jews as materially poor yet spiritually rich circulated widely among the leaders of American Jewry, no matter their political bent. In fact, so accepted was this conception of Eastern European Jewry that it appeared in the educational textbooks used to teach the next generation of American Jews about its history. Much like the cultural productions aimed at adults, these textbooks painted the shtetl as an idyllic refuge from poverty and oppression, where inhabitants revered learning more than gold and sacrificed their own needs in order to care for those poorer than themselves.

Textbooks focusing on Jewish history proliferated during the postwar years as supplemental synagogue schools provided record numbers of Jewish children with a religious education. The number of American Jewish children attending religious school more than doubled between 1948 and 1958, with an estimated 80 percent of them receiving some manner of a formal Jewish education as of 1959. Moreover, for the first time in American Jewish history, these schools did not primarily educate boys, as had once been the norm, but an equal number of girls as well.[25]

Though sponsored by different movements of American Jewry, the various Jewish history textbooks published during the postwar years presented their young readers with remarkably similar renditions of Eastern European Jewish history. In the early 1950s, Deborah Pessin published four volumes of *The Jewish People*, a textbook underwritten by the Conservative movement's United Synagogue Commission on Jewish Education. Over the course of the same decade, venerable Jewish educator Mamie G. Gamoran, a longtime member of Samson Benderly's Bureau of Jewish Education, composed a three-volume Jewish history textbook for the Reform movement's Union of American Hebrew Congregations. Libby Klaperman, who would become the national education chairman of the Women's Branch of the Orthodox Union, along with her husband Rabbi Gilbert Klaperman of the Modern Orthodox Rabbinical Council of America, also published a four-volume Jewish history series, *The Story of the Jewish People*, during the 1950s. Finally, in 1964, recognizing the need for a more concise, single-volume textbook, Behrman House reissued Rabbi Lee J. Levinger and Elma Ehrlich Levinger's 1928 *The Story of the Jew*, updated and revised by journalist Harry Gersh.[26]

While intended as historical lessons, these Jewish educational textbooks included a strong dose of moral instruction. They also portrayed the culture of Eastern European Jews as the wellspring of an authentic Jewish life that, in the words of Deborah Pessin's *The Jewish People*, "brought the teachings of Judaism to their highest peak." According to these texts, the rejection that these Jews faced at the hands of their neighbors enabled them to create a pure Jewish world, unaffected and uncorrupted by the influence of the surrounding culture. As Mamie Gamoran put it in her 1957 volume *The New Jewish History*, "Czars came and went. Laws were passed. . . . Events like these brought about some outward changes. But the inner life of the Jewish community hardly changed."[27]

Perhaps unsurprisingly for educational textbooks aimed at inspiring Jewish children to learn more about their religious heritage, all of these volumes stressed what had become a common trope in postwar portrayals of the shtetl: that the Jews who lived there prized Torah learning above money. "[In the shtetl] Torah is the greatest and most valuable possession of the Jews. Torah is more important than wealth," insisted Klaperman and Klaperman in *The Story of the Jewish People*. The Levinger text underscored that "study was the path to greatness, and knowledge the only lasting riches." By presenting this reverence for Torah as something different and surprising, the textbook educators implicitly taught their young readers that their own Jewish communities did not necessarily share the shtetl's noble values.[28]

These textbooks also stressed that only the men of the shtetl engaged in Torah study and benefited from the prestige afforded to the learned. Every one of these volumes illustrated this point through a description of marriage arrangements: "A fine young scholar could marry the daughter of a rich man," wrote Gamoran. Wealthy fathers would "go straight to the *Yeshivah* and seek out the most brilliant students" to marry their daughters, wrote Pessin, while the Klapermans noted that "a rich Jew will come to the synagogue seeking a groom for his daughter. He will want a Yeshiva bachur, a student of Torah." "The rich man, seeking a good match for his daughter, did not look first for the son of another rich man. He looked for a promising student," echoed the Levingers and Gersh in *The Story of the Jew*.[29]

This ubiquitous tendency to accentuate the way that Torah learning offered prestige exclusively to the men of the shtetl reveals as much about the gender norms of postwar American Jews as it does about shtetl history. Mentioning the desirability of Torah scholars as husbands would have been a handy way to illustrate the differences between the life of the shtetl and the culture of American Jews, since it was widely understood that the social prestige of middle-class American husbands hinged primarily on their capacity for successful breadwinning. These textbooks sent their students the clear, gendered message that, in an ideal Jewish society, men would be judged for their mastery of Torah rather than for their ability to earn and that marriage to wealthy women would be their prize for this accomplishment. For women, presumably, marriage to such a well-respected young man would have been its own reward.

These textbooks also idealized the shtetl as a place of extraordinary charitability, where economically insecure inhabitants gladly made sacrifices to ensure that their neighbors had what they needed to survive. Though they had to "save every kopek and groschen to provide food for their families," according to Gamoran, they nonetheless gave to the poor at every opportunity. "The givers were often close to poverty and beggary themselves. But charity was as important a part of their Judaism as worship and study, so they gave willingly," wrote the Levingers and Gersh in *The Story of the Jew*. Once again, these textbooks taught young readers that they, too, ought to prioritize philanthropic giving above the accumulation of personal wealth.[30]

Pessin's *The Jewish People* proved the most explicit of the postwar textbooks in its attempts to convince postwar American Jews to use "shtetl values" to guide their contemporary behavior. She enlivened her description of the *Va'ad Arba Aratzot*, the "Council of the Four Lands" that, from the sixteenth through the eighteenth century, had settled grievances among shtetl Jews, by imagining actual disputes that they might have adjudicated upon. The cases that Pessin invented to showcase the wisdom of the *Va'ad Arba Aratzot* included thinly veiled references to controversies that plagued American Jewry in the postwar years.

In a section titled "The Unfair Tax," for instance, Pessin presented a poor Jew who complained to the Va'ad about the way that taxation was handled in his shtetl. The leaders of his town had decided to raise money for communal institutions by taxing salt, a necessity that the poor had to pay for as well as the rich. After considering the matter, the Va'ad decided to tax meat instead of salt, as "the rich eat more meat than the poor" and would therefore "pay a higher tax than the poor." In this manner, Pessin presented the wise leaders who oversaw shtetl life as supporting the concept of progressive taxation. This was a rather pointed message to the children of American Jews, whose families were quickly moving into higher tax brackets and might resent having to pay more taxes than those poorer than themselves. In *The Jewish People*, Pessin argued, not particularly subtly, that the authentic Jewish values that developed in the shtetl demanded a system of taxation that expected more from the people who could afford it and did not place undue burdens on the poor.[31]

Pessin also argued a contemporary political issue in "The Stubborn Merchant," another case that her fictionalized Va'ad ruled upon. In this case, shtetl representatives complained that a merchant in their town was growing rich by doing business with Spain. "You mean that he finds it in his heart to send goods to a country that tortured and exiled our people?" asked the incredulous leaders of the Va'ad, and they encouraged the shtetl representatives to gently educate the man about the crimes that Spain committed against the Jews and ask him to reconsider his actions. In this scenario, of course, Pessin used the setting of seventeenth-century Poland to reference postwar controversies over whether Jews could do business with Germany in the wake of the Holocaust, even when such dealings might prove lucrative. Once again, Pessin educated American Jewish children to value principles over profit and made the case that Jewish values demanded that level of discernment.[32]

At the same time they portrayed the Eastern European shtetl as the source of authentic Jewish values and culture, postwar American Jews also imagined the historical, immigrant slums of the Lower East Side as another mythic, vibrant, and thoroughly Jewish space. Indeed, the sacralization of the shtetl and the Lower East Side were deeply connected, as postwar American Jews often portrayed the immigrant world of the Lower East Side as a continuation of shtetl life on more hospitable American soil.

There are sound reasons as to why American Jews turned to the history of the Lower East Side of Manhattan to represent their immigration experience. During the years of mass migration in the early twentieth century, New York attracted more Jews from Eastern Europe than anywhere else in the United States. Approximately three-fourths of these Jewish immigrants lived, at some point in their lives, within the three wards that later became known as the Lower East Side. Between the 1880s and the 1920s, this area had accrued over 1.5 million Jewish residents, the largest Jewish neighborhood the world had ever seen.[33]

The tendency among American Jews to revisit this neighborhood where so many Jewish immigrants settled did not begin in the postwar years. A nostalgic tourist market in what was then known as the "East Side" had emerged as early as the 1920s, as former inhabitants who had left the area for more desirable accommodations made pilgrimages back to the neighborhood to relive and reimagine their past. But it was not until the economic boom following the Second World War, as American Jews made their way incontrovertibly into the middle class, that the Lower East Side assumed a mythic place in the collective imagination of American Jews, regardless of whether they or any immigrant ancestor had actually resided in the neighborhood. Indeed, it was not until the 1960s, once the area was firmly entrenched in the psyches of American Jews as an important site of Jewish history, that the "Lower East Side" became the accepted name for the area. Before these years, American Jews had referred to the neighborhood by a variety of names, including not only the "Lower East Side" but also "the ghetto," "East Side," "old East Side," and "Delancey Street."[34]

Romantic portrayals of the neighborhood during its heyday as an immigrant enclave proliferated among postwar American Jews. Running throughout these depictions was the assumption that the poverty and isolation of the Lower East Side led directly to its richness and dynamism. The social marginalization of Lower East Side Jews, it was claimed, enabled a Yiddish-language literature, theater, and press to achieve new heights, while their poverty encouraged them to become labor activists who fought for a more just society. Additionally, writing from the vantage point of the flush postwar years, American Jewish memoirists, educators, and writers often described the squalid conditions of the immigrant Jewish slums not as a problem to be overcome, but rather as a source of vitality, pleasure, and fun.

Noted sociologists Nathan Glazer and Daniel Patrick Moynihan, for instance, described the working-class culture of the Jewish immigrants of the Lower East side as more natural, gratifying, and substantial than the middle-class life of upwardly mobile postwar Jews. In their 1963 best seller *Beyond the Melting Pot*, they argued that on the Lower East Side unassimilated, impoverished, and socially marginalized Jews effortlessly forged a successful balance between their Jewish particularity and a universalistic commitment to the progress of all mankind. "When the Jews were thus most Jewish, when they took their Jewishness for granted, they looked forward to a time when all barriers would be down and they could participate freely in the labor movement, business, politics, culture, and social life," they wrote. Glazer and Moynihan's study advanced the idyllic paradigm of a culturally pluralistic New York City, in which all New Yorkers would be equally invested in their ethnoreligious communities as well as in the betterment of society as a whole.

Poverty in the Postwar Jewish Imagination

Poor, immigrant Jews living on the Lower East Side, in the imagination of these scholars, had fulfilled this ideal, while their postwar descendants had yet to discover a "satisfying pattern of Jewish middle-class life."[35]

Guidebooks that directed sightseers to the Jewish Lower East Side also advanced the notion that middle-class Jews had lost something profound and authentic as they left their impoverished, immigrant neighborhoods. While African, Chinese, and Puerto Rican Americans outnumbered the Jewish residents of the Lower East Side by the 1950s, guidebooks such as Bernard Postal and Lionel Koppman's *The Jewish Tourist's Guide to the US* suggested places that tourists could still visit to experience a sense of the neighborhood as it was during the era of immigration. "The lower East Side has lost virtually all of the flavor that it was noted for when it boasted the world's largest Jewish community," they lamented, the result of Jewish migration to "the four corners of the five boroughs, Long Island, and Westchester county." The guidebook adopted a tone of elegy over this once-vibrant Jewish enclave, painting Jewish financial and physical mobility as a process of cultural loss rather than achievement.[36]

Kate Simon, who would later go on to write successful memoirs of her own immigrant Jewish childhood, romanticized the poverty of what she dubbed the "Old Jewish East Side" in *New York: Places and Pleasures*, a guidebook catering to artistic and intellectually minded travelers in search of off-the-beaten-track destinations. Simon carefully led her readers to the remaining establishments that reminded her of "the purity of the old era," and she celebrated the ways that they continued to flout middle-class conventions. With characteristic lyricism, she described the raucous atmosphere at Katz's delicatessen, with its "many strings of salami like a curtain of monster beads, the slices of meat for sampling flying across the counter, the eager noisy customers, the amiable countermen roaring bawdy gossip . . . the steamy, intimate air and speech" as a "modern Breughel." She is equally charmed by the owner of Ershowsky's Meat Market on East Houston Street, who admonished her for her polite manners: "Lady, do me a favor? Please don't say 'please' to me. I'll get used to it and I'll like it and soon I'll want everybody should say 'please' to me. And you know around here it's not a 'please' neighborhood, and I'll expect, and I'll wait, and they wouldn't say it, and all the time I'll feel terrible . . . so please don't spoil me, lady." As Simon described a New York City that bohemian tourists in search of local color might appreciate, the vestiges of an impoverished and marginalized American Jewish community were all that mattered; the lives and establishments of suburban middle-class Jews registered not at all. For Simon, as Jews became middle class they became both less authentic and less interesting.[37]

In a review of Simon's *New York: Places and Pleasures* that appeared in *Commentary* magazine, University of Pennsylvania professor Gerald Weales elaborated on the notion that the culture of middle-class Jews paled in comparison to that of their indigent forebears of the Lower East Side. Unlike Simon, however, Weales noted the irony of longing for the lively, immigrant culture of the Lower East Side even though crippling, desperate poverty wracked the neighborhood. Weales agreed with Simon that the Lower East Side theater scene had more cultural value than "the musical comedy written and performed for the Reform Community Center out of Long Island." Still, he could not "honestly say that the conditions that produced a flourishing Yiddish theater on Second Avenue are preferable to those that give the matrons the leisure to dabble in amateur show business. The balance of loss and gain is a difficult one to weigh."[38]

American Jewish educators joined Simon and Weales in celebrating the Yiddish-language arts and letters that thrived on the Lower East Side. They applauded this Yiddish culture not only for the quality of the work that it produced but also as proof that the immigrant Jews enjoyed a pure Jewish life, undiluted by even the language of the American majority. "Here [on the Lower East Side] they created a Yiddish-speaking world of their own," explained Naomi Ben-Asher and Hayim Leaf to young readers researching New York Jews in their 1957 volume *The Junior Jewish Encyclopedia*. In Pessin's *The Jewish People*, the Yiddish newspapers and theater of the Lower East Side represented "old institutions on new soil," direct, linguistic lines of connection between Eastern Europe and the United States. Yiddish represented "more than a language" to the immigrants of the Lower East Side, according to Klaperman and Klaperman in *The Story of the Jewish People*, as it was also "the stream in which Jewish culture passed from generation to generation." But in their quest for integration, regretted the Klapermans, American Jews had relinquished this valuable resource. "Alas, today, because there are fewer Jews who speak 'mama lashon' [mother tongue], the Yiddish theater is almost gone," they lamented.[39]

Journalists also mourned the state of the Lower East Side's Yiddish culture attributing its decline to Jewish upward mobility and assimilation. The *Forward* newspaper, the premier daily of the Jewish immigrants, had become "the victim of success," determined *Time* magazine in a 1962 article that noted the paper's dwindling circulation. And in *Commentary* magazine, Dan Wakefield mourned the "shrunken Yiddish literary world" that barely held on within the cafes and cafeterias of the Lower East Side, a mere "remnant of the spirit that pervaded the storied days" of the Jewish immigrants. The waning of the vibrant Yiddish culture that once existed on the Lower East Side seemed to represent the loss of a more genuine Jewish existence, uncorrupted by linguistic and cultural assimilation into the middle-class, American majority.[40]

Along with the decline of an intellectual and artistic life conducted in the Yiddish language, postwar Jewish writers also mourned the loss of the distinctly Jewish, radical labor movement of the Lower East Side. Indeed, scholars pointed out the symbiotic relationship and significant overlap between the Yiddish-speaking intellectuals and the labor activists who had once dominated the neighborhood. In contrast to the assumed anti-intellectualism of the "general labor movement" in America, on the Lower East Side "labor and the intellectuals never parted ways," claimed Abraham Menes, himself both a scholar, a founder of the YIVO Institute for Jewish Research, and a leader of Jewish Labor Committee. For Menes, this unique partnership between intellectuals and the activists of the Lower East Side had a significant impact not only on immigrant Jewish life but also on the wider culture, as together they demonstrated to the world that "there can be dignity in poverty."[41]

For Yeshiva University historian Hyman Grinstein, both the Yiddish culture of the Lower East Side and the committed labor activism of its inhabitants proved that "there was a brighter side to the life in the ghetto." Writing in a festschrift honoring venerable Jewish historian and Columbia University professor Salo Wittmayer Baron, Grinstein insisted that "a deepened social sense, a greater feeling of the equality of all men, and a flowering of Yiddish literature" did not only exist alongside the devastating poverty of the slums but "were also to some extent the products of the slums." Grinstein argued that there were cultural benefits to the social isolation and indigence of the Jewish immigrants. Emphasizing both the "light and shadows" of the immigrant enclave of the Lower East Side may have been Grinstein's way of honoring Salo Baron's call for a less lachrymose reading of Jewish history, but it also echoed a common tendency among postwar American Jews to insinuate that conditions of isolation and poverty were uniquely capable of producing more genuine Jewish lives.[42]

Romantic recollections of the ardent, working-class, labor activism of the Lower East Side also provided inspirational fodder for the declining numbers of postwar American Jews who continued to align themselves with the radical left. Michael Gold, one-time editor-in-chief of the *New Masses* and a longtime columnist for the *Daily Worker*, penned such an idealized paean to the poor Jews of the Lower East Side in the pages of the Communist-affiliated *Jewish Life*. Years earlier, in 1930, Gold had published his only novel, *Jews without Money*, a gritty, hard-edged memoir that spoke frankly about the hardships of growing up in the East Side slums. However, in 1954, in response to what he felt to be the middle-class bias of the official Tercentennial celebrations of Jewish life in America, Michael Gold penned a very different elegy to the immigrant neighborhood in which he had been raised, imbuing his depiction of the Lower East Side with a sentimentality that had never penetrated his earlier work. "I was brought up in the worst slum in America, yet my memories remain of a brave, neighborly, talented people who, though martyred by tragic poverty, yet knew how to laugh and sing and hope," wrote Gold. The East Side of his childhood, he insisted, "was a heroic battleground where the sweatshop slaves wrote poetry of protest and rose in a series of great, heroic strikes and political campaigns against their poverty." In contrast, he accused the middle-class Jews of the postwar years of creating a "degraded" Jewish culture and becoming "appeasers" of McCarthy's anti-Communist crusade.[43]

While some romanticized the lofty political and intellectual achievements of the Jewish denizens of the Lower East Side and attributed these accomplishments to their culture of poverty and marginalization, other postwar Jewish writers offered the impression that the bedraggled Lower East Side was simply a more exciting place—especially for children—than the antiseptic middle-class suburbs. This theme ran through the memoir of Samuel Chotzinoff, a noted musician, music critic, and director of the National Broadcasting Company's musical department. Chotzinoff published a short piece about his Lower East Side boyhood in 1954 for *Holiday* magazine, which he followed up with a full-length memoir, aptly titled *A Lost Paradise*, in 1955. While he had long since moved to safer and pricier neighborhoods uptown, his reminiscences of the immigrant slums described an area filled with a heightened sense of adventure. "Excitement lay in wait at the turn of a street corner, in the somber hallways . . . in manure-fragrant stables, in the rubble of demolished buildings, in open manholes," he wrote, as his nostalgic lens transformed evidence of the neighborhood's squalor into sources of pleasure. Other "excitements" that—at least in retrospect—offered young Chotzinoff "a delicious feeling of daring and fear" included "the spectacle of drunkards swaying and teetering and talking loudly to themselves," bedraggled prostitutes who would "threaten us grotesquely with their fists and lunge at us futilely as we came too close," or the sight of "a policeman forcibly propelling a drunk and twisting his arm until the wretch screamed with pain." Though many of Chotzinoff's recollected memories seemed to describe a very difficult childhood indeed, he nonetheless insisted that the Lower East Side had many advantages over his later dwellings in the more elegant neighborhoods of New York City. "In retrospect, no place else was so soul-satisfying as that corner of New York from the Brooklyn Bridge to Fourteenth Street and from the Bowery to the East River," he concluded.[44]

The idea that the Lower East Side slum provided children with a happier childhood than a middle-class upbringing also ran through Sydney Taylor's best-selling children's series, *All-of-a Kind Family*, published in 1951. Taylor herself had grown up on the Lower East Side and drew from her experiences to write the beloved series. The first installment of *All-of-a-Kind Family*, which included some of the first Jewish protagonists in American children's literature, won the first Isaac Siegal Memorial Award for Children's Books offered by the Jewish Book Council.

All-of-a-Kind Family told the tale of five spirited sisters named Ella, Henny, Sarah, Charlotte, and Gertie. In spite of the poverty and bleakness of their neighborhood, they managed to have an idyllic childhood. Though tight financial circumstances forced all the girls to sleep in one room, they "looked forward" to bedtime when they could think of games, tell stories, and surreptitiously nibble on the treats they purchased with their few prized pennies. Though they did not have money to pay for entertainment, the girls thought it "heavenly" to take out books from the free public library, a grand adventure to push through the crowded pushcart markets as they shopped for the Sabbath, and a rare treat to watch the horses of the carousel, even though they "knew there was no money to spare for such luxuries" as actually taking a ride. The costumes they made for the masquerade holiday of Purim out of old and borrowed clothes proved funnier and more creative than any store-bought getup, and though they lacked proper instruments, the orchestra they put together using pots and pans from their mother's kitchen could not have been more festive. Throughout this series, the privations of the Lower East Side offered the protagonists opportunities to experience excitement, warmth, closeness, and an authentic Jewish culture that seemed to elude the middle-class Jews of the postwar years.[45]

While the postwar American Jews who wrote about the heyday of the Lower East Side or the vibrant Jewish life of the shtetl had to draw from long-ago memories, those who wrote glowing reports of the land of Israel could access more recent information. Because of this, the comparisons they made between the supposedly vacuous, complacent life of middle-class American Jews and the presumably more meaningful, self-sacrificing, and austere life of Israeli Jews tended to be especially pointed. Many were quite critical of the American Jews who chose to remain in their home country rather than migrate to Israel, and some expressed guilt over their own choice to live in the comfort of American affluence rather than helping to build the new Jewish state.

Though, to the consternation of these critics, few American Jews would move to Israel during the postwar years, they showed their fealty to the new state in other ways. They contributed money to Israel on a broad scale, supplying the new nation with $400 million for aid, development, and defense between 1945 and 1948 alone. American Jews also incorporated the Jewish state into their ritual and cultural lives. Synagogues inserted regular prayers for Israel into their liturgy, while Jewish educators and religious leaders began to use the Israeli, rather than the European, pronunciation of Hebrew in their lessons and prayers. The Israeli flag began to appear alongside the American flag at Jewish gatherings and events, Israeli-made products became top-selling items at synagogue gift shops, and American Jews included sets of Israeli folk dancing into their bar mitzvah and wedding celebrations. Books and novels describing life in Israel appeared on the dockets of Jewish book clubs, while Jewish and non-Jewish Americans alike became caught up in a romanticized version of Israel's birth through Leon Uris's 1958 best-selling novel *Exodus*, as well as the 1960 film adaptation that starred Paul Newman as Israeli military hero Ari Ben Canaan.[46]

American Jews also showed their support for Israel by idealizing the lives of the Jews who lived there. In spite of Israel being a place to which postwar American Jews could—but largely chose not to—emigrate, depictions of the Jewish state touched upon many of the same themes that characterized recollections of the shtetl and the immigrant enclave of the Lower East Side, two destinations to which Jews could not return. Israel also seemed to represent a place where Jewish life flourished in all of its authenticity, uncorrupted by outside influences. For instance, Herman Wouk, the best-selling author of *Marjorie Morningstar* and himself an Orthodox Jew and a committed Zionist, claimed that Jews in the postwar United States could easily lose "our salt, our *tam* [lit. flavor]," by which he meant the fundamental qualities that made them Jewish. On the other hand, he maintained, Jews in Israel were in no danger of losing their essential Jewishness. "Every Israeli has *tam*," he declared, by simple virtue of living on Jewish soil in a Jewish land.[47]

Additionally, much as postwar American Jews imagined the Lower East Side to be the continuation of the authentic Jewish life of the shtetl, they also imagined the new state of Israel as being deeply intertwined with the legacy of Eastern European Jews. In addition to viewing Israel as the only current incubator of an authentic and undiluted Jewish culture, they also painted it as a "living memorial" where the survivors of the Holocaust could find their refuge and where the vanished culture of Eastern European Jewry could flourish anew. Jewish history textbooks of the postwar years portrayed the dramatic moment in which Holocaust survivors were finally able to enter the Jewish homeland as the ultimate triumph of Israel's new independence, firmly ensconcing the tragic history of Eastern European Jews into the establishment of the Jewish state. "The prophesy was fulfilled. The DP [displaced persons] camps were emptied at last," declared Gamoran in *The New Jewish History* as she described the first months of Israeli independence. "Even while the fighting was going on the Jews poured out of the DP camps and the broken cities and villages of Europe and made toward what was for them a truly Promised Land," echoed the Levingers and Gersh in *The Story of the Jew*.[48]

American Jewish leaders celebrated Holocaust survivors' entrance into Israel and the eagerness of Israeli Jews to help them rebuild their lives. At the same time, they often dismissed middle-class, American Jews' attempts to help Holocaust survivors with philanthropic dollars and to welcome those who had been allowed to enter the United States. Even before Israel achieved its independence in 1948, Rabbi Charles Shulman, a retired navy chaplain, Reform movement leader, and prolific writer on communal affairs, extolled the Jews who lived in Mandate Palestine for the significant help they offered the survivors and reprimanded American Jews for giving only what they could easily afford. At a 1946 Hadassah dinner, he informed his audience that the Jews in Palestine could "be like you. They can take it easy. . . . [Yet] they are not content to live at ease in Zion" while survivors of the European genocide languished in displaced persons camps and lacked a permanent home. "Unlike the American Jew," he continued, "the Palestinian [Jew] . . . knows he must be prepared to sacrifice. He will gladly reduce his own standard of living to help ease the suffering of those who survived."[49]

During a Yom Kippur sermon that same year, Shulman imagined how the Jews living in Mandate Palestine might berate their American counterparts for not being willing to give up their comforts to help the survivors of the Holocaust:

What do **you** do for them? Nothing. You write a check to an organization called the United Jewish Appeal and then you forget about them. What do I do? I leave my Palestine home and travel thousands of miles to come to them as a messenger of hope. I settle among them. I wipe away the tears from their eyes . . . I tell them that their Jewish people have not forgotten them. . . . I eat their meager rations with them. I hold out the promise of a new life to them. . . . You enjoy all your privileges without any cost to your pleasures or pursuits. You even eat a superior dinner as you hand out a little money for them.[50]

The notion that Israelis voluntarily and enthusiastically lowered their standard of living in order to accommodate the new immigrants flooding into the Jewish state inspired American Jewish writers and educators of the postwar years. Throughout the late 1940s and 1950s, Israel witnessed a mass influx of immigrants not only from Eastern Europe but also from Middle Eastern nations such as Iraq, Yemen, Egypt, and Morocco, where conditions had become less stable and often dangerous for Jews due to hostilities against the new Jewish state. The Israeli government instituted a strict ration system of food, clothing, and other supplies for all of its citizens during these years in order to ensure that the new nation could produce enough resources to sustain the hundreds of thousands of new citizens.

While many Israelis resented these austerity measures after years of war and hardship, American Jewish writers and educators described all Israeli Jews as exhibiting gallant forbearance as they enthusiastically reduced their own standard of living in order to provide for the new immigrants. Celebrating the sacrifices made by Israeli Jews as the Jewish state absorbed new citizens was a central theme that animated two books published by journalist Ruth Gruber during the 1950s, *Israel without Tears* (1950) and *Israel Today* (1958), an updated version of the earlier volume.

Gruber herself had a varied and illustrious career as a journalist and an advocate for Jewish refugees. Born to Jewish parents in 1911 in Brooklyn, New York, she earned her PhD at the age of twenty from the University of Cologne, where she was upended by the fascist rallies and demonstrations she witnessed. Upon returning to the United States she began a career in journalism and worked as a foreign correspondent specializing in fascist and Communist activity. Gruber's career as a reporter was replete with heroics; in 1944 she spearheaded a mission to rescue one thousand European refugees and bring them to the United States, and in 1947, on assignment for the *New York Herald Tribune*, she broke the story about the *Exodus* ship full of Holocaust survivors that British forces prevented from entering into Palestine. In the years after Israel became a state, Gruber covered every major wave of Jewish immigration into the country, concluding with the migration of Ethiopian Jews, which she wrote about in 1987.[51]

While Gruber certainly acknowledged that Israelis, like Americans, jumped at the chance to enjoy American-style luxuries when they could, *Israel without Tears* (1950) and *Israel Today* (1958) recorded Gruber's admiration for the way that the inhabitants of the young nation relinquished these creature comforts when faced with the challenge of providing for Jewish refugees from Eastern Europe and the Middle East. Her books recounted the many jokes that circulated through Israel regarding the citizenry's frustrations with the strict rationing they faced:

> Dov Joseph [then Israel's Minister of Supply and Rationing] received a telephone call. A voice said, "Minister, I think rationing is fine. The food restrictions are wonderful. People ought to be singing your praises all over the country."
>
> The Minister of Supply and Rationing was pleased. "I'm delighted to hear you say that," he said. "Would you be willing to travel around the country and tell people?"
>
> "I'd be glad to," the voice said, "but I have no strength."[52]

While this rather dark humor may strike contemporary readers as evidence that postwar Israelis had a hard time with the scarcity of goods available to them, for Gruber they proved that Israelis responded with "good humor" to the challenges they faced in a new and struggling country.[53]

Indeed, in Gruber's estimation, Israel's ingathering of the Jewish exiles represented "Israel's greatest achievement." And while she praised those American Jews who donated to the United Jewish Appeal to help make it happen, she made it clear that "the people of Israel themselves gave the greatest contribution and the greatest sacrifice." Only Israelis faced the "higher taxes, lower living standards, tent cities, and a return to rationing." In spite of this, there were "no protests, no cries of indignation." For Gruber, the Jews of Israel understood, as no other people did, that "there was no price on human life."[54]

Jewish history textbooks echoed Gruber's understanding of Israelis as being particularly selfless and ready to forswear personal comforts in order to bring more Jewish refugees into their country. "To take care of the immigrants means that every Israeli has to . . . accept limitations in food and clothes, and do without even the least luxury. This sacrifice the entire nation has made, and continues to make today," insisted Klaperman and Klaperman in *The Story of the Jewish People*.[55]

Fiction aimed at young American Jews also emphasized the eagerness of Israeli Jews to accept material deprivation as they welcomed new immigrants into their land. In 1951, for instance, Althea Silverman, a prolific writer of Jewish children's books, published *Habibi's Adventures in the Land of Israel*, which recounted the adventures of an American boy nicknamed Habibi (literally "my beloved" in both Hebrew and Arabic) who lived for a year in Israel with his parents. When they went to visit an orphanage, Batya, the fictional director, lamented that there were no extra beds to accommodate the boats of immigrant children who arrived in the country daily. Still, when thirty more young refugees suddenly appear, Batya and her staff selflessly gave up their own beds in order to welcome them: "No room? There is always room. We'll spread mats on the floor, in the cottages, the dining-hall, the workshops. . . . How can anyone say there's no room?"[56]

Similarly, when Habibi and his family visited a kibbutz near the Dead Sea, the residents were told that a shipload of refugees from Persia had just arrived in the country and needed a place to stay. Members of the settlement decided to take them in, although they lacked enough food or supplies. In order to ensure that everyone on the kibbutz would be provided for, many of the men volunteered to temporarily leave the settlement and their families in order earn extra money to support the new immigrants. After seeing such a remarkable display of selflessness, Habibi asked his father if he "would call those men heroes." "My son, I would indeed call them heroes," his father responded, letting young American readers know, in no uncertain terms, how they were supposed to feel about the self-sacrificing Jews of Israel.[57]

Nora Benjamin Kubie, another popular Jewish children's book author of the 1950s, took a different approach to Israel's postwar austerity measures in her 1953 volume, *The First Book of Israel*. The story followed Susan, a young, non-Jewish, American girl, who traveled to Israel with her family in order to visit David, a Jewish, Israeli boy her own age. What Susan discovers is that the sacrifices that David and his family must make in order to accommodate new immigrants end up making their lives uniquely meaningful and enjoyable. For instance, David and his family live in an apartment "we should think small for a family of four." However, "David thinks any room with no bed in it a waste of space, because there are twice as many people in his country now as there were a few years ago and there are hardly enough rooms to go around." The reader finds that David does not mind living in such close quarters because he "has the balcony on which to play. From there he can lean out and talk to his friends in the street without having to run down four flights of stairs." In Kubie's description, the shortage of indoor space only compels David to have more fun outdoors.[58]

Likewise, when Susan shares a Friday night supper at David's house, she discovers that the food shortages enhanced the pleasure of the Sabbath meal. Together, over a table "laid with a fresh white linen cloth, a bowl of flowers, silver candlesticks, a new-baked loaf of bread and a bottle of wine," they feast on stuffed fish, chicken, salad and stewed apricots. When Susan mentions that the family did not seem to be experiencing any limitations on food, David's mother informs her that they "don't eat so well as this always, for we have not yet raised enough food in our new country for all the people. But we save up all week so as to have a good dinner on Shabbat." Being able to enjoy a satisfactory repast only once a week made the diners appreciate it all the more. Implicitly, through such idealized vignettes of Israeli life, Kubie's book challenged its young readers to consider whether a life of abundance could be as profound as the relative austerity experienced by Jews pursuing noble ends in the land of Israel.[59]

Kubie was not the only American Jew to intimate that the lack of amenities made life in Israel more satisfying than life in America. Indeed, Rabbi Edgar Siskin, the spiritual leader of North Shore Congregation Israel, a wealthy Reform congregation in Glencoe, Illinois, made this idea explicit in a 1956 sermon. Life in Israel is characterized by "economic austerity, material and physical insufficiency. . . . Think of all the things we have and take for granted that the vast majority of the people in Israel do not have and have little hope of getting," he preached. "Yet," he continued, "their mood is buoyant and their spirit undefeatable." In contrast, he argued, "here, in the midst of unparalleled prosperity and opportunity, many of us lead a spiritually and culturally impoverished life." The notion that economic scarcity led to spiritual and cultural greatness while abundance led to complacency and despondency represented, according to Siskin, a "marvelous lesson" in how best to live a fully satisfying Jewish life.[60]

The (relatively few) American Jews who emigrated to Israel during the postwar years took such lessons deeply to heart. Journalist Ronald Sanders, who would later become the editor in chief of the Zionist-oriented *Midstream* magazine, visited Israel for the first time in 1960 as part of a yearlong fellowship from the Fulbright Foundation. There, he spoke with American Jews who had settled in the Jewish state and, upon his return to the United States, wrote about what had prompted their migration. Sanders concluded that part of Israel's draw for these "serious-minded young Americans" was that the country seemed "to offer an alternative" to an "overly comfortable way of life." American Jews discovered Israel "precisely in the era when rapidly spreading affluence was beginning to challenge the moral constitution of the Western countries," he surmised, and those who moved to Israel understood their ability to live without luxury as "an essential test in the continuing validation of . . . [their] soul."[61]

Nell Ziff Pekarsky, a former national president of Junior Hadassah who lived in Jerusalem for five years while her husband established a Hillel house at the Hebrew University, expressed embarrassment over the indulgences she had allowed herself when she still lived in the United States. Writing for *Hadassah* magazine in 1952, she described the kind of hardships she had to endure in Jerusalem: cutting short a parent-teacher conference because kerosene was suddenly available after two weeks of doing without and standing in line for hours to procure a new scrubbing rag to replace an old, shredded one. Having adapted to a life of rationing and endless queues for scarce goods, she found herself ashamed when she remembered "how much food I used to dump into the garbage can each day." Still, in spite of being a "spoiled American housewife," she expressed a certain amount of pride that she was able to manage as well as the Israelis: "If they could take it, so could I!"[62]

Shula Hirsch, a New York City schoolteacher, also saw moral value in Israeli austerity and felt guilt about not moving to the new state. As a child in Los Angeles, Hirsch had been intensely involved in Habonim, a left-wing Zionist youth group. Many of her peers in the movement had moved to Israel to start their own "American" kibbutz, Gesher Haziv. In 1962 Hirsch published *An American Housewife in Israel*, a book that humorously recounted her family's two-month trip to Israel, her fumbling acclimatization to her new surroundings, and her heartfelt longing for the more meaningful life in the land of Israel that she believed her friends had chosen. "The life they lead is exceedingly simple," she said of her Israeli friends. Though they had "no phone and no car," she insisted that they did not miss these luxuries. The palms of an old friend may have been "black from manual labor," but they were also "strong as a result of having built the land of Israel." Hirsch, for her part, often reported feeling like she was a "tremendous disappointment" for not having moved to Israel with her youth movement friends and that she was "letting the state of Israel down" by returning to her comfortable life in America.[63]

While these American Jewish writers admired all Israelis for their relatively humble lifestyles, the restrictive life of the "kibbutz," Israel's socialist farming collectives, held particular fascination. A society in which individuals neither had nor needed money, and in which everyone shared their property and labored for the good of the whole, often registered as the opposite of American materialism and the solution, as Ronald Sanders put it, "to the spiritual troubles of middle class life today." Even Ruth Gruber, who recognized that the postwar kibbutz was not the utopia that it often seemed to be, nonetheless maintained that the "stoic, Spartan life" of the kibbutz represented the "idealism of brotherhood and equality" and the "reflection of Israel's dream."[64]

Murray Weingarten, who had been a leader of the Habonim movement in the Bronx, moved to Israel in 1948 and helped found Gesher Haziv. In 1955 he published *Life on a Kibbutz*, a memoir of his experiences. In this book, Weingarten recollected some of the difficulties that he and his American-born peers faced as they established their collective farm. Chief among their challenges was a conscious struggle to give up their class privileges, to refrain from flaunting their personal connections to wealthy and influential individuals, and to remain laborers instead of the "managers" that their middle-class educations prepared them to be.[65]

Though Weingarten readily admitted that Gesher Haziv still had to work through many problems before it could be a fully satisfying endeavor, he nonetheless maintained that it provided him with the most ideal Jewish life. "I live in a kibbutz because it seems to me the most positive and satisfying way of life which I can lead, not only as a human being but specifically as a Jewish human being," he wrote. While he acknowledged that Jewish culture had the potential to thrive in the comfortable American diaspora, he nonetheless felt that "the big beautiful Jewish community buildings" in the United States "seem to me empty of content." In the end, he maintained that only the state of Israel provided "the opportunity for full and unhampered Jewish creativity which can at best enjoy only partial opportunity in the United States or elsewhere." For Weingarten, only Israel provided the setting for a wholly Jewish life, removed from the outside influences—both cultural and material—that could contaminate its authenticity.[66]

While relatively few postwar American Jews would follow Weingarten in his attempt to relinquish the comforts, privileges, and opportunities available to them in the United States, the notion that affluence and social acceptance compromised authentic Jewishness circulated throughout American Jewish communities. Their descriptions of the shtetl, the Lower East Side, and Israel described locales marked by economic scarcity and cultural isolation. In the imagination of postwar American Jews, however, the poverty and social marginalization that so often endangered Jewish communities and Jewish lives became positive forces that fostered a dynamic and vigorous Jewish culture. Postwar American rabbis, writers, thinkers and intellectuals wondered whether a healthy and authentic Jewish life could exist without hardship. As they romanticized less affluent and more isolated Jewish communities, they painted their own integration into American society as evidence of cultural dilution, and their economic success as evidence of complacency and spiritual vacuity.

As we will see in the following chapters, postwar American Jews often turned a disparaging eye on their own communities, lamenting their supposed retreat from the project of social justice, the purported emptiness of their spiritual practices, and their presumed departure from genuinely Jewish gender roles. As they did so, the romanticized, impoverished Jews of the shtetl, the immigrant slums, and the new state of Israel provided the foils against which they judged their own lives.

TWO

What Now Supports Jewish Liberalism?

Upward Mobility and Jewish Political Identity

In 1956 the office of public opinion research at Princeton University released a study that heartened Rabbi Harold Saperstein, a liberal Reform rabbi from Lynbrook, Long Island. Speaking from his pulpit in March of that year, Saperstein relayed the finding that, while wealthy religious groups tended to espouse more conservative political ideals than less affluent ones, Jews proved a notable exception. "They ranked highest in occupational and economic status—but instead of being lowest in liberal ideas they ranked highest," explained Saperstein. The reason for this, he surmised, lay in the Jewish "moral and ethical heritage . . . and this still strengthens us to be true to our convictions even when it means going contrary to the interests of our own economic group."[1]

Discovering that Jews continued to champion liberal ideals even as their fortunes grew must have offered considerable relief to Saperstein and other liberal Jewish leaders, many of whom had come to suspect that Jews were growing politically conservative as they moved to the middle class. This concern plagued not only the many liberal rabbis of the postwar years but also those Jewish intellectuals and activists outside the religious orbit who held deep commitments to liberal or, somewhat less commonly, leftist political values. These leaders feared that as Jews adapted to a conformist and complacent middle-class lifestyle in what they perceived as the Republican strongholds of suburbia, they would, inevitably, adopt conservative political views and shy away from social activism. That the actual picture of Jewish politics in suburbia did not necessarily match these leaders' projections did little to assuage their anxieties. Like the characters "Harvey and Sheila" in comedian Allan Sherman's 1963 parody of the Israeli folksong "Hava Nagila," they continued to believe that American Jews who had "worked for JFK" would certainly "switch to the GOP" once they owned a house and swimming pool.[2]

The purpose of the current chapter, however, is not to assess whether upwardly mobile American Jews grew more or less politically conservative as they enjoyed American prosperity and moved to the suburbs in the two decades following World War II. Rather, this chapter traces and analyzes the widespread fear, often expressed by the liberal and left-wing leaders of American Jewry, that American Jews would adopt conservative values as a result of their economic rise. For many of these leaders, the Jewish climb into to the middle class challenged their conceptions of what it meant to uphold "authentic" Jewish politics. After all, many liberal and left-wing American Jews viewed their left-of-center politics as a fundamental aspect of their Jewish identity, arguing that authentic Jewish morals, stemming from both the religious dictates of the biblical prophets as well as the history of Jews as a persecuted minority, demanded that Jews support social justice and the causes of the underdog. These leaders strongly identified with the Jewish history of poverty and exclusion that stood in tension with their present circumstances. Economic mobility, and the promise of becoming part of the privileged middle class, seemed to threaten this crucial aspect of Jewish difference.

Historians have spilled a great deal of ink over the origins, nature, and limits of Jewish liberalism during the postwar years. Most agree that liberal attitudes dominated during this period, with major Jewish institutions such as the American Jewish Committee, the American Jewish Congress, the Anti-Defamation League, and the National Council of Jewish Women advancing an agenda that backed individual rights and equal opportunity through means of legal reform. While they generally did not go so far as to promote civil disobedience, these organizations' active participation in the legal and educational struggles for civil rights, civil liberties, and the separation of church and state placed them decidedly on the left of the American political spectrum. Additionally, postwar polls generally found that most individual American Jews continued to express opinions to the left of other Americans. To give just one striking example, a 1952 Gallup poll revealed that while 45 percent of Protestants and 56 percent of Catholics agreed with Joseph McCarthy's anti-Communist crusade, only 2 percent of American Jews approved of McCarthy's mission and tactics.[3]

Scholars have also pointed out the limits to the liberalism of postwar American Jews, who tended to retreat from their political principles when they conflicted with their private interests. Northern Jews, for example, may have vehemently opposed the legal segregation of public schools that existed in the South, but many also defended their excellent neighborhood schools, even when the demographics of those neighborhoods produced all-white student populations. Widespread Jewish support for civil rights also did not stop them from migrating out of mixed-race neighborhoods into all-white suburbs when granted the opportunity to do so. While most postwar Jews supported liberal ideals, only a minority would make personal sacrifices to advance them.[4]

Additionally, a nascent Jewish conservatism also started to develop during the postwar period. Some of its most vocal spokespeople came from the group of intellectuals associated with *Commentary* and *Partisan Review*, later dubbed the "New York Intellectuals" by its most consistently left-leaning member, Irving Howe. The more conservative voices in the group included the cold warrior Lucy Dawidowicz, who throughout the 1950s emphatically denied the compatibility of Jewishness and Communism and accused the Jewish supporters of Julius and Ethel Rosenberg, the two American Jews convicted and executed for spying for the Soviet Union, of fomenting antisemitism. Also among the conservative-leaning group was *Commentary* editor Norman Podhoretz, who, in his influential 1963 essay "My Negro Problem—and Ours," used his experiences of childhood trauma at the hands of African American peers to justify his ambivalent feelings regarding Jewish civil rights activism in the postwar years.[5]

Although the liberal consensus of postwar American Jewry may have been more qualified than it appeared, this does not mean that Jewish upward mobility led directly to political conservatism. No evidence indicates that newly prosperous Jews were any less ideologically liberal or politically active than those Jews who did not share in their economic rise. In fact, less-well-off Jews, who were more likely to remain in urban neighborhoods during the postwar years instead of migrating to the tonier suburbs, tended to oppose civil rights reforms such as school desegregation more often and more vocally than their wealthy, suburban counterparts. Urban Jews lived in the areas most frequently targeted for desegregation, and while some staunchly supported the programs, many others felt that these experiments threatened the high quality of education that their children enjoyed in their local schools. Consequently, the less moneyed urban Jews proved more likely to join organizations like New York City's Parents and Taxpayers Association, which fought to maintain segregated neighborhood schools. Wealthier Jews, generally isolated from the day-to-day tensions of integration, had little reason to question the liberal stances of their communal organizations.[6]

Upward Mobility and Jewish Political Identity

Still, and in spite of the fact that most upwardly mobile, suburban Jews retained their liberal sympathies during the postwar years, observers of Jewish life continued to believe that they would not. Sociologist and Anti-Defamation League consultant Melvin M. Tumin, for instance, accused newly affluent American Jews of becoming "conservative, security-seeking, status-minded, and apolitical" as they attempted to "fit in to American life at its middle-class worst." Sociologists Nathan Glazer and Daniel Patrick Moynihan likewise predicted the inexorable wane of Jewish liberalism in *Beyond the Melting Pot*. In the initial years of Jewish economic mobility, they argued, "it seemed desirable that they should remain liberal and sympathetic to the needs of those who were still poor and deprived and those who came after them. . . . But what now supports Jewish liberalism?"[7]

The mass migration to the suburbs that Jews participated in during the postwar years seemed to bolster these prognostications of an inevitable decline in Jewish liberal values. Upwardly mobile Jews sought a standard of living that reflected their growing affluence and reflected their increased social acceptance. Suburbia offered these young, prosperous Jews the spacious homes, quiet streets, and lush, green backyards that had become popular markers of middle-class status in the postwar decades. While Americans of all stripes purchased suburban homes during the postwar years, Jewish suburbanization outpaced that of other Americans. An estimated two-thirds of American Jewry settled in the suburbs by 1960, as opposed to only one-third of the overall American population. In some areas, Jews moved to the suburbs in even greater concentrations than the national average. By 1959, for instance, 85 percent of the Jewish residents of Cleveland, Ohio, lived in the outlying areas of Shaker Heights, University Heights, Cleveland Heights, East Cleveland, and Euclid. And while the overall population of Long Island's Nassau County increased by 220 percent between 1940 and 1960, the Jewish population increased by an overwhelming 1,770 percent.[8]

Liberal Jewish leaders commonly blamed the suburban environment for leading Jews away from their political convictions. They were convinced by the "conversion hypothesis," a theory advanced by political scientist Robert C. Wood in 1958, which predicted that newcomers to suburbia would sever their old ties to left-leaning candidates and, in concert with their new neighbors, vote for the more conservative candidates of the Republican Party. Wood followed the conventional wisdom of the era, which assumed that the upwardly mobile residents of suburbia were more concerned about social status and pleasing the people around them than about individual integrity or political principles. Left-of-center politics, argued Wood, would remind new suburbanites, uncomfortably, of the working-class and ethnic backgrounds that they were eager to leave behind.[9]

Postwar records of suburban voting patterns, however, showed that instead of "converting" to the Republican party, new suburbanites tended to retain the political affiliations that they had known in the city. This trend certainly applied to Queens County, a suburban borough of New York City, in the 1952 local elections. That year, the areas of the county that had been settled before the war voted solidly Republican. In the districts where the newer, often Jewish, migrants had made their homes, the Democratic party dominated. Some of these new suburban votes even went to candidates in the Liberal and American Labor parties that leaned farther to the left than the Democrats. In the experience of essayist and author Sylvia Rothchild, the Jews who moved to her adopted suburban hometown of Sharon, Massachusetts, transformed local politics, causing the Democratic party to grow so large that it "disturb[ed] a predominantly Republican town which was once able to count up its dissenters without any trouble."[10]

On the national stage as well, American Jews continued to vote overwhelmingly for the candidates of the Democratic Party during the postwar years. In 1952, when the very popular Republican candidate Dwight D. Eisenhower ran for president against Democrat Adlai Stevenson, 77 percent of American Jews voted for Stevenson as opposed to 44 percent of the general population. When Eisenhower faced Stevenson once again in 1956, 75 percent of Jews continued to choose the Democratic candidate, though he garnered only 42 percent of the overall vote.[11]

In spite of these trends, liberal rabbis such as Albert Gordon and Harold Saperstein continued to agonize over whether American Jews would continue to uphold their political ideals once they settled into the middle-class, suburban milieu. They feared that suburban Jews, unwilling to risk their comfortable homes or social standing, would remain silent on such touchy issues as separation of church and state and racial integration in order to avoid conflict with their new, affluent, and often politically conservative, non-Jewish neighbors. Suburban Jews refrained "from taking any action or making any statement . . . not conforming to the mores of the larger community," claimed Albert Gordon, himself a pulpit rabbi in the suburb of Newton, Massachusetts.[12] Similarly, Rabbi Harold Saperstein, who had earlier applauded the Jewish tendency to maintain liberal ideals even as they grew more affluent, devoted his 1964 Rosh Hashanah sermon to encouraging his suburban constituents to pursue their politics openly and without fear of reprisal: "A question of church and state comes up—religion in the public schools. We feel

Upward Mobility and Jewish Political Identity

deeply about it. We're convinced that right is on our side. But the advocates of caution are quick to be heard." He urged the members of his Long Island congregation to base their political commitments on their sense of justice rather than on their fear of what their public activism would do "to the Jewish image in the eyes of the community."[13]

Echoing the tone of these rabbis, some of the Jews who wrote about their experience of moving to the suburbs reported that the culture of suburbia squelched the activist ethos and intellectual fervor that had animated the working-class urban enclaves of their youth. Nostalgia for the urban neighborhoods to which they never intended to return made the cultural gap seem even wider. For instance, Harry Gersh, a former leftist and labor activist who had lived in Greenwich Village and marched in May Day parades in the 1930s, moved to the suburbs upon his return to civilian life at the close of World War II. In a 1954 article for *Commentary*, Gersh described the contradictions of his comfortable, middle-class, suburban lifestyle. On the one hand, he gloried in his pleasant relationships with his neighbors, his spacious home and soft, green lawn, in his sense of effectiveness in small-scale local politics, even in the new, liberal-minded, group of friends that he found in his new hometown. But unlike some of his peers who "laughed off" their radical pasts, Gersh remained sympathetic to the "sound and decent values" that he had fought for in his youth. Now living among the "class enemies" that he had once struggled against so passionately, Gersh remained plagued by a sense that he had betrayed his former political convictions. "We now know (hope anyway) that the class enemy isn't the enemy we thought," wrote Gersh. "Sometimes we wonder."[14]

This feeling of disappointment over the supposed lack of an activist culture in the suburbs did not emerge only among former leftists like Gersh. Sylvia Rothchild, who often insisted that she belonged in the quiet, leafy suburbs and far away from the noise and squalor of her childhood home in Brooklyn, still complained about the lack of political and intellectual vigor among suburban Jews. She reported that the suburb in which she lived provided "no haven for serious people" and that its Jewish inhabitants used "words like 'serious,' 'cultural,' 'intellectual,' and even 'Jewish'" in a "derogatory sense" and refused to attend any activities that could be described in those terms. Instead, as Rothchild saw it, the Jewish inhabitants of her suburb valued middle-class sociability over political and intellectual pursuits. As someone who had been heavily involved in Zionist groups during her urban youth, she responded with dismay when representatives of the local Hadassah chapter informed her that "there were only a few people in the organization who were really concerned about Zionism" and that most participants joined the group only for social reasons.[15]

In his 1957 *From the Dark Tower*, novelist and biographer Ernst Pawel added to the chorus of critics who accused middle-class, suburban Jews of stifling their political convictions. Described by *New York Times* reviewer David Dempsey as one of the many books of the era that grappled with the problems of Whyte's *Organization Man* but with a "unique," Jewish "twist," *From the Dark Tower* leveled one of the most scathing invectives against the supposed political and social conformity of suburban Jews. Pawel drew inspiration for the novel from his own life experiences as a public relations executive at an insurance company and a resident of the Jewish suburban enclave of Great Neck, New York. It followed Abe Rogoff, a former leftist intellectual who settled down to a stable job at an insurance firm and a comfortable home in the fictitious suburb of Samaria Beach. As long as he made the effort to fit into the social and political life of the town, the members of his suburban community overlooked his past exploits as a revolutionary. After his boss committed suicide, however, Rogoff decided that he had abandoned too many of his principles in order to fit in with his company and his community. He angered Jewish and non-Jewish suburbanites alike by calling the town's plan for Civilian Defense against atomic bombs a farce, and then defending a local schoolteacher in danger of being fired for his Communist beliefs. In the end, having become a social pariah, he triumphantly escaped suburbia to become a local reporter in the Rocky Mountains. The novel represented, in the words of reviewer Harold Ribalow, the triumph of the protagonist's "Jewish morality" over the "goddess of success."[16]

In *From the Dark Tower*, Pawel painted the Jewish institutions of suburbia as primary agents of social conformity. The local rabbi and the members of the synagogue's men's club felt particularly threatened by the protagonist's unpopular political stances. Insisting that his renegade public actions threatened the welfare of the Jews of Samaria Beach, they offered Rogoff $50,000 to sell his house and move to another town. Real suburban rabbis, some of whom exhorted their congregants to a more confrontational political activism, bristled at Pawel's unflattering portrayal of their vocation. *From the Dark Tower*, complained Rabbi Harold Saperstein, "made the rabbi and synagogue represent the forces of conformity. . . . I do not agree." Instead, he hoped that the popularity of the synagogue in suburbia would lead to "dynamic change and creative development."[17]

In contrast to the picture painted by their critics, however, instances certainly arose in which suburban Jews took up the struggle for liberal causes when they moved to their new communities and refused to back down from their principles even when it caused tension with their non-Jewish neighbors. The separation of church and state emerged as an issue that raised the ire of many suburban Jews, especially as their children began to attend suburban public schools dominated by Christian students. While many suburban Jewish parents objected vehemently when the public schools required their children to recite the Lord's Prayer and participate in the school Christmas pageant, they also did not want their children to face social ostracism from their peers and disapproval from their teachers if they refused to participate.

At times, these suburban parents publicly challenged the Christian prayers and practices endorsed by their children's public schools. A not uncommon controversy erupted in Plainview, Long Island, in 1957, when Jewish parents objected to a school policy statement defending the inclusion of Christmas parties, nativity scenes, crosses and carols within the public-school curriculum. At a town meeting, a local rabbi tried to explain the position of the parents to a hostile audience of five hundred townspeople and was faced with heckling, boos, and antisemitic slurs. Letters in the local newspaper accused resident Jews of being "atheists" and "no-good communists." In the end, however, the Jewish faction succeeded in removing the overtly religious symbols, such as Nativity scenes and crosses, from their children's public education.[18]

Plainview did not represent the only suburb in which Jewish residents clamored for the separation of church and state, in spite of the disapprobation of some of their neighbors. In 1961 Jewish Telegraphic Agency reporter Boris Smolar offered a survey of the tensions that had surfaced in suburban communities when Jewish residents objected to Christmas celebrations being held in their children's public schools. "Neighbors, once friends, are not speaking to each other. . . . Children are warned against playing with other children whose parents clashed over the presentation of a Nativity play in public school," he noted. In some suburbs, according to Smolar's report, Jewish residents even called for a public meeting of "lay leaders from each church and synagogue in town, together with school officials," in which they "thrashed out their points of view frankly and vigorously," a tactic that he claimed had worked successfully to ease some of the bitterness that these conflicts had generated. Confronting violations of the separation between church and state, rather than tolerating them in deference to the Christian majority, seemed to be the order of the day for many suburban Jews in the postwar years.[19]

The suburban parents who struggled against the Christian customs that pervaded their local public schools acted in concert with national Jewish organizations such as the American Jewish Congress, which often took a leading role in the court cases that dealt with the separation of church and state. Lawyers from the American Jewish Congress became principal strategists in landmark Supreme Court cases like *McCollum v. Board of Education* (1948), which declared it unconstitutional for public schools to set aside "released time" for religious instruction; *Engel v. Vitale* (1962), which proclaimed it unconstitutional to require public school students to recite prayers composed by state officials; and *Abington v. Schempp* (1963), which made it illegal to require public school students to recite from the Bible. Indeed, Jewish organizational support for these cases proved so intensive and so public that, even though other, nonsectarian agencies like the American Civil Liberties Union had also played significant roles, critics tended to associate these cases with Jewish organizations alone. In fact, the editors of *America*, a Catholic newspaper that was opposed to the court's decisions, warned postwar Jews that their investment in this issue would certainly lead to antisemitism: "We wonder ... whether it is not time for provident leaders of American Judaism to ask ... whether what is gained through the courts by such victories is worth the breakdown of community relations which will inevitably follow them."[20]

Significantly, although leaders of the Jewish organizations believed strongly in the separation of church and state, they often proved more cautious about bringing these cases to court than some of the suburban Jews who were neither the leaders of defense organizations nor legal experts, but who nonetheless objected to the inclusion of Christian practices in their children's schools. No Jewish organization followed up with a complaint filed by a rabbi in West Hempstead, Long Island, regarding the practice of observing a period of silent prayer in his town's public schools, because the organizational leaders did not feel that the case would lead to a significant court victory. And the American Jewish Congress did not, at first, offer its support to the plaintiffs of the *Engel v. Vitale* case, which consisted of five parents from Long Island's New Hyde Park, all of whom were Jewish by descent though one defined himself as an atheist and another had joined a Unitarian church. Though the American Jewish Congress later reconsidered and did throw its weight behind the plaintiffs, the organization's legal department had initially shied away from *Engel* on the suspicion that the courts would find the state-sponsored prayer to which the parents had objected to be nonsectarian and innocuous. Indeed, the suburban Jewish plaintiffs, less aware of the legal intricacies underlying these cases and more idealistically devoted to the principle of the separation of church and state, proved bolder than the Jewish organizations in challenging laws that they believed to be unjust.[21]

Upward Mobility and Jewish Political Identity

While the separation between church and state occupied the attentions of many liberal Jewish leaders, no political issue ignited their passions more than civil rights. Support for the civil rights movement emerged as an essential component of postwar Jewish liberalism. Many postwar Jews supported civil rights not only out of concern for black Americans but also because they believed that Jews' own interests depended on a society free of racial prejudice. Jews also experienced discrimination in housing and employment in the United States, though not to the same extent as blacks. As many Jewish activists saw it, racists and antisemites were more often than not the same people, and it served the advantage of both Jews and blacks to fight discrimination and exclusion. "It is not always the same race, color, or creed that is subjected to abuse," observed Isaac Toubin, associate director of the American Jewish Congress, in 1953. "But this abuse, no matter what its target, always poses the identical threat to the achievement of a peaceful and just communal life."[22]

Of course, the civil rights coalition between blacks and Jews had never been as seamless as its promoters believed it to be. Most American Jews, after all, enjoyed the privileges of white skin and its related economic advantages, and many proved unwilling to risk these benefits for the sake of racial equality. Certainly, most Jews who lived in the south, no matter their personal beliefs, never felt secure enough in their own standing to overtly challenge the line separating blacks from whites. Even among some northern Jews, the feelings of solidarity with African Americans began to wear thin over the course of the postwar period, especially in the 1960s as the civil rights movement moved northwards and challenged the successful, and all-white, neighborhood public schools used by many Jews in northern cities.[23]

Even when we take these tensions into consideration, however, Jewish support for civil rights proved unique, significant, and widespread during this period, with both Jewish individuals and Jewish organizations playing substantial roles in the struggle. The many individual Jews involved in the civil rights movement included those who participated outside the auspices of the organized Jewish community, as well as those who represented Jewish communal and religious organizations. Although Jews constituted only 3 percent of the American population at the time, they made up an estimated two-thirds of the white freedom riders in 1961, and one-third of the white student volunteers who traveled to Mississippi for the freedom summer voter registration campaign of 1964. Prominent Jewish individuals active in the movement included Bella Abzug, who in 1950 tried to defend Willie McGee, an African American man who had been falsely accused of raping a white woman, and Andrew Goodman and Michael Schwerner, two activists murdered in Mississippi in the freedom summer of 1964. Jewish theologian Abraham Joshua Heschel walked alongside Reverend Martin Luther King Jr. during the march from Selma to Birmingham in 1965, and Rabbi Joachim Prinz, president of the American Jewish Congress, equated his own experiences in Hitler's Germany with the plight of African Americans when he delivered a speech at the 1963 March on Washington.[24]

Jewish organizations also mobilized in support of civil rights during this period. The American Jewish Congress, in particular, invested heavily in the legal battles against race-based segregation, and employed more civil rights lawyers on its staff than did the Justice Department during these years. The extent of the cooperation between the American Jewish Congress and the NAACP was such that in 1947 the two groups shared briefs, reports, and confidential project notes along with monthly luncheons at the American Jewish Congress offices.[25]

Jewish and African American organizations worked in tandem to combat segregation in every aspect of American life, targeting the beaches, restaurants, housing developments, and sports leagues that continued their restrictive policies. In 1950, for instance, the Minnesota Jewish Council, aided by the Anti-Defamation League and the American Jewish Congress, successfully integrated a local beach. In 1946, in coalition with the United Public Workers of America, the NAACP, and the Civil Rights Congress, the American Jewish Congress sued restaurants in Atlantic City, New Jersey, that had refused to serve African Americans attending the United Public Workers' annual convention. And beginning in 1947, the United Auto Workers, NAACP, and the Anti-Defamation League launched a widespread campaign using advertisements, legal pressure, and picketing to desegregate the American Bowling Congress, which voted to end its whites-only policy in 1950.[26]

Many of the Jewish leaders who spearheaded and supported this investment in civil rights believed that Jewish experiences of marginalization and exclusion made it imperative for American Jews to fight against discrimination targeting any other minority group. But the Jewish migration to suburbia, which occurred simultaneously with an influx of African Americans into neighborhoods once dominated by Jews, made these liberal leaders suspect that American Jews lacked dedication to the cause. They watched in horror as Jewish urbanites seemed panicked to sell their homes rather than live in a mixed-race area. According to Marvin Braiterman, a Baltimore attorney and a leader of the Reform Movement's National Commission on Social Action, the migration of Jews to affluent, racially homogeneous suburbs constituted a "moral disaster." Liberal leaders of American Jewry began to suspect that the Jewish dedication to the civil rights movement, a commitment that they viewed as the only authentically Jewish response to racial injustice, amounted to little more than lip service.[27]

As urban Jews began their migration to the suburbs, liberal rabbis, educators, and communal professionals faced the often wrenching decision of whether to follow their constituents and move their synagogues to new suburban locales, or instead to remain in their urban surroundings. To relocate these institutions just as African Americans entered the neighborhood seemed to them a betrayal not only of the less affluent Jews who could not easily afford to move to the suburbs but also of their commitment to racial integration and civil rights. Those who remained in the city, however, faced the prospect of dwindling membership and the resulting loss of dues and resources necessary to sustain their functions and services.

The breakdown of the Jewish enclave that once thrived in Boston's Dorchester neighborhood may be one of the most dramatic, and certainly one of the most studied, cases of an urban Jewish neighborhood that did not survive the transformations of the postwar period. In the early and mid-1950s, when some Jews in the neighborhood had only just started to move to outlying suburbs, the leaders of two of Dorchester's Jewish schools and three of its synagogues calculated that the area would soon be bereft of Jews and announced plans to move to the burgeoning suburbs of Brookline and Newton. As local Jews followed the institutions upon which they depended, the predictions of these leaders became self-fulfilling prophesies that hastened the dissolution of their community. The Dorchester neighborhood changed rapidly as these institutions left the area. In 1950, more than fifty-thousand Jews lived in walking distance of Mishkan Tefila, the most prominent Conservative synagogue in the area. By 1960, two years after Mishkan Tefila moved to Newton, only seventy-five hundred Jews remained in its vicinity. Over the course of that one decade, the area changed from being two-thirds white to 71 percent black.[28]

Even though Jews migrated en masse to the suburbs, they did not necessarily relinquish their political or even material ties to the city. As Lila Corwin Berman has demonstrated in her study of postwar Detroit, postwar American Jews often nurtured a "metropolitan" identity that emphasized the connections between city and suburb. Some, like Detroit's Temple Beth El, encouraged suburban constituents to drive to the urban core when they wanted to access religious services. Other congregations that could afford to do so maintained both suburban and urban synagogue buildings. To give just one example, the leaders of Congregation Rodeph Shalom, a Reform

Temple located in North Philadelphia, refused to sell their urban edifice as their constituents left for the suburbs. Instead, in 1949, they opted to build a suburban extension in Elkins Park, Pennsylvania, to serve the everyday needs of their congregants. The congregation retained its North Philadelphia location for formal events, interreligious "goodwill" services, and urban-outreach programs that served the growing African American population of North Philadelphia.[29]

The rabbis of the Brooklyn Jewish Center, an urban congregation affiliated with the Conservative movement, tried to stem the tide of Jewish migrants from Brooklyn to Long Island by appealing to their liberal sentiments and their commitments to civil rights. In a 1952 discussion session on the topic of "changing neighborhoods," Associate Rabbi Benjamin Kreitman informed the group that the rapid demographic shifts in this area occurred because "the Jews who brought the idea of brotherhood into the world have not been able to apply these principles into their own community relations." He argued that if Jews had been more serious about ideals of integration and equality—principles that, he believed, Jews themselves had invented—their neighborhood would have been more stable and the survival of the congregation less precarious.[30]

Rabbi Israel H. Levinthal, the senior rabbi of the Brooklyn Jewish Center, also begged his congregants not to leave the area in order to avoid living side by side with new, African American residents. "I, too, have noticed an exodus on the part of some of our people and, to be very frank with you, it has pained me greatly," he wrote in a letter to a constituent, later reprinted in the congregational newsletter. He insisted that he had no issues with congregants who moved to the suburbs for what he called "valid reasons," such as a desire for more living space, a driveway, and a leafy backyard. But he felt a sense of "indignation" when Jews left the neighborhood to avoid living among black neighbors, "because we then become guilty of that very offense for which we blame others when it affects us."[31]

Rabbi Levinthal's belief that some of his congregants had what he considered "valid" reasons for their migration to the suburbs underscores the intertwined nature of racial prejudice and upward mobility during this period. Presumably, even a committed liberal like Levinthal would have thought it reasonable for one of his constituents to move because they wanted the quiet streets, velvety lawns, and spacious living rooms that only suburbia could offer, even if these areas officially or unofficially excluded racial minorities. Levinthal harbored no resentment against congregants who moved to all-white areas, as long as they did not move specifically because these neighborhoods excluded blacks. But at a time when middle-class lifestyles linked so closely to white-skin privilege, liberal Jews could not always tell where upward mobility ended and racism began.

Jewish leaders at the time debated whether the move to suburbia indicated a Jewish eagerness to "escape" racial tensions or whether racial segregation represented an unfortunate but inevitable result of their upward mobility. When Marvin Braiterman accused suburban Jews of "escapism" in 1959, for instance, Rabbi Albert I. Gordon rushed to their defense. "There are many . . . more important reasons why Jews began moving to the suburbs . . . [such as] the increasing number of marriages, larger families, changing housing needs, improved economic income, better transportation and the desire for improved status," he argued during a speech of the forty-sixth annual meeting of the Anti-Defamation League. Like Levinthal, Gordon refused to castigate suburban Jews for migrating to racially exclusive suburbs, as long as economic mobility, rather than racism, motivated their move.[32]

But while Gordon excused American Jews for moving to racially homogeneous suburbs, other liberal Jewish leaders proved less forgiving. Albert Vorspan, who founded the Reform Movement's Commission for Social Action in 1953 and would serve as its director for the next forty years, berated suburban Jews for retreating from the racial crisis. "Jews, carrying their synagogues on their backs, have long since fled from these seamy problems [of racial integration] to the nirvana of monochromatic homogenized neighborhoods in the middle- and upper-class reaches of suburbia," he railed. Unlike Levinthal and Gordon, Vorspan did not exempt suburban Jews from their moral and ethical responsibility to fight for civil rights simply because they did not live in neighborhoods where those tensions had surfaced most acutely; indeed, he viewed involvement in this struggle as a Jewish imperative. "We cannot delude ourselves into thinking that our smug suburbs will ride out the tornado of racial change whipping through the world. They won't," he warned. And those who were content to remove themselves from struggles for racial justice, he added, should "cleanse [their] prayer books of those words like justice and brotherhood" and "stop pretending to be Jews."[33]

Other Jewish leaders joined Vorspan in castigating middle-class, suburban Jews for professing support for racial justice but being unwilling to make personal sacrifices to achieve it. When sociologist Marshall Sklare revealed preliminary findings from his study of the Jews of Highland Park, Illinois, a wealthy suburb of Chicago, he found that one-half of his informants considered it an "essential moral affirmation" to work "for the equality of Negroes," and an additional third deemed it highly important. However, in spite of these stated beliefs, Sklare found little evidence that those suburban Jews had made any practical effort to assist African Americans in purchasing homes in their all-white neighborhood. Sklare's findings horrified Rabbi Arnold Jacob Wolf of Congregation Solel, Highland Park's most politically active Reform synagogue. "Can we escape the conclusion" that a typical Jew in our area "is likely to be a rich, important, liberal—hypocrite?" wondered Wolf in his congregational bulletin.[34]

Wolf felt, quite keenly, the uncomfortable dissonance of being a liberal leader who lived and worked in a racially segregated, affluent suburb. Upon being offered the James M. Yard Brotherhood Award of the National Conference of Christians and Jews, Wolf wryly noted, "I acknowledge with pride that I have, indeed, spent some fifteen hours last year in the Negro ghetto of Chicago, that I have signed four petitions and joined three boards." However, he continued, "I still live in [the suburb of] Winnetka and the only colored person I see regularly is my cleaning woman (I wonder what she would think of the award!)" Along with other liberal Jewish leaders, Wolf suspected that his own middle-class lifestyle, imbricated in long-standing legacies of racial discrimination, compromised his commitment to social justice.[35]

While most suburban Jews were not forced to grapple with the severe racial tensions that embroiled their urban counterparts, the suburban environment did not entirely isolate them from issues of racial integration. In a few cases suburban Jews even braved censure and assault from racist neighbors as they welcomed African Americans into their once segregated neighborhoods, and liberal Jewish rabbis delighted in showcasing these exceptional instances. In one well-publicized example, Jews in Levittown, Pennsylvania, defended an African American couple, William and Daisy Myers, who sought to move to their community in 1957. The local Jewish Community Council released a public, written statement welcoming the Myers into their town, and Jewish residents continued to support them even after segregationists painted Ku Klux Klan symbols on the home of a Jewish family that had befriended the couple. "These Jews in Levittown were really practicing the teachings of our great religion," declared Rabbi Earl S. Star of Philadelphia's Congregation Rodeph Shalom in his congregational newsletter. And Rabbi Albert Gordon, in his study of Jewish suburbia, cited this incident as a hopeful sign that suburban Jews "may ultimately . . . take the lead in the fight against social inequities and in behalf of civil rights."[36]

But few suburban Jews had the opportunity to prove their commitment to civil rights through such dramatic showdowns. Many of their communities simply did not become racially integrated during the postwar period; in others, African Americans moved in without fanfare, prompting little reaction from residents, Jewish or otherwise. This, for instance, is what happened in Winnetka, Illinois, in 1963, when a black librarian quietly moved into town. "We had a drink and a talk and that is probably the way the whole thing really ends," explained Rabbi Wolf. "Someone will move in, and you will mix a martini and lend a lawnmower. But the Kingdom of God . . . will be a step closer."[37]

While most middle-class suburban Jews were content to profess support for civil rights without doing much to achieve it, a few, particularly religious leaders and students, traveled South from their middle-class communities in order to engage more directly in the struggle. When these Jewish activists talked about their experiences, some cited their dissatisfactions with the middle-class suburban milieu as an element that pushed them southward. When Albert Vorspan reported on the activities of a group of rabbis who traveled to St. Augustine, Florida, to participate in a civil rights sit-in, he mentioned that the rabbis had been drawn south partly out of "escapism" from the "antiseptic middle-class establishment of synagogue life." In Vorspan's estimation, these rabbis had wanted to participate directly in the civil rights struggle rather than preach to cautious board members and congregants who may have believed in racial equality but seemed reluctant to make sacrifices or change their behavior in order to bring it about.[38]

Ellen Lake, a student at Radcliffe who had been raised in the affluent Westchester suburbs of New York, also felt that the activist community in Mississippi modeled a set of ideals different from and more authentic than what her suburban Jewish community had to offer. "In the freedom struggle I found the only real thing that I could see in our society," she explained while participating on a panel of Jewish activists in 1965. "People who I've grown up with have standards mainly of incomes and money and a very shallow type of success, I didn't see really anything to be proud of in this kind of Judaism and in going to Mississippi I found a great deal to be proud of."[39]

As Jewish liberals worried that economic security would squelch the political passions of American Jews, Jews farther to the left of the liberal majority may have had the most difficult time adapting to the transformations of upward mobility. It proved a struggle for Jewish leftists to accept the new, middle-class status of a growing majority of American Jews. After all, in the immigrant era, even though most Jews had never been official members of the Socialist Party, the strong influence of the Jewish labor movement and the enormous popularity of the Yiddish-language, socialist *Forward* newspaper had worked quite effectively to develop a robust, working-class consciousness among American Jews. Later, during the depression of the 1930s, a small yet vocal Communist contingent also had an important, if controversial, influence on Jewish political sensibilities.[40]

During the postwar years, Jewish leftists saw their institutions weaken and their influence wane. In the early decades of the twentieth century, Jewish socialists and Communists had built a dynamic infrastructure of secular Jewish institutions that included newspapers, labor organizations, Yiddish schools, camps, resorts, cultural programs, and cooperatives that provided housing and insurance. At the end of World War II, about fifty thousand American Jews still belonged to the Jewish People's Fraternal Order, a mutual-benefit organization sympathetic to Communism. The group provided low-cost health insurance for its members, sponsored Yiddish schools and a children's summer camp called Camp Kinderland, and offered financial backing to Jewish-Communist newspapers like *Jewish Life* and the Yiddish-language *Freiheit*. Even after the New York State Department of Insurance forced the Jewish People's Fraternal Order to cease its role as an insurance broker because of its political affiliations, the organization, which split into men's and women's divisions called the Jewish Cultural Clubs and Societies and the Emma Lazarus Foundation of Jewish Women's Clubs in the early 1950s, continued to support its aging membership through cultural activities, demonstrations, and social events.

Thousands of non-Communist Jewish socialists, somewhat protected from the McCarthyist investigations that targeted their Communist rivals, also belonged to the Workmen's Circle fraternal organization, which offered its members insurance and cultural activities. They sent their children to the Workmen's Circle Yiddish-language "folk" schools and to its summer camp, Camp Kinderring. They also continued to read the venerable *Forward* newspaper, still in operation as a Yiddish-language daily.[41]

These institutions on the Jewish left saw their membership age and their overall numbers dwindle during the postwar years. Between 1946 and 1958, for instance, the proportion of American Jewish children studying in secular, leftist Yiddish schools declined by half, leaving those schools to serve less than 2 percent of the overall population of Jewish schoolchildren. How did Jewish leftists respond to these changes, and to a Jewish community that seemed to be abandoning radical—if not liberal—politics as they moved into the middle class?[42]

Certainly, many factors in addition to upward mobility contributed to the decline of the Jewish left in the postwar years. Disappointment with the Soviet Union, the nation that Jewish Communists had looked toward for political inspiration, represented one factor that led some Jews away from the left. While the Nazi-Soviet Pact of 1939 had already weakened the resolve of many Jewish Communists, Khrushchev's 1956 admission of Stalin's crimes, the "doctor's plot" that falsely accused Jewish physicians of murdering Soviet officials in 1952–53, and the discovery that thirteen prominent Yiddish poets, artists, and academics in the Soviet Union had been arrested in 1948 and murdered by Stalin in 1952, convinced others to break with the Left during the postwar era.[43]

Also contributing to the decline of the American Jewish Left was the terrifying anti-Communist investigations of the 1950s, which were believed by many American Jews to specifically target Jewish individuals, communities, and organizations. Though only a minority of the American Jewish population had ever been members of the Communist Party, more conservative Americans often linked the liberal causes espoused by mainstream Jewish organizations—such as civil rights and civil liberties—to Communist ideals. Finally, and most insidiously, the image of the Jew as a subversive Communist had long been a trope in antisemitic literature. It had appeared in the *Protocols of the Elders of Zion*, the 1903 Russian forgery that had popularized the notion of an international Jewish conspiracy for global domination; in Adolf Hitler's 1925 biography *Mein Kampf*; in the writings of American antisemites such as Henry Ford and Father Coughlin in the early part of the twentieth century; and in the statements of postwar antisemites like Congressman John Rankin of Mississippi, who claimed that "communism is Yiddish" and that "every member of the Politburo around Stalin is either Yiddish or married to one." The antisemitic slurs uttered by the rioters who attacked the left-wing attendees of a 1949 Paul Robeson concert in Peekskill, New York, along with the high-profile, 1953 execution of the Jewish couple Julius and Ethel Rosenberg on charges of spying for the Soviets, provided further reasons for American Jews to fear that non-Jewish Americans might associate Communism with Jewishness.[44]

While Senator Joseph McCarthy himself, the politician who spearheaded the anti-Communist investigations, tended to target mainline Protestants rather than Jews, anecdotal evidence indicates that both state and federal anti-Communist inquiries disproportionately focused their efforts on Jews. These investigations often left their subjects without careers, struggling for income, and ostracized by their friends and communities. In 1953, for instance, the U.S. Navy dismissed Jewish scientist Abraham Chasanow after antisemitic neighbors fabricated accusations that he had associations with Communists, though the Navy later apologized and reinstated him in 1954.

Every one of the New York City schoolteachers fired for security reasons during the Cold War was Jewish. And known antisemites infamously hijacked the 1950 Senate confirmation hearings of Anna M. Rosenberg, who had been nominated for the position of assistant secretary of defense, by falsely accusing her of being a former member of the Communist Party. Though she was subsequently cleared of the charges and confirmed by the Senate, the postwar wave of anti-Communism had produced a climate in which reputable government agencies took the rantings of antisemites seriously, as long as they were couched in the vocabulary of Cold War fears.[45]

In this climate of suspicion, mainstream Jewish organizations worked hard to dissociate themselves from Communism, sometimes compromising their support of civil liberties in the process. The American Jewish Committee and the Anti-Defamation League purged former Communists and Communist-sympathizers from their organizations, shared files with the Federal Bureau of Investigation and the House Un-American Activities Committee, and encouraged local Jewish community councils to expel left-wing groups from their ranks. Jewish organizations, including the American Jewish Congress, Hadassah, and the Federation of Jewish Philanthropies of New York all ended their relationships with the Social Service Employees Union that represented their clerical workers because of its alleged Communist ties. Undoubtedly, some of the people who made these decisions truly believed that Communists within the American Jewish community posed a threat to their organizations. More of them were apprehensive, with good reason, that a stronger stand in defense of the radical Jewish Left could have discredited their work on behalf of the liberal goals that fueled their political agenda. At worst, such a stance might have prompted the government to investigate or even dissolve the organizations in question, or it may have sparked a new wave of American antisemitism and compromised Jews' newfound security and acceptance. Supporting the Jewish Left in midst of a vehement wave of American anti-Communism presented risks that mainstream Jewish organizations proved unwilling to take.[46]

While disillusionment with the Soviet Union, government harassment, and the rejection of the mainstream Jewish community certainly weakened the American Jewish Left, many observers of postwar Jews believed that the upward mobility of American Jews, above and beyond any other factor, tore away at their political attachments. The middle-class affluence and social acceptance of postwar American Jews, they reasoned, made them less amenable to revolutionary or radical political changes that would put their newfound gains at risk. "The Jewish community, which had once been largely working

Upward Mobility and Jewish Political Identity

class," had become "almost entirely middle class," explained Nathan Glazer in 1957. "How could such a community maintain its attachment to . . . socialist, secular, Jewish movements?" Glazer, who himself had moved away from the radical politics of his youth before embarking upon a successful career as a sociologist and public intellectual, may have been commenting on his own political trajectory as much as on the choices of Jews in general.[47]

Those Jews who remained leftists, a group that included socialists, Communists, and "fellow travelers" who agreed with many of the ideals of Communism but did not officially join the party, felt particularly disoriented by the prosperity of the postwar years and the resulting changes in Jewish political expression. Though these Jewish leftists did not represent a unified group in any sense, and tensions between socialists and Communists had caused acrimony in Jewish leftist unions, schools, camps, and fraternal organizations since the 1930s, they nonetheless experienced a similar sense of unease regarding the growing affluence and middle-class orientation of American Jews. After all, many members of this avowedly secular contingent of Jews based their sense of Jewishness largely on being political and social outsiders rather than on the religious definitions that they so emphatically disavowed. Many saw their Jewish identities and their affiliation with the working class as inextricably intertwined.

As the income of secular Jewish leftists began to rise in the postwar years along with the earnings of other Americans, these activists struggled over the question of how to express themselves as Jews. Some of these Jewish radicals solved this identity crisis by modifying their political ideology, rethinking their wholesale rejection of the synagogue, and joining the liberal, anti-Communist consensus adopted by the majority of American Jews during the postwar years. Others, such as New York intellectual Irving Kristol, went so far as to embrace the Cold War and, eventually, neoconservative politics as they moved into the middle class. But those Jews determined to remain radicals faced a particular struggle over how to sustain a Jewish secular, leftist and working-class identity in postwar America.

The pages of *Jewish Life*, a Jewish-Communist newspaper that changed its name to *Jewish Currents* in 1956 after breaking with the official Communist Party, reveal the strategies used by some Jewish leftists to maintain their ethnic and class affiliations despite their changing economic circumstances.[48] In July 1952, for instance, the paper printed the unusual story of Abraham and Rebecca Perel, a professional couple who opted to rejoin the working class of their childhoods. Leaving behind their lucrative, postwar careers, they decided to pursue factory work in a New England mill town.

The Perels' return to the working class not only made them feel like more effective activists but also like better Jews. As Jewish members of the working class, they considered themselves to be in a particularly advantageous position to fight antisemitism among those working people who believed all Jews to be exploitive, middle-class manufacturers. They recounted with pride their resolution "never to let any anti-Semitic remarks go unchallenged" and noted incidents where they had the opportunity to tell their fellow workers about "the Jewish working people in our country . . . and how they are among the most outstanding fighters for the rights of working people." Eventually, they claimed, they managed to convince their coworkers that "making prejudiced remarks about different nationalities resulted in playing one worker against the other" and weakened the strength of the union.

As the Perels described their fight to end antisemitism among their fellow workers, they also insinuated that they served the Jewish community better than the Jews of the middle class. They felt disgusted by what they deemed to be the trivial concerns of the other Jews who lived in their small, New England town, who squabbled over "whether Reform or Orthodox Judaism" provided the best vehicle for being a "good Jew," and who were "astounded at the mere suggestion" that there was "any anti-semitism in the town." The Jewish middle class, they believed, had become not only spoiled by its money but also deluded as to the marginal position of Jews in the United States. The Perels insisted that their working-class lifestyle offered them a way, and perhaps the only way, to advance not only the class struggle but also the authentic political interests of American Jews.[49]

Certainly, most Jewish leftists did not follow the Perels in rejecting financial security once they achieved it. However, many continued to cling to their working-class identities long after their professional choices and achievements would have convinced most people of their middle-class status. In 1954, for instance, *Jewish Life* made the argument that Jewish white-collar professionals, including those in high-income careers such as doctors, dentists, and lawyers, were "little better off than workers" in terms of their economic security and outlook for the future. Though thin on evidence, the article nonetheless claimed that "the overwhelming majority of the Jewish people require a New Deal approach and not a Hoover-Eisenhower 'trickle-down' approach to meet the present economic problems," and placed even the most financially secure American Jews squarely into the coalition of people who would benefit from economic reform. While most Americans had come to classify themselves as middle class by the postwar years, even if they did not earn what was officially considered a "middle-class" salary, many Jewish leftists continued to consider themselves "working class," even as they enjoyed the economic prosperity of the postwar years. For these Jewish radicals, class identity had become more a matter of self-understanding than a reflection of profession, income, or any other measure of empirical evidence.[50]

Postwar Jews on the left also tended to emphasize the importance of those American Jews who remained in the working class and encouraged the many Jews who had made the upward climb to follow the political lead of those who had not. Readers exhorted *Jewish Life* and, later, *Jewish Currents* to continue writing for the "remaining plebians" in the Jewish community. "Jewish workers are still the only class in Jewish life capable of consistent, clear-sighted, militant policies in defense of the Jewish people as a whole," declared editor Morris Schappes. Other articles noted that the Jewish history of discrimination and prejudice made even those Jews of the middle class more amenable to radical politics, though they warned their readership that the activism of these affluent Jews might be limited to genteel, nonconfrontational organizational work rather than the grassroots resistance and direct action demanded by the working-class left.[51]

The anti-Communist Jewish Left, whose constituents vehemently rejected the Communist leanings of *Jewish Life* and largely affiliated with the Workmen's Circle fraternal order, struggled to attract new members among young, upwardly mobile Jews more likely to own factories than work in them. William Stern, then the National Director of the Workmen's Circle English-language division, was tasked with the job of convincing young Jews to join the organization. In a regular column in *The Call*, a magazine sponsored by the Workmen's Circle, he detailed the challenges of promoting socialism among a new generation of middle-class Jews: "The young man who dislikes being identified with 'workmen,' and the one who immediately thinks of communism when he hears the term 'workmen,' are more than likely not qualified intellectually or ideologically for Workmen's Circle membership," he admitted. But even those Jews who agreed with the political bent of the Workmen's Circle were, by midcentury, generally not workers themselves. "The worker of yesterday may today have become a business man [*sic*] or a professional," confessed Stern in 1957. "And the new member is only sometimes a working man. He is more likely what we would call middle class."[52]

Workmen's Circle leaders like William Stern strained to justify how an organization primarily made up of middle-class Jews could claim to function as a labor organization. Accepting that the upward mobility of American Jews was unlikely to end, he envisioned a Jewish labor movement in which "labor" referred to the sympathies, rather than the identities, of the constituents. For contemporary members of the Workmen's Circle, he explained to one confused interlocutor, "the term 'labor' is no longer meant in its literal and limited sense." He, along with other Jewish socialists, suggested that the Workmen's Circle must reorient itself to attend not to particularly Jewish causes but instead to universal issues of social justice from which midcentury Jews did not necessarily suffer. Partnering with other liberal and leftist organizations who specialized in these questions, they reasoned, ought to be a key component of the Workmen's Circle's future activities.[53]

Not all of the organization's members agreed that the mission of the Workmen's Circle ought not to prioritize the needs of Jews, even if those Jews happened to be middle class. "Are we content to see the Workmen's Circle as just an auxiliary of other liberal, socialist, or civil rights organizations?" asked Allen Flexser, a member of branch 1052. Instead, he maintained that the organization ought to do more to promote "our secular Jewish heritage" among members. Is Ginsberg from branch 1049 went so far as to suggest a "rapprochement" between the secular Workmen's Circle and religious Jewish groups, arguing that both constituencies could address the spiritual and ethical vacuity of the new generation of middle-class American Jews.[54]

For the many postwar Jews leaders who subscribed to a liberal, or, less often, a left-wing political ideology, upward mobility proved disorienting. Before the bulk of American Jewry had achieved financial security, and in the years when antisemitism had placed debilitating social and economic limitations upon American Jews, the political struggles of the underdog also advanced the economic and social interests of American Jews themselves. But as Jewish fortunes rose and antisemitism declined in the postwar years, it seemed that the material and social interests of American Jews might have been better served by a more conservative political stance. For all the significant differences between liberal and leftist Jewish leaders, they held in common a belief that American Jews were morally obligated to continue upholding the politics that supported the poor and disenfranchised. The increased economic profile of American Jews seemed to threaten this commitment.

For many of the postwar Jews staunchly committed to liberalism or the Left, the prospect that Jews would abandon left-of-center politics seemed unthinkable. For these Jews, political ideals did not necessarily exist separately from Jewish identity; rather, these beliefs constituted an integral part of what they believed made them Jewish. In their view, the upward mobility that challenged these ideas imperiled the very essence of Jewishness. As these activists defended liberal and leftist Jewish politics against the impact of upward

Upward Mobility and Jewish Political Identity

mobility, they felt themselves to be the protectors of Jewish authenticity and Jewish difference in a middle-class American culture that threatened to absorb it.

Postwar affluence challenged not only the ways that American Jews configured their political views, but also their relationship to the Jewish religion. We turn now to Jewish leaders who defined their Jewish identities primarily in religious terms, uncovering their concerns about how upward mobility transformed, and perhaps corrupted, American Judaism.

THREE

Pathfinders' Predicament

Negotiating Middle-Class Judaism

"We at Solel are proudly building a beautiful temple in which to pray," proclaimed Rabbi Arnold Jacob Wolf, the spiritual leader of Congregation Solel, in his congregational newsletter in 1962. In spite of Wolf's declaration of pride, however, the ensuing paragraphs of the newsletter revealed a strong sense of ambivalence regarding his congregation's construction project. "When it is ready . . . will we have forgotten what we built it for? Or will our Temple, like so many others of our time, be an empty monument, a spectacular frivolity?" Wolf wondered.[1]

Solel, a Reform Congregation in the suburb of Highland Park, Illinois, represented a somewhat unusual synagogue on the postwar American scene; in the words of Rabbi Wolf, it was "a Temple for people who didn't like Temples." Proudly nonconformist and critical of most of the other suburban synagogues of their day, the members of Solel endeavored to free their congregation from what they believed to be the problems endemic to middle-class American Judaism. Decrying their peer institutions as overly large, anonymous, and more concerned with wealth and social status than spiritual concerns, the members of Solel instituted regulations to distinguish themselves from other affluent postwar synagogues. They limited their membership to 425 families to encourage a sense of intimacy among congregants, disallowed social clubs such as sisterhoods and men's clubs in order to discourage distractions from religious pursuits, expected members to participate in their "experimental" prayer services and rigorous adult education seminars, and banned bar mitzvah celebrations that, members felt, had become ostentatious displays of wealth. Finally, while Solel had been an independent congregation since 1957, its members had initially balked at the prospect of

Exterior of Congregation Solel Building, 1963.
Courtesy of Congregation Solel, Highland Park, Illinois.

constructing their own synagogue building out of concern that such a project would detract from their religious mission. Wolf chose to name this maverick group of suburban worshipers "Solel," taken from the Hebrew word for "pathfinder" or "trailblazer," out of the conviction that they were paving the way for a new and more authentic Jewish congregational life in the prosperous postwar suburbs.[2]

This chapter details the widespread communal discomfort surrounding the religious culture of middle-class American Jews and the particular ways in which a self-consciously critical congregation like Solel responded to these concerns. While most postwar American congregations did not follow Solel in steeling themselves against the normative institutional patterns of affluent suburban synagogues, the anxieties articulated by Rabbi Wolf and his constituents reverberated widely among postwar American Jews and especially among the rabbinic leadership. After all, as American Jews benefited from the economic prosperity of the postwar years, they also placed, in the words of prominent Jewish intellectual Lucy Dawidowicz, "an unmistakable middle-class stamp on their . . . beliefs and observances." Long-accustomed to thinking of social exclusion and economic need as integral components of a genuine Jewish identity, American Jewish leaders did not necessarily feel comfortable with a postwar American Judaism that reflected acceptance and affluence rather than marginality and want.[3]

Rather than viewing the developing middle-class Jewish culture of the suburbs as evidence of vitality and devotion, rabbis often interpreted the innovations of postwar suburban Jews as proof of complacency and a lack of commitment. The spate of modern, air-conditioned synagogues cropping up in postwar suburbia and the lavish catered receptions that commemorated the bar mitzvah and other Jewish lifecycle events emerged as symbols for what seemed to be the superficiality and inauthenticity of Jewish life in midcentury America.

American Jewish rabbis—even those as celebrated for their iconoclasm as Solel's Arnold Jacob Wolf—played a contradictory role in these critical assessments of the religious culture of postwar American Jews. Even as they accused their constituents of corrupting Jewish life with an unseemly focus on money and status, rabbis invested deeply in the establishment of the new, and distinctly middle-class, Jewish culture being forged in postwar America. They depended on the higher salaries that their newly affluent congregants could offer them and helped raise funds for the synagogue structures in which they would conduct religious services and teach classes. Their critique of postwar American Judaism represented not just indictments from above but also self-censure from within.

The concerns of postwar rabbis over the spiritual health of postwar American Jews stood in contrast to their rising rates of religious affiliation. American Jews participated enthusiastically in what became known as the "religious revival," in which Americans of all backgrounds joined religious institutions in unprecedented numbers. While the nation's population grew by 19 percent in the 1950s, the number of people who affiliated with a church or synagogue increased by more than 30 percent. The U.S. government encouraged this popular upswing in religion as it disseminated Cold War rhetoric that pitted the "godless" Communists of the Soviet Union against god-fearing, and therefore presumably morally superior, Americans. For instance, President Eisenhower justified adding the words "under God" to the pledge of allegiance in 1954 by pointing to the "spiritual weapons" that Americans might wield against those "deadened in mind and soul by a materialistic philosophy of life." Eisenhower also afforded synagogue-goers an honored place alongside churchgoers within the camp of American believers, declaring in 1952 that "our form of government makes no sense unless it is founded in a deeply felt religious faith, and I don't care what it is." Although few American Jews articulated their decision to join a synagogue using Cold War arguments, one must nonetheless understand their tendency toward affiliation within a political climate that defined religious belief as an essential component of being American.[4]

While American Jews did not attend prayer services as regularly as their Christian counterparts, they, like other Americans, displayed skyrocketing levels of congregational membership during the postwar years. In the late 1950s, 60 percent of American Jews, or more than 3 million Jewish individuals, belonged to a synagogue, which represented the only time since the colonial period when more than half of American Jewry chose to affiliate. In 1956–57 alone, American Jews established twenty new Modern Orthodox synagogues, twenty new Reform synagogues, and forty-one Conservative synagogues. Moreover, as a 1956 study of Jews living in the Washington, D.C., area revealed, Jews proved more likely to affiliate with congregations as their incomes rose. It would seem that in this respect, upward mobility enhanced Judaism in America.[5]

In spite of the enthusiasm of newly prosperous Jews for synagogue membership, not all of their leaders believed in the legitimacy of this "religious revival." Like some Protestant thinkers, including Martin Marty, Peter Berger, and Gibson Winter, and some Catholic leaders such as Andrew M. Greeley, they questioned the depth of religious feeling that accompanied the revival. The Jewish critics, however, had additional and distinct reasons for doubting the value of the postwar upswing in religious affiliation. They contended that for American Jews, the conspicuous increase in religious affiliation signified an attempt to remake Judaism into something more recognizable and acceptable to the Christian majority and a means of fortifying Jews' own entry into the middle class. Increasing rates of involvement in the synagogue and its activities seemed to boil down to a crass attempt, as Julian Greifer of the National Association of Jewish Center Workers put it, to "look our Methodist neighbors in the eye."[6]

Jewish leaders who distrusted the religious revival often took their cues from sociologist Will Herberg. In his best-selling 1955 study *Protestant, Catholic, Jew*, Herberg contended that while middle-class Americans did not easily tolerate differences in language, politics, or dress, they welcomed variations in religious belief. Herberg therefore reasoned that as the descendants of European immigrants became ensconced into the middle-class mainstream, they tended to eschew those symbols of ethnic particularity that isolated them from the majority and turned instead to the socially acceptable arena of religion as the one way in which they continued to express their cultural particularity. According to Herberg, the quality of this religious revival grew increasingly "secularized," demoted to a utilitarian tool that would help its practitioners secure a middle-class status.[7]

In *Children of the Gilded Ghetto*, an influential 1961 sociological study of Jews in the Detroit area, Judith R. Kramer and Seymour Leventman applied Herberg's analysis more specifically to the Jewish case, accusing postwar Jews of degrading their religious practices as they sought admission into the middle class. Kramer and Leventman admitted that postwar Jews proved unlikely to relinquish their Judaism, as their religious affiliations did not "restrict their life chances" or threaten their financial status in any way. Still, the sociologists took little consolation in American Jews' continued commitment to their ancestral religion. Instead, they claimed that upwardly mobile Jews had modified their observances "in the direction of greater conformity to those of the dominant society" and, in the process, "reduced" these practices to "an occasional acknowledgement of synagogue and ritual." In their opinion, mid-century Jews may have continued to offer a nominal fealty to their religion, but the thin quality of their observances reflected their desire for success and acceptance rather than true commitment to Judaism. The result was a Judaism that included just enough ritual to "assuage the conscience," bled of authenticity and depth.[8]

This suspicion that religious affiliation signified little more than conformity to middle-class convention led postwar rabbis to dismiss the significance of their climbing synagogue membership rolls. In a 1957 article for *Congress Weekly*, Rabbi Charles Shulman, a Reform rabbi from Riverdale, New York, argued that suburban Jews regarded their synagogue affiliation as a "badge of respectability" aimed at impressing their churchgoing neighbors. For Shulman, this affiliation represented "the psychological tribute that the minority pays to the majority." This could not be, he added, "the most desirable form of Jewishness." Similarly, in a 1962 high holiday sermon, Conservative Rabbi Philip Lipis expressed amazement over the growth of new synagogues on Chicago's North Shore, but he warned his congregants against becoming "dazzled" by this expansion. Rather than being moved to the synagogue by a genuine interest in religion, Lipis charged that the suburban Jews of the North Shore flocked to the synagogue in "lamblike conformity" to the social mores of affluent suburbanites.[9]

The leaders of the maverick Congregation Solel, for their part, made the decision to restrict their congregational membership just as this communal critique of the "religious revival" reached its height. They, too, were suspicious of the notion that affiliation equaled commitment. Limiting their membership, according to a 1958 statement of the board of directors, enabled them to cultivate a "cohesive" congregation devoted to the specific, spiritual values of Solel rather than to the idea of belonging to a synagogue. Rabbi Wolf insisted that they needed to maintain a smaller congregation in order to "keep the members' needs visible and to keep the rabbi's services from becoming ludicrously theoretical." Dismissing critics who accused them of "snobbism," the leaders of Solel felt strongly that only a small and steadfast congregation would keep them from losing their "particular individual identity" and becoming "just another institution."[10]

For the many Jewish leaders who did not view high membership rolls as evidence of authentic religious commitment on the part of American Jews, the postwar building boom of new, large, and expensive suburban synagogues seemed nothing less than a grand farce. American Jews engaged in unprecedented levels of synagogue construction during the postwar years, building or rebuilding more than one thousand religious edifices between 1945 and 1965. From 1945 to 1950 alone, Jews spent between $500 million and $600 million on new synagogue structures, located mostly in the new Jewish communities mushrooming in suburbia. The editors of *The Reconstructionist* included themselves among the critics who denied that this building boom signaled a true commitment to religious ideals. Rather, they lamented that "so much of our [synagogue] growth reflects the general bourgeois character of suburbia, along with the specific weaknesses of Jewish religious and cultural life in America."[11]

Suburban congregations built their synagogues in the modern architectural styles popular at the time. These modern designs, which emphasized abstraction and simplicity, struck both supporters and detractors as utterly novel. In form and in function, these buildings contrasted sharply with the stately, neoclassical designs of 1920s-era urban synagogues, as well as with the modest, store-front synagogues that had been a ubiquitous part of the urban Jewish streetscape during the immigrant period.

Supporters of modernist architecture drew on sociological, aesthetic, and practical justifications for constructing their new suburban synagogues in this style. They lauded the simplicity of the new synagogue structures, their "clear, crisp lines," and the ways in which they harmonized with the small scale and low density of suburban building patterns. Architect Eric Mendelsohn, a refugee from Nazi Germany, contended that the "human scale" of modernist buildings would prove particularly adept at nurturing a democratic civil society where totalitarianism could not thrive. And when the Reform movement published a guidebook on new synagogue building in 1954, it recommended turning to modernist aesthetics specifically to differentiate the new institutions from the urban synagogues of the past and to emphasize their cutting-edge dynamism.[12]

Still, and in spite of the impassioned supporters of modern architecture, critics targeted every aspect of these new, postwar, suburban synagogues, from their design, to their interior decor, to the various recreational and educational facilities they housed. To many critics, these buildings simply did not feel like proper synagogues. Indeed, they disparagingly compared these synagogues to nonsacred structures, implying that the buildings imparted little of the feeling of sanctity normally associated with places of worship. In assessing the newly built synagogues of suburban Queens, for instance, *Commentary* magazine's Morris Freedman described one as "a great white building looking somewhat like a bank," and another as "reminiscent of a modern college auditorium—plain, high, out-thrust front with rows of steps leading up." Julian Greifer charged that the new synagogues being built outside Philadelphia resembled "suburban shopping centers in their modern, functional, and sprawling appearance." Rabbi Benjamin Kreitman of the Brooklyn Jewish Center summed up the debate as follows: "Is the mood and feeling of timelessness with which we approach faith and worship jarred by these contemporaneous designs, or do they help religion to keep in step with the times?"[13]

The comfort and modern amenities that characterized suburban tract houses also became a priority within the sanctuaries of suburban synagogues. Suburban congregations, wrote art historian and journalist Alfred Werner, demanded large windows "so that the prayerbook can be read without strain," "good acoustics so that the sermon can be heard," "comfortable pews," and a "seating arrangement such that the ceremonies . . . can be observed by every participant." Congregations bought their pews from companies like American Seating, which offered both "full-upholstered, folding, individual seats for greater comfort and convenience" as well as cushioned pews "equipped with arm-rests." They outfitted the sanctuary floors in wall-to-wall carpeting, hid speakers and microphones in the lecterns, and installed air conditioners, still considered an uncommon luxury in those years, to cool the sanctuary in the warmer months. They commissioned well-regarded modern artists to design the stained-glass windows, the arks that held the Torah scrolls, and the eternal light that shone above it.[14]

Congregations fashioned their new synagogues to accommodate not only their religious worship but also their social pursuits. Ballrooms, which provided an elegant setting for weddings, bar and bat mitzvahs, club meetings, and fundraising dinners, became a central feature of these structures, and fees for catering services often earned a significant proportion of a synagogue's yearly income. Congregations rarely spared any expense in their installation of these catering facilities. In his assessment of the social hall in a suburban Queens synagogue, for instance, Morris Freedman described a grand room "the size of a basketball court, and two stories high," which included a stage with "balconies, a small grand piano, curving metal staircases, and an elaborate switchboard" that controlled the public-address and lighting systems. Aside from the ballroom, this synagogue had also included a cloakroom, a stainless-steel professional kitchen, and a bride's room "with thick, flower-embossed carpeting, pink-and-silver-papered walls, a pink brocade sofa, and a combined vanity and sink covered with pink formica and topped by a big, professional dressing-room mirror." Critics found it incongruous that these synagogues devoted so much structural space to social rather than religious pursuits and questioned whether these ballrooms truly reflected the spirit of an authentic Judaism. "Who could imagine a ballroom adjoining the Altneuschul in Prague [a well-known synagogue dating back to the medieval period]?" mused Jewish architect Alfred Werner.[15]

Opponents of these newly constructed suburban synagogues denigrated them as "country clubs," charging that their social functions had entirely eclipsed their religious services.[16] Journalist and editor Ruth Gay argued that, instead of meeting the spiritual needs of American Jews, postwar suburban synagogues represented "secular monuments—symbolic of the prosperity and security of the Jewish community of America." While admitting that they offered their congregants a space in which to educate their children and raise money for worthy causes, Gay nonetheless insisted that true religious expression, which she defined as heartfelt prayer, remained "absent" from these synagogues' activities. Sociologist Nathan Glazer agreed, remarking that "the children almost certainly went to the school, the teen-agers very likely went to the dances, the women probably joined the sisterhood, the men possibly joined the brotherhood. And last—and the rabbi often asked himself if it was also not least—were the religious services, poorly attended by a core of old-timers and the merest scattering of young people."[17]

Wealthy postwar congregations literally built their low expectations for weekly worship attendance into their synagogue structures. Synagogue architects grappled with the dilemma of building an edifice that could accommodate the large groups who came to worship on the high holidays but did not feel cavernous and empty the rest of the year. Trude Weiss-Rosmarin, founder and editor of the *Jewish Spectator* magazine, reported on an architect who had devised a system of rollaway partitions and movable walls to add fourteen hundred extra seats to the main chapel when needed for the high holidays. For Rabbi Israel Levinthal of the Brooklyn Jewish Center, the sliding walls of these "new and expensive" sanctuaries represented a "sad commentary of the status of our religious life."[18] For some observers, these new and, as the editors of the *Reconstructionist* journal termed them, "schizoid" synagogues served as monumental, costly testimonies to the religious shortcomings of suburban Jews.[19]

Whether it took place on sparsely attended Sabbaths or the packed high holidays, rabbis and intellectuals agreed that the prayer Jews experienced in sumptuous, state-of-the-art postwar synagogues lacked the intangible "spirit" that they believed to be characteristic of a more authentic Judaism. This sentiment certainly ran through the writing of Lucy Dawidowicz, whose career as a journalist, historian, and public intellectual had been profoundly shaped by the year that she spent as a student of Jewish studies in Vilna between 1938 and 1939, just before the Nazi takeover. Upon her return, Dawidowicz often bemoaned a middle-class, American Jewish culture that, in her estimation, paled in comparison to what was lost in the Holocaust.[20]

For Dawidowicz, the amenities of postwar American synagogues detracted from the depth and meaning of the prayers that took place within them. In her 1960 description of the Conservative Jewish Center in Garfield Hills, a suburban section of Queens, New York, she had the following to say about the quality of the prayer that took place in these institutions: "Decorum prevails, in dress and manners. The service is marked by dignity and evokes a fairly high degree of participation during responsive readings and communal singing. Cantor, choir and organist provide some pleasant music." While enjoyable enough, Dawidowicz maintained that the services lacked *kavvanah*, the "direction, inspiration . . . [and] awareness of the meaning of prayer." To illustrate her point, she quoted Rabbi Abraham Joshua Heschel, the preeminent Jewish theologian of the postwar years, who in 1953 had offered a similar description of how postwar American Jews worshiped: "Our services are conducted with pomp and precision. The rendition of the liturgy is smooth. Everything is present: decorum, voice, ceremony. But one thing is missing: Life." For Heschel and Dawidowicz, both of whom nurtured deeply felt connections to the destroyed and decidedly less prosperous Jewish communities of Eastern Europe, social integration and middle-class manners had drained American Judaism of its lifeblood.[21]

Conservative Rabbi Samuel Schafler agreed with Heschel and Dawidowicz that the comforts of the new postwar synagogues, with their cushioned seats and air conditioning, prevented Jews from experiencing genuine worship and repentance. In the pages of *Mas'at Rav*, a booklet distributed to rabbis and other Jewish professionals by the Rabbinical Assembly of the Conservative movement, he crafted one of the most searing rabbinical condemnations of suburban synagogues:

> An elderly Jewish woman finally agreed to listen to the pleadings of her children and came for the holidays to worship with them in their new suburban synagogue. Her children very proudly pointed out all the beauties and glories of their new synagogue. And they asked their mother what she thought of their synagogue's striking and beautiful architecture, what did she think of the wonderfully comfortable seats, and the air conditioning, and the marvelous hazan [cantor], and the eloquent Rabbi, and, of course, the mother agreed that all was really very beautiful indeed. She had but one minor comment: *Alles is shein, ober men ken nisht vainen dorten* [Everything is pretty, but a person cannot cry there].[22]

For Schafler, the creature comforts incorporated into postwar synagogues prevented worshippers from engaging in serious contemplation and atonement for their misdeeds. Tellingly, Schafler delivered his message through the conceit of an elderly Jewish woman who had refrained from moving to the suburbs along with her upwardly mobile children. Indeed, elderly Jews proved more likely to remain in urban areas in the postwar years after their children migrated to the suburbs, and less likely to adopt the trappings of a middle-class lifestyle. In the imagination of rabbis like Schafler who criticized the religious practices of the Jewish *nouveau riche*, elderly Jews seemed inclined toward earlier, presumably more authentic iterations of Judaism. They would not be able to find what they were looking for in the sumptuous synagogues of suburbia.[23]

What Rabbi Schafler left unspoken in his critique of the suburban synagogue, however, is how he might have characterized his own participation in the postwar Judaism that he found so wanting. After all, Schafler's own congregation, Temple Gates of Prayer in Flushing, New York, had completed its synagogue building in 1960, just a few years before the publication of his heart-wrenching anecdote. Temple Gates of Prayer's new construction boasted the same state-of-the-art architecture and comfortable seating that, in Schafler's story, had so distracted the elderly Jewish woman from having a genuine religious experience. Implicitly in this anecdote, Schafler questioned his own role as the "eloquent rabbi" who failed to move the elderly woman to tears, and who seemed to embody just another one of the meaningless luxuries that American Jews installed in their expensive new synagogues.[24]

Similarly, in 1950, Rabbi Max Gruenewald, the rabbi of Congregation B'nai Israel in Millburn, New Jersey, and a former rabbi and Jewish communal leader in Mannheim, Germany, composed his own pointed critique of suburban synagogue construction. In an article for the *Reconstructionist*, Gruenewald questioned the ethics of building a rash of new and expensive synagogues during the decades immediately following the Holocaust, when survivors of the genocide in Europe continued to depend on the largesse of American Jewry for their most basic needs. New Jewish congregations, insisted Gruenewald, had a moral obligation to balance their need for a synagogue with their responsibility to support those who survived. He proposed that congregations planning to build a temple ought to set aside a meaningful proportion of the expenses and donate it to the United Jewish Appeal. Certainly, he felt, these congregations could sacrifice what he viewed as the unnecessary luxuries of their new synagogues, such as air-conditioning or gilded social halls, in order to help rebuild the lives of those who had suffered so greatly. In this way, he believed, the structures themselves would serve as a fitting "tribute to those who perished" as well as a "contribution to those who build anew."[25]

Significantly, Gruenewald neglected to mention in the *Reconstructionist* that his own congregation, Temple B'nai Israel, had broken ground for a new synagogue building just a few months before his critique was published. Gruenewald's concerns about the ethics of postwar synagogue construction, therefore, need to be understood as something more complicated than a condemnation of American Jewish priorities. Implicit in this article was a personal interrogation of his own role in an affluent Jewish society that used its wealth for its own comforts and conveniences instead of making sacrifices for people who may have needed those resources more. His denunciation of postwar synagogue construction, written in the midst of his own congregation's building campaign, contained more than a measure of self-critique.[26]

The process of raising money to build, expand, and renovate synagogues also drew criticism from observers, who felt that unscrupulous fundraisers disrupted relationships between congregants in their quest for the bottom line. Sylvia Rothchild, who often wrote about her frustrations with suburban Jewish life, expressed fury over the tactics used by the professional fundraisers that her synagogue hired to gather the monies for an extensive renovation. In a congregation that had no history of offering special privileges to wealthier members or major donors, Rothchild reported that the solicitors began their campaign by classifying all members according to their assumed wealth, and then proceeded to invite the most affluent congregants to exclusive soirees and gatherings. Additionally, even though their rabbi had promised not to "pressure" potential donors, the fundraisers publicized all donations and expected a "minimum" contribution from every member, whether or not they believed in the necessity of the renovations or felt that they could comfortably afford it. While the campaign leaders dismissed complaints over their methods as "an excuse for selfishness," Rothchild sympathized with the "deeper concerns" of the critics. These campaign drives, she believed, led "not to any meaningful renewal of the temple but to further pressure, divisiveness, and distortion of values."[27]

But even when they were not enmeshed in the challenges of building a new edifice, critics still complained that suburban synagogues operated too much like profit-earning institutions. Although the practice did not originate in postwar suburbia, they lambasted these synagogues for charging steep fees for high-holiday attendance and showering honors and leadership positions upon the richest members. While few postwar congregations would have turned away a potential worshiper because of an inability to pay, the fees that they expected constituents to disburse for building campaigns, temple membership, and high-holiday seating assumed that their members enjoyed relatively high levels of income. Even in the midst of unprecedented communal wealth, however, not all Jewish suburbanites could easily afford the expense. In 1957 *American Judaism*, a popular magazine sponsored by the Reform movement, printed a letter written by a suburban Jewish woman of relatively modest means complaining about the high costs of synagogue membership. The fees required from her local suburban synagogue, she reported, included $120 for membership dues, $25 for high holy day tickets, $75 for Hebrew school tuition and supplies for her two children, $10 for her husband to join the men's club, and $7.50 to join the sisterhood. The letter writer lamented that the final cost of $242.50 that she would need to fully participate in her local synagogue, a sum that would be equivalent to over $2,000 in 2015 dollars, represented more than her family could comfortably afford. Though she wanted to join the temple, she refused to ask the board of directors to lower her costs, as she recognized the members of the board as friends and neighbors and would be embarrassed to "plead poverty" to them.[28]

While some reactions to this letter writer suggested that she buy fewer cigarettes and magazines or that she forgo the men's club and sisterhood, most acknowledged her concern that suburban synagogues did not make themselves accessible to congregants of lesser means. Rabbi Eugene Lipman and Myron Schoen, director of Synagogue Activities and director of Synagogue Administration for the Reform Movement's Union of American Hebrew Congregations, labeled the fiscal program described by the anonymous letter writer as "old fashioned," "inefficient," and "immoral." Instead, they advocated for a single membership fee that would include access to all of the services of the temple. This fee, they added, should be based on a sliding scale and graduated according to the income of each family. Similarly, a reader from Bay Shore, Long Island, characterized a uniform scale of dues as "Un-Jewish," adding that "those who can bear a greater share of the burden ought to do so." According to these commentators, Jewish ethics demanded that all Jews, regardless of income, have equal access to spiritual services. That many suburban synagogues set their fees based on an assumption of affluence, and in doing so possibly shamed those who could not afford to pay, seemed to contradict what these critics understood to be authentic Jewish values.[29]

◆ ◆ ◆

Such was the state of communal ambivalence over synagogue construction and administration when the board of directors of Congregation Solel decided to think seriously about building its own synagogue in October 1960. The initial plans of the congregation's founding members had certainly not included this major undertaking. Started in 1954 as the suburban "extension service" of the Kehilath Anshei Maarav (KAM) synagogue, a Reform congregation in the Hyde Park neighborhood of Chicago, its earliest members did not, at first, intend to form an independent congregation. Instead, they preferred to retain the part-time services of Rabbi Jacob Weinstein, their beloved rabbi from KAM, who agreed to travel back and forth between his urban congregation and this new satellite group on the suburban North Shore. However by 1957, as the suburban extension grew, the members realized that they could no longer function with part-time rabbinical support. They amicably broke with KAM and hired Arnold Jacob Wolf as their spiritual leader.[30]

Rabbi Wolf appealed to the emergent congregation for being "the type of person who was not ordinarily a rabbi." Born in Chicago in 1924 and ordained in 1948, Wolf was taking doctoral courses in Semitics at the University of Chicago at the time of his hire. He impressed the hiring committee with his intellectual pedigree, his sophisticated sermons, his willingness to experiment with synagogue conventions, and his outspoken political convictions. Over the course of his fifteen-year tenure at Solel, he became active in the civil rights movement and Vietnam War protests and hosted such high-profile speakers as Dr. Martin Luther King Jr. and the Chicago Seven at the congregation. In later years, he would go on to become one of the most prominent Reform leaders in Chicago, taking on the pulpit of KAM in 1980.[31]

While Rabbi Wolf supported his congregation's inclination against constructing a new synagogue, by 1960 Solel's board of directors had started to question the wisdom of not having its own building. For years, board members had been experiencing problems with the spaces they leased for their services and religious school. The congregation had become embroiled in a dispute with the Winnetka Masonic Lodge, where it often held services, over the state of the carpet, and tensions had increased between the teachers of the Solel's religious school and the administrators of the Ravinia public school who rented them space on Sunday mornings. The director of the religious school also felt that the lack of a building "profoundly hampered" Solel's educational mission, as educators could not permanently display student work or easily organize extracurricular activities.[32]

The practical justifications for building a new synagogue stood in conflict with members' reservations about how such a project might compromise the high ideals that distinguished their congregation. "We wanted to avoid the trivial, the irrelevant, and the mechanical in synagogue life," read a 1961 report of the committee on building plans, a document aimed at delineating the advantages and disadvantages of a construction project. "Would a building as such have the tendency to confuse brick and mortar with religion? We have boasted that we were a congregation of people and not a temple of stone—would a building alter this concept?" Added to these concerns was the worry, expressed by some members of Solel's board of directors, that a congregation with limited membership would find it impossible to pay for such an expensive project. In need of more funds, it might be forced to take in "not congenial members who agree with Solel's ideas but any member who is willing to support the Temple," warned one of the detractors.[33]

In the end, and in spite of their trepidation, the board of directors decided that the congregation ought to erect a building of its own. However, in keeping with the members' self-perception as an a typical institution, they attempted to go about this project in a way that distinguished them from their peer institutions. First, in response to their perception that most suburban synagogues included unnecessary luxuries, they committed to a building that contained "no frills" and did not budget in a spacious lobby area, a social hall, or air conditioning into their architectural plan. At first, they also balked at the extra expense of constructing an "expandable" sanctuary, but decided in the end to incorporate this feature in order to continue their tradition of allowing anyone, paid members or not, to worship with them on the high holy days.[34]

Solel leaders also maintained that suburban Jews used new synagogue construction as an opportunity to broadcast their personal prosperity, and they took steps to prevent this from happening with their new structure. They refused to incorporate memorial spaces and items marked with the name of the donor, such as "stained glass windows, dedicated rooms, halls, and ark." According to the board, these dedications served the egos of individual donors rather than the spiritual purpose of the congregation and therefore proved "contrary to our avowed purpose."[35]

The Solel board also wanted to avoid hiring the professional solicitors that middle-class, suburban institutions often used in order to gather funds for their expensive construction projects, and which had garnered criticism in the Jewish press for pressuring congregants to contribute in public, often embarrassing, ways. Instead, they decided that volunteers from the synagogue would manage the fundraising themselves, in hopes that this would help maintain the intimacy and cordiality of their congregation throughout the building process.[36]

While the Solel board members vowed to not to repeat what they deemed to be the unsavory practices that plagued other synagogue building campaigns, the difficult task of construction would eventually challenge all of their high ideals. The building project started off with promise, however. Five members agreed to donate a tract of land on Clavey Road in Highland Park upon which the congregation could situate the new edifice. Soon after, the board of directors' executive committee efficiently organized teams of volunteer solicitors to ask members for donations to pay for the construction. In the fall of 1961, they began to train these volunteers through a series of what they called—perhaps facetiously—"indoctrination meetings." Over the course these trainings, the volunteers practiced how to explain to potential contributors why the congregation needed a building, to answer the concerns of members who balked at the size of the budget, and to counter the complaints of those who accused the board of directors of making unilateral, undemocratic decisions as they embarked upon the building campaign.[37]

The final costs of Solel's building, originally projected at $750,000, ultimately came to $816,000—just over 6 million in 2015 dollars. Though Solel's board of directors initially insisted that all donations would be voluntary and that no one would put undue pressure on members for funds, they did not shy away from requesting quite substantial donations from the membership. They drew up confidential reports categorizing members according to how much money they made and determined their entreaties accordingly. The board antic-ipated that only the wealthiest of the congregation's 413 families would donate hefty donations of $7,500 to $10,000 (between $60,000 and $80,000 in 2015 dollars). However, they had high expectations of the bulk of the membership as well, projecting that 277 members would donate between $1,000 and $3,000 ($8,000 and $24,000 in 2015 dollars) to the cause. Perhaps unsurprisingly, the congregational board did not, at first, meet these ambitious fundraising goals; as of February 1962, they had raised only $693,000 toward their objective.[38]

When faced with a budget deficit it soon became apparent that the con-gregation would have to sacrifice some of its principles in order to meet the practical needs of construction. Because of the need for larger donations, board members began to reconsider their opposition to installing personal memorials in the building. Some proposed setting up "only one large plaque" on which donors could be listed, and others suggesting that a "memorial tab-let" in the library could be erected "without great fanfare." Another board member recommended increasing the size of the membership in order to help pay for the expenses, in spite of their earlier commitment to remaining a small and intimate congregation. Finally, in 1963, after acrimonious debate among the board members, they resolved that donations to the building fund would no longer be optional and that members of the congregation who did not comply would be asked to resign from Solel.[39]

Rabbi Wolf, for his part, became deeply embroiled in these fundraising efforts. While in May 1960 he had boasted rather gleefully about their "hole-in the wall, almost startlingly disreputable" offices and the "portable boxes" that housed their religious school materials, he became an active supporter of the building campaign and reassured the board about the ethics of the process. When board members balked at compelling members to donate more than they felt comfortable with, Rabbi Wolf assured them that "some pressure upon people to meet their obligations was a religious duty." He handpicked certain members of the congregation to be invited to an exclusive "Building Fund Luncheon" aimed at convincing them to donate additional monies to "finish the job" of funding the new synagogue. Though he certainly expressed concern that the building might represent "an end rather than a beginning" to their congregational mission and cautioned his constituents that "one of Parkinson's Laws is that beautiful buildings mark the end of a group's authen-ticity," Rabbi Wolf also played a significant role in making the new synagogue possible.[40]

While the congregation finally met its fundraising goals in October 1963, the increased pressure to contribute to the building campaign certainly caused tension among the members. One congregant, miffed that his initial contribution was deemed "insufficient" by a volunteer solicitor, informed the board in no uncertain terms that he and his family would not "justify ourselves, nor give a detailed report of explanation of why we cannot give more," and berated the board for committing to a $750,000 building project before considering "that there are people of moderate circumstances in this congregation." Another congregant bristled at being told that he ought to contribute between $1,500 and $2,000, instead of the $300 that he had originally pledged, and accused the Solel leadership of being a "wealthy board" and "not a true representation of the membership." This member further complained that the building plans were "too ostentatious" and that the "whole concept of Solel had undergone a change for the worse." In response, the board debated whether to "reassign" this congregant to a more effective team of fundraisers or, instead, to "give him a good kick in the ass and be rid of him."[41]

In the midst of this unpleasantness, some congregants put together a musical program entitled "Songs to Throw Out Building Fund Solicitors By" that they performed at Solel's annual congregational meeting in 1963. While lighthearted in tone, the musical skits reveal the congregation's ongoing struggle to remain true to ideals as it struggled to collect money for the new temple. Singing to the tune of *South Pacific*'s "There Is Nothing Like a Dame," for instance, the amateur performers celebrated their rich intellectual life and bemoaned their lack of funds:

> There's lots of books at Solel
> And nothing looks like Solel.
> We've got guts at Solel,
> And some nuts at Solel.
> We've gone in hock for Solel
> Sold our stock for Solel . . .
> We still need dough for our chateau, Solel.

Another song reworked the words of "Home on the Range" to acknowledge the friction that had arose between congregants over the course of their fundraising venture:

> Solel's home by the ditch
> Takes the poor but it favors the rich.
> We all gave our shirt,
> We gave till it hurt,
> Except for that son of a ——[42]

Negotiating Middle-Class Judaism

While Solel's building campaign certainly tested the congregation's conviction to resist the conventions of middle-class American Judaism, some members nonetheless maintained that, in the end, the project had enhanced, rather than detracted from, their congregational mission. Hal Barkun, for instance, a board member and strong supporter of the new building, thought it quite admirable when members committed their resources to the purpose of holiness and worship. In a poem that appeared in the congregational newsletter in 1962, he insisted that the new synagogue provided an opportunity for middle-class Jews to devote "our good Jewish brains, our warm Jewish hearts, and yes, our Jewish money, for something beyond the marketplace." Instead of using their newfound wealth for personal luxuries or self-aggrandizement, he believed that the new synagogue allowed them to "raise a finger toward God."[43]

◆　◆　◆

As American Jews endeavored to build new synagogues and debated the ethics of the process, they also expressed related concerns over the life-cycle events that Jews celebrated inside of these synagogues. As with the synagogue structures themselves, ambivalence over the growing opulence of Jewish life-cycle receptions became enmeshed with the ambivalence regarding American Jews' upward mobility and its impact on their religious traditions. For the rabbis and intellectuals who were uncomfortable with these events, the lavish affairs that had become the norm among middle-class, postwar Jews represented an egregious distortion of authentic Jewish customs and religious practice. These celebrations seemed to prove that middle-class prosperity had corrupted the religious life of American Jews, leveling an assault on both the dignity and the authentic meaning of sacred rituals.

No Jewish life-cycle celebration drew more ire from postwar critics than the bar mitzvah, an event that marked a boy's entrance into religious maturity at the age of thirteen. American Jews initiated the custom of holding sumptuous social gatherings in honor of the occasion, although some of the synagogue-centered rites date back to the medieval period, and Jews living in the German Empire formalized the ritual in the sixteenth century. The boys denoted their new position by publicly reading from the Torah or Haftorah (prophetic writings) for the first time and, beginning in the seventeenth century, delivering a speech that demonstrated their religious knowledge. As a bar mitzvah, literally a "son of the commandment," a boy assumed responsibility for the full array of religious rituals, which included wearing ritual garments such as *tefillin* (phylacteries) during times of prayer, and joining a *minyan* (prayer quorum) three times a day. The record of how this ritual spread into Eastern Europe and the Sephardic world remains unclear, but it probably did not happen until the eighteenth and nineteenth centuries.[44]

By the time that Eastern European Jews began to migrate in large numbers to the United States at the turn of the twentieth century, the bar mitzvah had become a firmly established ritual. But whereas in Eastern Europe the immediate family might have embellished the bar mitzvah observance with a light repast, Jewish immigrants in America transformed the party into a larger social event. In the years before World War I, the families of American bar mitzvah boys would host luncheons for guests at their homes. By the 1920s, those who could afford it invited friends and family to bar mitzvah "affairs," complete with a banquet and orchestra, at catering halls and hotels. For American Jews, a party following the service had become part of the event.[45]

The rapid economic expansion of the postwar years saw an increasing number of American Jews able, and eager, to celebrate the occasion of the bar mitzvah with great fanfare. They incorporated fanciful, often expensive flourishes into their parties never seen before. During the decades after World War II, bar mitzvah receptions commonly featured a six-course meal, sculptures of the bar mitzvah boy made of ice or chopped liver, baseball or luau-themed decorations, dancing girls, comedians, and elaborate Torah-shaped cakes upon which relatives of the bar mitzvah solemnly lit candles.[46]

Interestingly, while some form of a bat mitzvah ceremony for girls became commonplace during the postwar years, American Jews of this era tended not to invest the bat mitzvah with the same expensive embellishments of the bar mitzvah reception. As Jenna Weissman Joselit, a historian of American Jews' material culture, noted, "fanciful decorations, elaborate partying, and excessive gift-giving" rarely accompanied a girl's bat mitzvah during this era. Instead, celebrants commonly gathered for a modest "fellowship hour" after the synagogue service, opting for restraint rather than extravagance as they rejoiced in the girl's coming of age. Consequently, the opulent bar mitzvah, rather than the understated bat mitzvah, emerged as the primary target for those who criticized the religious practices of postwar American Jews.[47]

In fact, for journalist Stanley Meisler, the evolution of the American bar mitzvah both mirrored and demonstrated the upward mobility of American Jews. In the pages of the *Reconstructionist* in 1960, he compared his own bar mitzvah reception, "a buffet dinner on a paper plate eaten at a small East Bronx apartment," to that of his younger brother's celebration, which featured showgirls, a comedian, and a sit-down dinner at a Broadway nightclub. And while Stanley's gifts had amounted to a mere $125, the younger Meisler collected $1,200 in checks and saving bonds. The author attributed this escalation of the bar mitzvah festivities to the greater income enjoyed by his family's social circle in the fourteen years since he had celebrated his own bar mitzvah milestone. The differences between the two parties underscored his family's ascendancy into the middle class.[48]

As bar mitzvahs grew more lavish, many non-Jewish Americans would prove curious about the extravagant parties that Jews threw for their teenaged sons. The opulent bar mitzvah emerged as a topic of general, sometimes contemptuous interest in the public discourse. This national curiosity regarding bar mitzvah receptions exacerbated the worries of Jewish leaders over the propriety of these parties and the message they sent to non-Jewish Americans.

The national press began to report on bar mitzvah affairs in 1952, when *Life* magazine published "*Life* Goes to a Bar Mitzvah," a feature article highlighting the reception of Carl Jay Bodek, the son of a wealthy Philadelphia contractor. The article dutifully mentioned Carl's recitation from the Torah, but devoted its most detailed and ebullient coverage to the "lavish party" that followed the service. Underneath photographs of Carl cutting his Torah-topped cake and dancing with his father and rabbi, the magazine reported that the party, which "was held in large tents erected on Bodek's seven-acre estate," employed the services of three orchestras and a string quartet, eighteen waiters, and four Pinkerton detectives to "guard the 310 guests' furs and jewels." *Life* also published a photograph of Carl surrounded by the presents he received, including "seven suitcases, four toilet sets, a set of golf clubs and a traditional present, a gold watch." That a popular, national magazine like *Life* would publish descriptions of a bar mitzvah reception that seemed extravagant even by postwar standards contributed to fears that these large parties might potentially contribute to antisemitic stereotypes of Jewish wealth, greed, and vulgarity.[49]

Herman Wouk's 1955 description of a bar mitzvah reception in his best-selling novel *Marjorie Morningstar* added to public interest in the celebration. Wouk's novel detailed the elaborate catering flourishes at Marjorie's brother's bar mitzvah banquet, a party that included "the flower-decked ballroom, the spacious dance floor, the waiters in blue mess jackets, the murmuring orchestra behind potted palms, the fine linen and silver on the tables, the camellias by each lady's plate." The climactic moment of the party occurred when the bar mitzvah boy entered the ballroom, accompanied by a flaming cauldron of brandy sauce that the headwaiter poured on top of each guest's slice of grapefruit. Wouk enlisted one of his characters, Mr. Goldstone, to mock the showiness of the event: "Caterers, restaurants, great angle they got," said Mr. Goldstone. "Anything they can set fire to they charge ten times as much. Set fire to a twenty-cent flap jack, crepes suzette for two dollars. Maybe we could use it in our store, Mary. Sell a pair of flaming shoes, fifty dollars instead of five dollars."[50]

After the publication of *Marjorie Morningstar*, Jewish leaders criticized Wouk for his portrayal of a bar mitzvah, insisting that he had made "a sacred occasion seem comical." Wouk defended his description in *This Is My God* (1959), a book that explained his own religious beliefs and practices:

> In my novel, *Marjorie Morningstar*, I did my best to portray a bar-mitzva with accuracy and with affection. I thought I succeeded pretty well, but for my pains I encountered the most bitter and violent objections from some fellow Jews. . . . We Jews are a people of great natural gusto. In the freedom of the United States, where for the first time in centuries we have known equality of opportunity, we have made of the bar-mitzva a blazing costly jubilee. I do not see anything wrong with that. The American coming-out party is not too different.[51]

The criticism Wouk received for his portrayal of an opulent bar mitzvah pointed to the unease American Jews felt over the consumption and display associated with these parties. Though the postwar years saw a marked decrease in American antisemitism, many Jews continued to feel threatened by negative publicity. To have such a gaudy celebration featured in a best-selling book widely read by non-Jews made them feel self-conscious and even angry with Wouk for exposing a contentious issue. To wit, upon reading that Herman Wouk did not see any problem with American bar mitzvahs becoming a "blazing costly jubilee," UAHC president Maurice N. Eisendrath acidly responded, "he wouldn't."[52]

Two years after the release of *Marjorie Morningstar*, bar mitzvahs entered the public arena once again during a 1957 New York State Supreme Court case. The case involved the parents of a twelve-year-old boy who sought to pay for their son's bar mitzvah reception with the $600 that he had been awarded in a personal injury lawsuit. Because of the son's young age, the courts had the power to decide whether or not to release the child's funds for this purpose. Justice Samuel H. Hofstadter, who presided over the case, seized the opportunity to make a statement on what he felt to be the abuses of bar mitzvah celebrations: "The Bar Mitzvah ceremony is a solemnization of a boy's becoming a 'son of the commandment' and should encourage him in the path of righteousness. It was never intended to be a vehicle for mere entertainment and display. . . . It would be more fitting if the funds were utilized to initiate or continue his education in faith and morals," Hofstadter stated, though he finally allowed the parents to use $200 of their son's award to pay for the party.

This court case provoked wide comment among American Jews in the late 1950s. According to the editors of a synagogue newsletter in Westchester, New York, the case served as a reminder that "the religious significance of the occasion was to be emphasized" over the "celebration and the reception." Rabbi Albert Gordon of Newton, Massachusetts, cited the case as an example of what he called the "false values" that he felt had infiltrated into the bar mitzvah rite. Justice Hofstadter's admonishment of Jewish parents contributed to the notion that bar mitzvah receptions had become a very public disgrace.[53]

Concerns over the opulence of bar mitzvah parties loomed particularly large in the Reform movement, as the shapers of classical Reform in America had tried to eliminate the ceremony altogether. These nineteenth-century leaders promoted the rite of confirmation over what they considered to be the archaic bar mitzvah service. In their view, confirmation, a ritual that annually honored a cohort of teenagers who completed a course in religious education, improved upon bar mitzvah in numerous ways. First, the service honored the accomplishments of both boys and girls while the bar mitzvah celebrated only boys, and so confirmation felt more in tune with the Reform movement's official policy of equality between the sexes. Additionally, many Reform leaders had felt that boys of thirteen lacked the maturity to be initiated as full, adult participants in Jewish religious life, contending that confirmation, which consecrated older teenagers between the ages of fourteen and sixteen, more effectively served this purpose. The confirmation ceremony, they believed, emphasized a more modern, egalitarian, and sensitive approach to Judaism.[54]

By the postwar era, however, the bar mitzvah celebration had become common practice even among Reform Jews. According a survey conducted by the movement's National Federation of Temple Brotherhoods, 92 percent of Reform Temples celebrated bar mitzvah in 1953, while a poll taken in 1960 reported that 96.4 percent of Reform congregations commemorated the event. The Reform movement's adoption of the bar mitzvah ritual, instituted by the demands of the laity rather than by the recommendations of the clergy, caused consternation among many Reform rabbis. As the invention of the bat mitzvah ceremony for girls nullified complaints regarding the gender bias of the bar mitzvah ritual, condemnation of lavish receptions became a primary concern for those rabbis who continued to oppose incorporating the ritual into Reform Jewish practice. One such rabbi, Joshua Trachtenberg of Teaneck, New Jersey's Temple Emeth, told *Time* magazine in 1959 that the superficiality of the bar mitzvah ritual typified the inherent dangers of the Reform movement's return to ritualism. He characterized bar mitzvah as an "empty ceremonial" followed by a reception that displayed "the conspicuous waste which is the hallmark of such celebrations."[55]

The Conservative and Orthodox movements had never promoted the practice of confirmation as a replacement for bar mitzvah, though some Conservative synagogues had instituted both celebrations. Nonetheless, rabbis within the Conservative and Orthodox movements joined their Reform colleagues in their frustration with bar mitzvah receptions. In 1961, for instance, Conservative rabbi Elias Charry derided the bar mitzvah gathering as "an elaborate and costly birthday party at which the chief celebrants are the adults and the poor bar mitzvah boy is the real victim," and he went so far as to suggest that his movement deemphasize or even exchange bar mitzvah in favor of an initiation rite geared toward sixteen-year-olds. That same year, Modern Orthodox rabbi Leonard Gewirtz argued that American Jews had reduced bar mitzvah to "an occasion to show off their wealth, often with a general disregard for Jewish religious practice."[56]

Generally, in all the movements of American Judaism, even those rabbis who disapproved of bar mitzvah celebrations bowed to their congregants' strong preference for the rite and continued to sanction the ceremony. In this climate of anxiety over bar mitzvah parties, however, both the Conservative and Reform movements imposed standards for synagogue decorum aimed at toning down the receptions. The Conservative movement's standards for synagogue practice, adopted by the biennial convention of the United Synagogue in 1955, gently, and somewhat vaguely, reminded constituents that the receptions following bar mitzvahs and weddings would be considered a "seudah shel mitzvah," a religiously commanded meal, and must therefore be in consonance with the religious spirit surrounding the event.[57] Leaders of the Reform movement instituted more stringent guidelines in 1964, when the Central Conference of American Rabbis adopted a report that lambasted the "steady and alarming deterioration in the character of the Bar Mitzvah 'affair.'" The report warned constituents that the "extravagant consumption, the conspicuous waste, and the crudity" of these parties "were rapidly becoming a public Jewish scandal." To counter these trends, these leaders instructed members of the Reform movement to keep the receptions "simple," to offer entertainment "in keeping with the occasion," and to ensure that all of the festivities "be dignified and in good taste."[58]

Already troubled by what they perceived to be the excess of bar mitzvah parties, rabbis grew irate when rituals invented by bandleaders and caterers began to take on religious significance for the celebrants. Long Island's Rabbi Harold Saperstein expressed his astonishment when a congregant wanted his spiritual guidance in deciding which relatives should light particular candles on her son's bar mitzvah cake. "She couldn't understand when I told her that lighting candles at the Bar Mitzvah reception was not part of any Jewish tradition but a gimmick introduced by caterers and band leaders in recent years."[59] He found himself even more disturbed, however, when he witnessed another ceremony in which a small girl carried a *tallis* (prayershawl) into the banquet hall that the parents subsequently placed on the shoulders of the bar mitzvah boy. This ceremony, he felt, exploited Jewish symbols for the entertainment of the guests, "as though there had been no Bar Mitzvah [in the synagogue] and this made it holy."[60] As new customs like the candle-lighting ceremony began to take hold among postwar American Jews, their rabbis feared that these recently invented rituals would detract from the older, rabbinically sanctioned bar mitzvah practices. While meaningful to many of their constituents, rabbis dismissed them as inauthentic, not to mention expensive, intrusions into the bar mitzvah milestone.

Rabbi Erwin L. Herman, director of regional activities for the UAHC, believed that upwardly mobile Jews proved particularly susceptible to the lure of gaudy affairs as a means of publicly affirming their new financial status. He directed his vitriol at bar mitzvah caterers, whom he accused of taking advantage of American Jews' social insecurities. He lambasted the caterer as "the shepherd who leads us with uncomplaining conformity down the road of social acceptance. We have been good sheep—and like good sheep, we have been clipped. Enough! It is time to state without equivocation that we have had it, and to admit that we have been had, in the process." He implored American Jews to look toward other ways to celebrate and affirm their rising fortunes.[61]

Indeed, many postwar rabbis enjoined their upwardly mobile constituents to use their new wealth in ways they deemed more consistent with Jewish ethics and values. These rabbis feared that bar mitzvah parties reflected social posturing rather than what they considered to be more proper Jewish values, such as charity, education, or a commitment to serving the larger Jewish community. Chicago's Rabbi Ira Eisenstein, for instance, argued that the bar mitzvah party actually contradicted the ethical ideals that the synagogue hoped to transmit to its youth. "In school we try to inculcate the power to discriminate between what is important and what is trivial, between the good and the merely glittering," he wrote in his Temple Bulletin. "Then comes the bar mitzvah party which so often neutralizes all that the school has attempted to teach, and influences the child to believe that ostentation is better than modesty, and that money spent on elaborate entertainment is better than money spent on books or charity to the synagogue."[62]

Religious leaders sought to educate their constituents on how to use their money appropriately and attempted to steer them toward expenditures they deemed more worthy than the bar mitzvah party. Rabbi Edgar Siskin of Glencoe, Illinois, for instance, used the issue of bar mitzvah as a springboard from which to discuss financial ethics. In his Rosh Hashanah sermon in 1963, he implored parents of bar-mitzvah-aged youth to "stand up for decent moral values" and refrain from spending large sums on a reception. Instead, Siskin urged them to donate to humanitarian and religious causes such as promoting peace and civil rights, giving aid to Israel and their local synagogue, and providing sustenance for the impoverished Jews of the Near East and Eastern Europe.[63]

Similarly, Rabbi Roland Gittelsohn, then the leader of a congregation in Rockville Center, Long Island, suggested to his congregants that it would be more in keeping with Jewish values to forgo the large bar mitzvah reception in lieu of a contribution to the synagogue. As he told his congregants during a 1950 sermon, "I can think of no better way to reinforce the real religious emphases of your son's Bar Mitzvah . . . than by taking the additional money you might have spent for a public spectacle and giving it in honor of the Bar Mitzvah to your Congregation's building fund."[64]

Gittelsohn's request that his congregants contribute to the building fund rather than pay for a bar mitzvah contained more than a measure of irony, since postwar rabbis commonly lambasted middle-class American Jews for the spate of new synagogues that they had funded during these years. Synagogue members received conflicting advice over what their leaders considered to be worthy expenditures that reflected authentic Jewish values. And this tension, in turn, reflected the investment of postwar rabbis in the culture of affluence they decried. They may have disapproved of the luxuries of postwar synagogues, but they also helped gather funds for them. And while they may have criticized the excesses of the bar mitzvah ritual, they also officiated at the ceremonies and used them as a way to encourage these youths and their families toward greater involvement in Judaism and Jewish life.

Religious leaders were not the only ones who saw the potential of the bar mitzvah ceremony to increase commitments to Jewish life, if only it could be rid of its excesses. Secular Jewish educator Mark Millstone, a leader in the socialist Workmen's Circle Yiddish school system, insisted that nonreligious Jews had "a right to fashion [their] own version" of the ceremony. He called for a bar mitzvah "stripped of its commercialism and its keeping-up-with-the-Joneses" that would stress cultural and ethical Jewish traditions rather than religious ones. As a celebration of a "3000 year old moral and ethical legacy," Millstone insisted that a secular bar mitzvah could be a "source of inspiration and a rich emotional experience" for children and parents alike.[65]

Other celebrants tried to enrich the bar mitzvah by incorporating the State of Israel into the festivities. Some celebrants traveled to Israel in addition to, or in lieu of, a reception. Others joined the Jewish Agency's "National Bar Mitzvah Club," launched in 1962, which aimed to "enhance meaning of the Bar and Bat Mitzvah ceremonies" by enlisting participants into a three-year educational course before taking them on a study tour of Israel at the age of sixteen.[66]

The editors of the *Reconstructionist* applauded this trend of including Israel into the bar mitzvah rite. In 1963 they congratulated New York senator Jacob Javits on taking his son to Israel on the occasion of his bar mitzvah and expressed their hope that this would become a model for other bar mitzvah celebrations. "Considering what some *bar mitzvah* parties cost these days, the trip would be a bargain," they gushed. "And consider the difference to the boy: instead of being exposed to the eating, drinking and dancing, which have nothing whatever to do with his entrance into the household of Israel, he would find himself upon the soil where the words he chants echoed millennia ago." In suggesting that bar mitzvah be celebrated with a trip to Israel rather than a party, the editors of the *Reconstructionist* joined the chorus of religious leaders who disparaged the content of bar mitzvah celebrations rather than the actual expense. After all, travel to the Middle East also required a significant financial investment. Within these conversations, it was not Jewish affluence itself but the ways that American Jews had chosen to use their resources that provoked anxiety. They hoped that Jews would choose to invest their wealth in causes that seemed to them to reflect authentic Jewish values rather than in bar mitzvah receptions, which struck them as a frivolous waste.[67]

◆ ◆ ◆

Solel entered its own congregational debate over bar mitzvah as condemnations of the rite circulated widely among postwar American Jews. Unsurprisingly, the idealistic members of Solel responded to these concerns over bar mitzvah celebrations in a somewhat different way than their peer institutions did. While the leaders of other congregations tried to convince their membership to tone down or limit the opulence of their bar mitzvah celebrations, Solel's board of directors opted to disallow the ceremony and its attendant receptions altogether.

Solel had not always prohibited its members from celebrating the bar mitzvah. Between 1957 and 1959, families could arrange bar mitzvahs for their sons and bat mitzvahs for their daughters, provided that they adhered to the strict sumptuary standards instituted by the board of directors. However in the spring of 1959, the board decided that it would benefit the congregation to abolish the rite rather than regulate it.

While the members of Solel's board of directors proved quite unanimous in their antipathy toward a ritual that they felt had become an embarrassment to American Judaism, they remained concerned about the feasibility of banning it entirely. Some pointed out that certain members had joined the congregation specifically because they wanted their children to participate in the bar mitzvah ceremony, while others feared that they would not be able to gain or keep new members as long as they did not provide that service. One congregant wondered whether they had an ethical obligation to provide bar mitzvahs to those families who expected it "on traditional grounds."[68]

The case against continuing their bar mitzvah program proved more heartfelt and idealistic than the practical arguments leveled in its favor. Board members denigrated the ceremony as one of the "mechanical" activities that detracted from their spiritual mission and argued that more children were "hurt than helped by it."[69]

The leaders of Solel's religious school and worship committee felt particularly strongly about discontinuing bar mitzvah at Solel. According to the director of the religious school, preparing for the ritual failed to advance the main educational goals of the educational program, which emphasized conversational Hebrew rather than chanting from the Torah. The head of the worship committee pointed out that bar mitzvahs proved an "interruption and a distraction" from heartfelt prayer, producing a "child centered atmosphere" that altered the contemplative mood of the service.[70]

When the ban on bar mitzvah provoked opposition from some of congregants, the board crafted a report carefully explaining their position to disgruntled members. The "ostentatious displays of wealth and bad taste" associated with the bar mitzvah were, they insisted, anathema to Solel's identity as an intellectual and nonconformist congregation. The responsibility of a maverick synagogue like Solel to "guard against" such superficiality and showiness, they affirmed, was as "essential" as it was "difficult."[71]

Solel's board of directors held fast to the resolution against bar mitzvah just as it was suffering through the throes of its stressful campaign to raise funds for a new building. Though board members abandoned some of their high ideals as they raised money for Solel's expensive new edifice, they would not compromise with regard to their bar mitzvah policy. If the lack of a showpiece building would no longer distinguish them from the mainstream, middle-class synagogues that they so disdained, they would, at least for a time, remain distinctive in what Rabbi Wolf termed their "extreme solution" to the problem of the bar mitzvah.[72]

◆ ◆ ◆

Throughout the postwar years, American Jews used their new affluence to transform the texture and feel of their religious lives, building showpiece, modern synagogues and hosting lavish lifecycle receptions that reflected their unprecedented financial mobility. The time, energy, and resources that American Jews poured into their places of worship and coming-of-age celebrations revealed their continued commitment to Judaic practice. It signified their willingness to publicly assert their Jewish difference in front of non-Jewish neighbors in their new, suburban communities.

But many midcentury Jewish leaders did not regard these changes as symbols of vitality. Rather, as American Jews developed a religious culture that harmonized with their new prosperity and social status, they viewed these innovations as evidence of corruption and decline. Postwar rabbis questioned the authenticity and sustainability of middle-class Judaism, even as they worked to create it.

The suspicion that American Jews would not succeed in building a viable religious culture that could thrive in an atmosphere of prosperity struck an acute note of alarm among their leaders. Many accepted Herberg's influential 1955 argument that American middle-class norms encouraged the descendants of European immigrants to suppress ethnic markers like language and dress and instead to express their distinctive identities through their particular forms of religion. Indeed, increasingly during the postwar years, the evidence seemed to bear out Herberg's theory. Secular forms of Jewish expression—such as fraternal orders, secular Yiddish schools, leftist organizations, and Yiddish arts and letters—declined, and religious affiliation became a primary way through which American Jews marked their difference from other Americans.

But just as the process of upward mobility required American Jews to articulate their Jewishness through religious practices, it also, in the eyes of their leadership, rendered their religious lives superficial and inauthentic. The last bastion of Jewish distinctiveness seemed to be crumbling. For these leaders, and for all those American Jews who valued the continuity of Jewish life in America, the situation seemed quite dire. In various ways, they struggled to build a middle-class Jewish culture that felt substantive, authentic, and capable of nurturing new generations of committed, American Jews.

Congregation Solel represented an uncommon example of a postwar congregation that tried to resist what members viewed as the foibles of middle-class American Judaism. As much as possible, the congregation endeavored to maintain integrity and vibrancy in an affluent suburban environment that seemed to encourage superficiality and complacency.

Members of Solel need not have worried about their congregation's viability as a middle-class, suburban synagogue; sixty years later, it remains a dynamic institution still serving the affluent North Shore of Chicago. They did not succeed, however, in creating an institution that, for the long term, could resist the norms of middle-class Jewish life. Solel no longer limits its membership, it long ago reinstituted its bar and bat mitzvah program, and its building, having undergone various renovations, now includes air conditioning and a capacious reception area. Nothing along these lines substantially differentiates Solel from its peer congregations along the North Shore. But even if the members of Solel did not blaze permanent alternative paths in suburban Jewish life, the record of their attempts to do so remains a significant marker of the concerns and ambivalence of upwardly mobile Jews during the postwar era.

As postwar Jewish leaders examined the religious culture of middle-class American Jews and found it wanting, they also interrogated their own family life and gender roles. In this area as well, they imagined that their economic rise had degraded institutions and relationships crucial to the future and integrity of American Jewry. We now turn to the question of how and why these leaders came to believe that Jewish attitudes toward gender, along with politics and religion, had been compromised by the process of Jewish upward mobility.

FOUR

What Kind of Job Is *That* for a Nice Jewish Boy?

Masculinity in an Upwardly Mobile Community

In a popular joke that circulated among American Jews in the late 1950s, three Jewish mothers conferred with one another about their sons' career choices. One mother proudly stated that her son recently graduated from law school and accepted a job at a prominent law firm for a salary of $12,000 a year. The second mother happily reported that her son owned a flourishing dry goods business that brought in more than $25,000 a year. The third mother retained an embarrassed silence throughout the conversation. Finally, upon the cajoling of her companions, she admitted that her own son entered the rabbinate and earned an annual salary of only $4,500. Her friends exclaimed, "What kind of job is *that* for a nice Jewish boy?"[1]

This joke found its audience among a community wrestling with shifting conceptions of masculinity in the wake of the rapid upward mobility that characterized the years after World War II. Though it exaggerated postwar Jews' actual attitudes toward the rabbinate, the joke played with the growing assumption that a "nice Jewish boy"—that is to say, a Jewish man who dutifully lived up to the expectations of his family and his community—needed to be an upper-middle-class breadwinner. It achieved its humorous effect by intimating that the rabbinate, traditionally a position of prestige for Jewish men, had lost much of its luster in the new, affluent world of American Jews because of its comparatively low earning potential. The joke underscored a widespread perception that postwar Jews had betrayed older and more Jewishly authentic notions of appropriate masculinity as they adopted high earning power as the sole measure of male success.[2]

The notion that joining the middle class had somehow stifled the lives of Jewish men did not appear only in jokes. Indeed, for many American Jewish novelists, intellectuals, and rabbis of the 1950s and early 1960s, the challenges facing newly affluent Jewish men were no laughing matter. The pressure to become a prosperous breadwinner, they contended, had turned Jewish men into soulless moneymakers and stripped them of their idealism, their intellectual curiosity, their bravery, even their authentic Jewish identity. This concern became a key component of a specifically Jewish, and profoundly gendered, critique of upward mobility.

Jewish leaders were not the only Americans who worried about middle-class men in the postwar years. Many best-selling journalists and social critics concluded that the swelling American middle class suffered from a crisis in masculinity. David Riesman's *The Lonely Crowd* and William H. Whyte's *The Organization Man*, for instance, can be read not only as jeremiads bemoaning the state the American middle class in general but also as specifically gendered laments over the status of American men. The comfort and security of a middle-class lifestyle, according to these works, had transformed capable, self-assured, individualistic American men into soft, conforming suburbanites. In their view, American men who had once conquered the frontier and won two world wars, had by the 1950s decided to don their grey flannel suits and meekly follow the dictates of the corporation and the suburb. "What has happened to the American male?" wondered the historian and cultural critic Arthur Schlesinger Jr. in a 1958 cover story for *Esquire*. Once "utterly confident in his manhood," he argued, the American man had become nervous and effete, a victim of the affluent society.[3]

After absorbing the critiques of middle-class masculinity that filtered through American society in the postwar years, the Jewish leaders profiled in this chapter built on those ideas to create a distinctly Jewish conversation. Their discussion mined Jewish cultural symbols and interpreted the events of Jewish history to imagine alternative models of masculinity from which American Jewish men might draw inspiration. They populated their speeches and writings with valorized images of Jewish men who did not readily conform to the ideal of the middle-class breadwinner, such as intellectuals who opted for scholarly careers over lucrative ones and tough Israeli soldiers who seemed to choose heroism and self-sacrifice over the selfish pleasures of affluence. They extolled what they believed to be the more authentic Jewish masculinity of less prosperous Jewish men, and questioned the upward mobility that, to their minds, had steered American Jewish men away from more satisfying life choices.

The ability to live up to the heteronormative, middle-class ideal of becoming a male breadwinner with a dependent wife and children was a relatively new phenomenon for many American Jewish men. Most of them were the children or grandchildren of turn-of-the-century immigrants from Eastern Europe who, at least in the early years of migration, could not have survived on the financial contributions of only one earner. Most immigrant Jewish families, therefore, depended not only on the income of men but also on the earnings of their wives, who took boarders into their homes and worked in modest family businesses. Additionally, they relied on the income of unmarried daughters and sons who added to the family coffers by working in factories.[4]

With limited ability to achieve a sense of self-esteem through their earning capacity, the social and political ideals of the working class and a cultural respect for intellectualism offered immigrant Jewish men other avenues by which to gain a sense of accomplishment in the American milieu. Male Jewish immigrants who had not achieved economic security could still pride themselves in being fearless organizers and dedicated strikers fighting to ameliorate the conditions of the poor. Others managed to build a sense of self-worth through their intellectual pursuits, often looking down on more financially solvent peers, whom they derisively referred to as "allrightniks," for their presumed lack of knowledge and taste.[5]

As Jews became more financially secure over the course of the twentieth century, these alternative avenues for social status diminished, and the expectation that Jewish men would become high-earning professionals or businessmen steadily increased. Since postwar societal norms prescribed racial and gender segregation in the workplace and reserved the most prestigious and lucrative jobs for light-skinned men, the upward mobility of all American Jews hinged on the opportunities available to young Jewish males. Jewish men took advantage of these prospects, flocking to high-paying, high-status positions in fields such as medicine, law, and engineering. In the years directly after World War II, 13.8 percent of Jewish men worked in a professional field, as opposed to 8.8 percent of non-Jewish men. By 1957, the rate of Jewish male professionals had swelled to 20.3 percent, in contrast to 9.9 percent of non-Jewish men.[6]

While the popularity of professional careers grew among American Jewish men in the postwar years, the majority of Jewish men continued to own or manage businesses. Although many of these businessmen earned salaries comparable to or greater than those of the professionals, the relative popularity of business as an occupational choice for Jewish men declined over the course of the period as growing numbers chose the more prestigious professional jobs. While 55.6 percent of Jewish men had been self-employed at the onset of the postwar period, 31.8 percent of Jewish men continued to own their own businesses by 1957.[7]

These trends proved even starker among native-born Jewish men whose parents had also been born in the United States. Sociologists Judith Kramer and Seymour Leventman separated out this younger cohort in their 1961 survey of Jews living in the metropolitan Detroit area. They found that among this group, 46.5 percent of the men worked in professional fields such as medicine, law, engineering, or scientific research, while another 31 percent owned or managed a business. Only 7.1 percent worked as craftsmen, foremen, peddlers, or service workers.

Indeed, by the postwar period, it seemed that not only American Jews but also the general American public assumed that all Jewish men earned comfortable middle-class incomes. *Look* magazine declared in 1955, for instance, that the "the Jewish working-class has all but vanished" and that the [male] Jew is "a businessman, a doctor, a lawyer, an engineer."[8]

As the expectation that American Jewish men would become middle-class breadwinners grew, so did the vehemence of the Jewish writers, intellectuals, and religious leaders who disapproved of this standard. Philip Roth's best-selling 1959 novella *Goodbye, Columbus* represents what might be the best-known articulation of this dissatisfaction with middle-class models of masculinity. The work proved controversial among American Jews for its satirical, and often disparaging, take on middle-class Jewish life; indeed, as Roth himself recalled in 1963, critics accused him of being "self-hating," "tasteless," and of adding "fuel" to the fires of antisemitism. Still, despite the unease expressed by some postwar Jews over books that represented their community in a less than ideal light, the National Jewish Book Council recognized *Goodbye, Columbus* as an important expression of postwar Jewish concerns, awarding it the National Jewish Book Award for fiction in 1960.[9]

Goodbye, Columbus follows protagonist Neil Klugman's romance with Brenda Patimkin, a young woman whose family had moved from the working-class Jewish enclave of Newark, New Jersey, to the affluent suburb of Short Hills. Klugman, himself a Jewish, working-class resident of Newark, is tempted by the prospect of marrying Brenda, giving up his low-paying job at the Newark Public Library, and joining Brenda's father in his prosperous business. However, he sees something limiting, even unrefined, about the role of middle-class earner promised to him by Brenda and her family.

Roth fashioned his protagonist according to the Jewish cultural ideal of the financially insecure, male intellectual. Neil Klugman majored in philosophy in college, works in a library, and bears a last name that literally means "smart" or "clever" man in Yiddish. Even though the wealth of Brenda's family makes Klugman feel insecure, his intellectual prowess allows him to feel some sense of superiority over Brenda's affluent, although less culturally sophisticated, family. "Do you know Martin Buber's work?" Neil asks Brenda's Orthodox, religiously committed mother in an attempt to build common ground.

> "Buber . . . Buber," she said, looking at her Hadassah list. "Is he orthodox or conservative?"
>
> " . . . He's a philosopher."
>
> "Is he *reformed*?" she asked, piqued either at my evasiveness or at the possibility that Buber attended Friday night services without a hat, and Mrs. Buber had only one set of dishes in her kitchen.
>
> "Orthodox," I said faintly.[10]

While Brenda's mother condescends to Neil because of his lack of wealth, Neil looks down on her for religious attachments that, to him, feel less substantive than his own engagement with the intricacies of Jewish philosophy.

If Neil finds Brenda's mother's lack of intellectualism laughable, he recoils from the coarse, aggressive masculinity modeled by Brenda's businessman father. The warehouse of Patimkin Kitchen and Bathroom Sinks is an all-male world from which Neil feels entirely alienated. From the posters of scantily clad women on the walls –"women so dreamy, so fantastically thighed and uddered" that even the very heterosexual Neil "could not think of them as pornographic"—to the commanding tone of Mr. Patimkin as he orders his employees about, Neil cannot relate to the patterns of masculinity displayed by Brenda's affluent father. He imagines himself working for Mr. Patimkin and failing miserably in his manly duty to manage the workers as they unloaded enamel sinks from the company's trucks:

> Suppose Mr. Patimkin should come up to me and say, "Okay, boy, you want to marry my daughter, let's see what you can do." Well, he would see: in a moment that floor would be a shattered mosaic, a crunchy path of enamel. "Klugman, what kind of worker are you? . . . Don't you even know how to load and unload?" "Mr. Patimkin, even breathing gives me trouble, sleep tires me out, let me go, let me go . . . "[11]

Although Neil feels insecure about his presumed inability to conform to the assertive businessman's model of masculinity demanded by the Patimkins, he is never entirely sure that he wants to give up his values for theirs and implores Mr. Patimkin to "let him go." By the end of the novel, when Neil finds Brenda willing to acquiesce to her parents' demand that they stop being sexually intimate, he determines that he can no longer accept these challenges to his own conceptions of masculinity, which included the right to premarital, sexual relationships. Consequently, he ends their relationship and embraces his choice to be a thinker rather than an earner. In the last paragraph of the novella, he has left Brenda and returned to the intellectual haven of the library, "back in plenty of time for work."[12]

Much as Philip Roth satirized the lack of intellectualism among middle-class Jews in *Goodbye, Columbus*, literary scholar Morris Freedman also doubted whether young Jewish men continued to value scholarly pursuits as they sought more remunerative careers. In 1951 Freedman was teaching courses at City College while earning his doctorate in English at Columbia University. In an article entitled "The Jewish College Student, 1951 Model: Is the Old Idealism and Zeal for Learning Gone?," he discussed what he felt were the changing aspirations of Jewish students at City College, the all-male institution at which he himself had been an undergraduate. Freedman maintained that before the war, the young Jewish men studying at City College had been idealistic about their intellectual interests, caring little about how their coursework might enhance their future job prospects. But after World War II, he lamented, Jewish students pursued degrees only as a means to achieving professional success: "The avid 'grind' reaching out to embrace diverse fields of learning . . . has given way to the college man of as few intellectual parts as he can get away with, choosing his career with calculation and shrewdness but not heart, instinct, devotion, or a sense of sacrifice," complained Freedman.[13]

According to Freedman, the masculine role models that Jewish City College students sought to emulate had shifted between the time that he was undergraduate and the postwar years. He recalled that during his time at the school, students regarded philosophy professor Morris Raphael Cohen as the "Paul Bunyon of Jewish intellectuals." Just as American boys delighted in stories about the physical power of the giant lumberjack, City College students exchanged tales of Cohen's "gigantic mental prowess" with "loving exaggeration." But in the 1950s, he complained, the Jewish student admired only the "practical men, the rich, the successful" and had little respect for "highbrows" like "Lionel Trilling, Ernest Nagel, Alfred Kazin, or Sidney Hook." Freedman, himself a scholar who aspired to the intellectual circles of Trilling and Kazin, felt threatened by these shifts in masculine ideals. He perceived a loss in social status as higher-earning businessmen and professionals came to dominate Jewish communities and commanded the respect of Jewish students.[14]

Contrary to Freedman's claim that postwar Jews no longer gave scholars like Morris Raphael Cohen the respect they deserved, however, *The Eternal Light*, a radio show produced by the Conservative movement's Jewish

Masculinity in an Upwardly Mobile Community

Theological Seminary of America, broadcast a program to honor Cohen and his accomplishments in 1953. The radio script represented Cohen as the antithesis of the upwardly mobile male breadwinner, portraying him as a man who refused lucrative and prestigious career opportunities in order to uphold his principles. In the following section of fictionalized dialogue, for instance, Cohen turned down a high-status university position after being pressured to change his identifiably Jewish name:

> Dean: I have been authorized to offer you a position on our faculty.... The salary, I may add is as high as that offered by any University in the country.
> Cohen: It's a tempting offer.
> Dean: There's just one small matter ... that is, the faculty clubs limit their membership.... It's not a question of congeniality, its more a matter, for example of your name.
> Cohen: My name is an old one, borne by the hereditary high priests of Israel.... The first words I spoke were in Yiddish and the first I read were in the Hebrew of the Bible and the Commentaries. These things are a part of me and I have no desire to change them, even if I could.
> Dean: I am afraid you misunderstand me, Dr. Cohen.
> Cohen: No, I understand you very well, but I will not let it spoil my temper. Good day.[15]

The Eternal Light dramatized the life and choices of Morris Raphael Cohen as a cautionary tale for those American Jewish men who might have been tempted to abandon their values and attenuate their Jewishness in exchange for wealth and stature. Indeed, by celebrating Cohen's refusal to grab at the chance of economic advancement and cultural assimilation into the American elite, the radio script offered a critique of the middle-class, male breadwinner as the ultimate ideal for American Jews.

The Eternal Light continued to provide counterimages to the ideal of the affluent, male breadwinner in 1959, with a script that dramatized the challenges of a fictional high school teacher named Dave Gorman. Though struggling to make ends meet on his modest income and complaining to his wife that "it's easy to run through a teacher's salary," Gorman remains an idealist who believes he can inspire his students to greatness. He encourages one of his students, an aspiring poet named Frank Miller, to apply to a university where he can work on his writing. Frank's businessman father disagrees with Gorman's advice and angrily confronts him.

Miller: That's what I want you to do. Get him to give up the idea of going to college to—to fool around with poems and stories!

Dave: You are asking a very difficult thing. . . . I'm your son's teacher, Mr. Miller. I'll tell you what I want for him. I want to help him make the most of himself, the most of what he really is. . . . I think you also want the same thing.

Miller: You listen to me, Gorman! I'm not sending my son to college to be an academic bum, a Phi Beta Kappa without a decent suit of clothes, a . . . a . . .

Dave: A teacher?

Miller: Who are you to decide that you're right and I'm wrong? I can buy and sell you a dozen times over![16]

With this exchange, *The Eternal Light* pitted two ideals of masculinity against each other. Mr. Miller demands that his son become a high-earning businessman like himself, while the son's teacher, Mr. Gorman, encouraged him to choose a lifestyle of intellectualism and modest earnings. The script ends before the son actually makes his choice. However, the way the script characterizes the two men who embody these opposite ideals, portraying Dave Gorman as thoughtful and articulate and Mr. Miller as bombastic and ill-mannered, clearly indicates the path that the authors of *The Eternal Light* would have wanted young Frank to take.

Much like the male intellectuals who believed that their work no longer garnered the respect it deserved, rabbis, too, lamented what they viewed as the diminishing prominence of their own venerable profession among postwar American Jews. At a time when only men could join the American rabbinate, rabbinical complaints over their loss of status served as an implicit challenge to the changing ideals of Jewish masculinity in an upwardly mobile community.

For instance, Rabbi Edgar Siskin of Glencoe, Illinois, devoted his 1952 Rosh Hashanah sermon to bemoaning the lack of social stature claimed by rabbis in the postwar years. "In the Jewish tradition, the [religious] scholar occupied the highest rung on the communal ladder . . . he was accorded more honor and status than anyone else," he preached. However, complained Siskin, as American Jews have "assimilated the success ethics of America," the rabbi has "almost been lost in the shuffle . . . treated with a mixture of amusement, pity and disdain." To postwar rabbis, who had presumably decided against more remunerative careers in favor of religious leadership, this perceived lack of respect for their positions as scholars and leaders felt quite personal. They urged their constituents to return to what they believed to be more authentic Jewish values that prioritized learning over wealth, and to allow rabbis to reclaim what they felt was their rightful place as the most respected members of the community.[17]

Rabbis of the postwar years often complained that wealthy business-men and male professionals had come to dominate American synagogues, a realm in which, they felt, the rabbi should certainly hold ultimate authority. In 1962, for instance, Maurice N. Eisendrath, president of the Reform move-ment's Union of American Hebrew Congregations, declared that the "cult of mammon" had invaded American synagogues. The wealthiest members of postwar congregations, he complained, had effectively edged out their rabbis from a decision-making role and rarely deferred to their expertise. In con-sequence, he believed that American synagogues suffered from a veritable "dictatorship" of the financially successful.[18]

Not only did rabbis worry about their own diminished status among a wealth-conscious population, but some also feared that they themselves had become corrupted by models of masculinity that prioritized affluence over spirituality, service, and scholarship. According to Rabbi Simon Greenberg, vice-chancellor of the Conservative movement's Jewish Theological Semi-nary, postwar rabbis often felt guilty when they accepted posts in flush sub-urbs that offered them a high salary and middle-class standard of living. If a rabbi "has attained reasonable physical comfort and economic security, he suspects himself of having fallen prey to the fleshpots," wrote Greenberg in the pages of *Conservative Judaism* magazine. Such rabbis, according to Greenberg, feared that their attachment to these comforts compromised their integrity. "Visions of a Jeremiah, an Amos, an Akiba, an Israel Salanter, a Herzl, a hum-ble chalutz, constantly haunt him," wrote Greenberg, referring to a series of iconic male figures from Jewish sacred texts and Jewish history who had re-linquished social acceptance and financial security to pursue their high ideals.

Greenberg's article revealed the competing models of masculinity that rabbis negotiated during the postwar years. While they may have wanted to model their lives after men who had been financially insolvent proph-ets, scholars, and idealists, they also felt the lure of the material and social rewards that would come from a successful pulpit in a wealthy commu-nity. Greenberg's lament underscored the often-conflicted role of postwar American rabbis, who were both dependent on their affluent congregants for their own income and security and yet critical of communal values that seemed to prioritize wealth over more spiritual concerns and honored the businessman over the rabbi.[19]

In addition to bemoaning what they perceived to be the diminished prestige of male scholars and rabbis, American Jewish leaders looked to the nascent state of Israel for alternative models of Jewish masculinity that that seemed to contrast sharply with the image of the middle-class breadwinner. Certainly, the Zionist project's preoccupation with Jewish masculinity has been well documented. Early Zionists such as Theodor Herzl and Max Nordau had internalized antisemitic conceptions of Jewish men as passive, overly intellectual, weak, effeminate, and in possession of an uncanny and unnatural knack for business. These early Zionist theorists aimed to transform Jewish men from scrawny moneymakers into a new breed of what Nordau termed "Muscle Jews," ready to use their physical might to reclaim their ancestral homeland. In later years, the Zionist culture that emerged in the State of Israel retained this focus on aggressive masculinity and emphasized military heroism and physical strength as the ideal among its male citizens.[20]

American Jewish men also wrestled with long-standing, antisemitic stereotypes that painted them as physically weak, cowardly, and preternaturally good with money. Indeed, during the immigrant era, American Jews had expressed hope that the freedom found on American shores would transform the Jewish man from "a shrunken, wizened creature afraid of his own shadow to a being unafraid, buoyant, and erect." By the 1930s, American-born Jewish sportsmen like boxer Barney Ross and baseball player Hank Greenberg challenged widespread misconceptions regarding the physical inferiority of Jewish men. Likewise, the 550,000 Jewish soldiers who served in the U.S. Army during World War II also helped to convince more of the American public, and American Jews themselves, that Jewish men could live up to American ideals of masculine toughness.[21]

In spite of these developments, however, some American Jews continued to fear that Jewish men had not sufficiently demonstrated their capacity for strength and heroism. This concern proved especially evident in discussions over Jewish upward mobility, as the proliferation of professional, breadwinning Jewish men—who seemed to live up to the 1950s cultural specter of the "man in the grey flannel suit"—seemed to reinforce stereotypes of Jewish men as greedy, puny, and cowardly.

But if the lifestyles of middle-class American Jews did little to disprove preconceptions of the weakness of Jewish men, romantic visions of the tough, male, Israeli soldier certainly did. Idealized images of Israeli soldiers circulated among American Jews in the postwar years, and several American Jewish writers used these images of Israeli men to castigate the choices of their middle-class, American counterparts.

For instance, Ben Hecht, a noted Hollywood screenwriter, playwright, and proponent of a militant, revisionist Zionism, often portrayed the men fighting for the Jewish state as tougher, braver, and more idealistic than their well-to-do American coreligionists. In the years before Israel achieved its independence, Hecht penned the forceful rhetoric of the American League for a Free Palestine, an organization that supported the Irgun, the underground Zionist organization that carried out guerrilla warfare against the British authorities who then controlled the area. His propaganda materials, which appeared in Broadway plays, in newspaper advertisements, and organizational pamphlets, not only valorized the strength and bravery of the Jewish men who performed terrorist acts aimed at unseating the British mandate but also painted American Jewish men as deficient, even effete, in comparison.

On September 5, 1946, *A Flag Is Born*, a play written by Hecht and produced by the American League for a Free Palestine, opened in New York's Alvin Playhouse. The play featured three Jewish survivors of the Holocaust: the sick and dying Tevya, played by Paul Muni; his wife Zelda, played by Yiddish theater actress Celia Adler; and a bitter young man named David, played by a then-unknown Marlon Brando. Tevya and Zelda, who recoil from David's anger and budding propensity for violence, end up meeting their deaths in an abandoned Jewish graveyard in Europe. The young David is about to follow suit by committing suicide, when he encounters three male soldiers from Palestine who rehabilitate him by convincing him to join the underground army. These soldiers reignite David's will to live not only by promising him an independent state but also by modeling for him an aggressive, militant, Jewish masculinity: "Come David, Saul and the Maccabees live again in Palestine. Their strong arms are bared again. . . . The manhood the world took from us roars again in Palestine."[22]

As *A Flag Is Born* valorized the "muscle Jews" of Mandate Palestine, it simultaneously rebuked wealthy Jewish men from America and England for their supposed timidity and lack of aggression. David spoke directly to middle-class Jews in one of the most memorable speeches of the play: "Where were you—Jews? Where were you when the killing was going on? When the six million were burned and buried alive in the lime pits, where were you? . . . Strong Jews, rich Jews, high-up Jews; Jews of power and genius! . . . Where was your cry of rage that would have filled the world and stopped the fires? Nowhere!"[23] To Hecht, middle-class Jewish men lacked the heroism of the men who fought for a Jewish state. Perhaps if they had been less respectable, less wealthy, and more prone to manly belligerence, he implied, they could have stopped the Holocaust from happening. Hecht's rhetoric proved effective,

Still from *A Flag Is Born*, 1946.
Used with permission from Getty Images.

and members of the audience of *A Flag Is Born* rushed to respond to an appeal made after the show to donate money to the Irgun for "armament, supplies and survival."[24]

Hecht also drew comparisons between the supposed weakness of American Jewish men and the toughness of Jewish militants in Palestine within the pamphlets he distributed to American Jews in hopes of raising funds for the Irgun. One such brochure took the form of a letter written by Hecht "to the Terrorists of Palestine," in which Hecht explained why, in his opinion, many American Jews did not support the Irgun's guerrilla attacks.

Masculinity in an Upwardly Mobile Community

Those American Jews who denounced the terrorists, Hecht claimed, included "practically all the rich Jews of America, all the important ones, all the influential ones." "Jewish wealth and respectability," wrote Hecht with acid sarcasm, "are fearlessly rushing sandwiches" to the Jewish survivors of the war, instead of purchasing weapons with which they could secure a state. In Hecht's view, these well-off Jews' "exhibition of weak stomachs, weak minds and weak spines" contrasted sharply with the "brave men" of the Irgun, who continued to fight "despite torture, calumny, low supplies and overwhelming odds." He enjoined American Jewish men to reclaim their masculinity by using their wealth to arm terrorists instead of buying foodstuffs, items stereotypically associated with nurturing femininity rather than aggressive masculinity, for the starving survivors of the Holocaust.[25] Hecht's fundraising propaganda went so far as to equate donating money for arms with actual, physical attacks. "*Now* is the time to throw another punch, the strongest one you can. $250 saves a life. . . . *Hit hard to save more lives,*" insisted one 1947 advertisement printed in *PM Magazine*. Hecht's rhetoric offered affluent American Jewish men a way to identify with militant Zionist fighters from the safety of their middle-class homes.[26]

In 1951, four years after Israel became an independent Jewish state, the well-known novelist and Zionist Meyer Levin joined Hecht in contrasting Israeli men to well-off American Jewish men supposedly weakened by virtue of their middle-class lifestyles. In a satirical short story, "After All I Did for Israel," Levin mocked an American Jewish businessman who had organized a fundraiser for Israel and invited an idealistic, young soldier from the Israeli army to speak to the crowd. Instead of simply thanking the Americans for their time and money, the soldier encouraged the Americans to move to the Jewish state. Levin described the response of the well-to-do audience as follows: "I don't think many people really knew what he was saying; they were just looking at him, what a fine example of Palestine youth, and every one of the women was figuring maybe he would fall in love with her daughter and she'd put him through medical school and since the war was won over in Israel, he wouldn't have to go back, and she could set him up in a fine downtown practice."[27]

Levin's story painted the fundraising activities of wealthy American Jews as laughable and even hypocritical, as they willingly donated their excess money to Israel but balked at the idea of moving there themselves. The author scoffed at the notion that an Israeli war hero would consider relinquishing his ideals and leaving his homeland to become a wealthy professional. Indeed, in Levin's story, the move went the other way. Instead of the soldier moving to America, the soldier convinced the son of the American businessman to give up his professional prospects and relocate to Israel. American Jewish men, implied Levin, had two models of masculinity they could follow; they could pattern their lives after the somewhat ridiculous, affluent breadwinners, like the American Jewish businessman who had organized the fundraiser, or they could follow in the steps of the Israeli soldier, move to the Jewish homeland, and live a life of rugged, heroic idealism. For Levin, relocating to Israel clearly represented the more admirable choice.

Novelist Leon Uris crafted the consummate, and certainly best-known, male Israeli hero with Ari Ben Canaan, the protagonist of his 1958 best seller *Exodus*, which dramatized the story of the Israeli struggle for independence. Topping the U.S. best-seller list for close to five months in 1959, Uris's influential narrative played a determinative role in generating American sympathy for Israel and convincing the U.S. public that the Jewish state represented a beacon of civilization in a hostile and backward Middle East.[28]

In addition to the impact that *Exodus* had on the American view of Israel, however, it also revealed some of the anxieties of both the author Uris and of the many American Jews who, in the words of rabbi and scholar Arthur Hertzberg, adopted the novel as their "bible" during the postwar years. Certainly, the lives of the fictional Israeli heroes of *Exodus* could not have diverged any further from the circumstances of American Jews. Although a relatively small proportion of actual Israelis lived in the socialist agricultural collectives known as *kibbutzim* and *moshavim*, nearly all of Uris's Israeli characters lived in these settlements, fearlessly building successful farms out of dry, desert land as they resisted Arab attacks. Moreover, as Uris made clear, these valiant *kibbutz* dwellers performed this back-breaking labor without the incentive of personal gain, since even after years of hard work, "even the clothes on their back" did not belong to them but to the settlement as a whole. As Uris romanticized the selfless accomplishments of these Israelis, he leveled a tacit reproach at his American Jewish readers who enjoyed affluence and security as Israelis made sacrifices on behalf of the Jewish state.[29]

Of all of the heroic characters created by Uris in *Exodus*, none matched the figure of the intrepid soldier, Ari Ben Canaan. The paradigmatic representative of what Paul Breines has termed the "tough Jew," Uris portrayed Ari as something of a superman. "Six feet tall," "hard and powerful," and with "the strength of a lion," Ari could work for days without sleeping, outsmart British blockades, repel Arab attacks on the borders of the new state, and bear pain that "could have killed an ordinary human being." And for all of his talents and abilities, Ari had no desire for affluence or luxury. He longed only for the Israeli state to be militarily secure, so that he could "come home" to his farm and "work on his land."[30]

Masculinity in an Upwardly Mobile Community

With the character of Ari Ben Canaan, Uris provided American Jews with a model of Jewish masculinity that diverged quite sharply from the ideal of the middle-class breadwinner. Indeed, when she first met Ari Ben Canaan, the American nurse Kitty Fremont pointed out the ways in which he differed from the Jewish men that Kitty had known in America: "This Ben Canaan doesn't act like any Jew I've ever met," she noted. "You know what I mean. You don't particularly think of them in a capacity like this . . . or fighters . . . things of that sort."[31]

Uris articulated the significance that tough Israeli soldiers like Ari Ben Canaan presumably had for American Jewish men through the voice of a minor yet important character, the grizzled American ship captain Bill Fry. Fry appears in the novel when he smuggles ships loaded with Jewish refugees through the British blockade in the years prior to Israeli independence. When asked why he, as an American Jew, opted to engage in this struggle, he explained that while he "loved America" and "wouldn't trade" what he had there for "fifty Palestines," he still felt invested in the cause of the Jewish state because it offered him a more heroic model of Jewish masculinity that countered stereotypes of Jewish cowardice. "All my life I've heard I'm supposed to be a coward because I'm a Jew," clarified Frye. But the tough, male soldiers fighting for a Jewish state make "a liar out of everyone who tells me Jews are yellow. These guys over here are fighting my battle for self respect." For Uris, the success of the State of Israel had become a priority for American Jewish men specifically because it allowed them to claim a militant masculinity. This fight for the Jewish state, Uris intimated in *Exodus*, offered a narrative through which American Jewish men could overcome stereotypes of cowardice and greed and garner the admiration of the non-Jewish world.[32]

Sociologist Marshall Sklare interviewed professional Jewish men who, much like Uris, Hecht, and Levin, also believed that the tough masculinity and military success exhibited by Israeli soldiers had a salutary effect on the relationship between American Jews and non-Jews. In 1958, Sklare queried the Jewish inhabitants of Highland Park, Illinois, about their feelings toward Israel. One prosperous accountant opined that the victories of Israeli soldiers convinced non-Jews that "Jews have the guts to stand up and fight—that the Jew is a *man*, not just a merchant." The revealing, gendered language chosen by this respondent underscored the ambivalence felt by some postwar American Jewish men as they pursued, and often excelled at, middle-class occupations that offered them financial security in the United States but did little to assuage antisemitic stereotypes of Jewish men as effete, greedy, and uncannily good with money. Tough Israeli soldiers, in the mind of this accountant, had proved the manliness of all Jewish men, in a way that American Jewish men, for all of their economic success, had not.

Another one of Sklare's respondents, a wealthy lawyer, expressed a certain amount of guilt over his feeling that the toughness and bravery of Israeli men had afforded Jewish men in America a measure of respect that they had not earned. "I think the Gentiles admired what the Israelis did," stated this informant. "I think we got something we didn't deserve from it," he added, when non-Jewish approval of Israel's military prowess "spilled over to us." His response, once again, revealed the ambivalence of middle-class, American Jewish men who had chosen careers that offered them comfort and security, instead of following Israeli men who, in the minds of their American Jewish counterparts, eschewed the prospect of affluence to pursue a path of national service and military heroism.[33]

While the figure of the tough Israeli soldier seems, in some ways, to represent the polar opposite of the stereotype of the brainy, male Jewish scholar, among postwar American Jews these contrasting models of masculinity shared an important commonality. They both represented an alternative to the expectation that all Jewish men would inevitably become the stable and successful breadwinners of their families by devoting their lives to pursuing high-paying careers in medicine, law, or business. To those upwardly mobile Jewish men bristling under middle-class gender norms, both models of Jewish masculinity seemed like inspiring ideals, indeed.

The perception that American Jewish men lacked the toughness of Israelis, along with the notion that American Jews no longer respected male rabbis and intellectuals, underscored a similar, and deeply gendered, ambivalence over Jewish upward mobility in the postwar years. The rabbis, writers, and intellectuals profiled in this chapter, and even those everyday denizens of Jewish suburbia who answered Marshall Sklare's questionnaires or circulated uncomfortable jokes regarding the lowered prestige of the rabbinate, understood that a middle-class milieu placed new pressures on American Jewish men to choose high-income careers. To be clear, most American Jewish men embraced the opportunity to run successful businesses, earn professional degrees, and take in salaries that propelled themselves, and their families, into the privileged world of the middle class. However, at times, they also experienced these demands as limiting and restrictive.

While Jewish men joined many other Americans as they fretted over a supposed crisis in masculinity caused by unprecedented postwar prosperity, the Jewish Americans profiled in this chapter did not rely on best-selling social critics to analyze their economic climb. Instead, they adopted a particularly

Jewish lexicon through which to interrogate their rising financial status and middle-class identity and developed a distinctively Jewish set of alternative masculine ideals. The history, collective memory, and shared mythology of the Jewish people provided them with a rich array of symbols through which to express deeply felt concerns about becoming part of an affluent middle-class majority. The tendency to turn to their Jewish heritage for a language of critique emerged as one important way that postwar American Jews remained culturally distinct as they embraced the American middle class.

Significantly, the texts that idealized Jewish male soldiers and intellectuals also imagined a world in which Jewish women were either absent or marginal. Morris Raphael Cohen, upheld as the paradigmatic Jewish intellectual in so many of these discussions, worked in the all-male world of City College, an institution that did not admit women until four years after his death. Likewise, the American Jewish rabbis who bemoaned their loss of status during the postwar years worked within a field that did not yet admit women into its ranks. Finally, while images of female Israeli soldiers sometimes did appear in books like Uris's *Exodus*, these women fighters were almost always eclipsed by the powerful men who controlled both the battlefield and the narrative. While the men who formulated this gendered critique of Jewish upward mobility may have resented the expectation that Jewish men serve as breadwinners in middle-class families, their criticisms did not challenge the male dominance that characterized those families.

Still, no less than American Jewish men, American Jewish women in the postwar era also faced new expectations regarding their proper roles in the middle class community. Developing alongside these postwar critiques of Jewish masculinity was another, related conversation about American Jewish women and the lives that they could, and should, be leading as they moved into the middle class. It is to this tense and conflicted conversation that we now turn.

FIVE

Hadassah Makes You Important

Debating Middle-Class Jewish Femininity

In 1957 Hadassah, the Women's Zionist Organization of America, attempted to recruit middle-class Jewish homemakers by promising them a way to make an impact on the world beyond the confines of their comfortable suburban homes. "Hadassah Makes You Important!" trumpeted one 1957 membership brochure above a photograph of a well-coiffed housewife sporting manicured nails and gold-knot earrings. Indirectly challenging postwar middle-class conventions that limited women's activities to hearth and home, this campaign sent a message to upwardly mobile Jewish women that involvement in Hadassah would offer them the kind of substance and fulfillment that they could not attain through household responsibilities.[1]

While this particular Hadassah campaign encouraged potential members to pursue activities outside of the home, American Jewish women during the postwar period received many, and often conflicting, messages about how they ought to conduct their lives as they entered the middle class. No less than American Jewish men, American Jewish women also faced new expectations regarding their proper roles in a middle-class community. As postwar Jewish men felt pressure to become breadwinners, the mores of the middle class stipulated that married women limit their interests to the needs of home and family. Jewish women received mixed messages from their leaders as they negotiated their responses to these middle-class prescriptions for domesticity. Some Jewish leaders supported middle-class gender ideologies, and warned Jewish women against spending too much time away from domestic responsibilities. Others, including the leaders of Hadassah, encouraged Jewish women to defy postwar gender norms and to engage, fully and deeply, in the public sphere.

"Hadassah Makes You Important" brochure cover, 1957.
Used with permission from American Jewish Historical Society, New York and Boston.

Significantly, both those leaders who believed that Jewish women needed to contribute to the world outside of their homes and those who feared that they were spending too much time away from their families all tended to agree that the rising affluence of American Jews posed a threat to Jewish women and the Jewish families they were supposed to be raising. Some leaders believed that those middle-class Jewish women whose husband's salaries allowed them to retreat from public engagement did not lead productive and meaningful lives. Others maintained the opposite: that Jewish housewives spent too much of their energy away from domestic pursuits and that their unpaid organizational work endangered the cohesion of the Jewish family. Jewish women, therefore, faced contradictory advice, counseling, and directives over how to negotiate their roles in an upwardly mobile community.

Postwar expectations of women's domesticity differed from what had been expected of Jewish women earlier in the century. While American Jewish women had left wage work upon marriage as early as the immigrant era, they still contributed to the family economy in other ways, caring for boarders in their tenement apartments and laboring in family businesses. The income generated by married Jewish women, however, no longer seemed necessary once Jewish men were in a position to support their families on their own. Upwardly mobile Jewish families could now afford to subscribe more fully to domestic norms that testified to their middle-class status. Indeed, married Jewish women tended to retreat from wage work at slightly higher rates than their non-Jewish counterparts. In 1957, 27.8 percent of married Jewish women worked for wages, as opposed to 29.6 percent of non-Jewish women. This disparity intensified among married women with children under the age of six, when only 11.8 percent of Jewish women, as opposed to 17 percent of non-Jewish women, worked outside of the home.[2]

But even after their families could afford to survive on the earnings of a sole, male, breadwinner, married Jewish women rarely restricted their activities to the domestic sphere. In addition to the nearly 28 percent of married Jewish women who continued to contribute to the family income, middle-class Jewish women worked without wages for a variety of causes. They became leaders and activists on behalf of both Jewish and nonsectarian causes, and their unpaid labor served as the backbone of local civic institutions.[3]

The postwar suburban environment supported the trend of unpaid communal leadership for both Jewish and non-Jewish women. While men spent the bulk of their time pursuing professional goals in the city, women sustained the institutions serving their home communities. The gender patterns of

suburbia, therefore, offered unprecedented opportunities for women to become leaders in religious and civic life. Though the status and monetary rewards continued to go to men, women spearheaded and maintained the local
infrastructure of the postwar suburbs.[4]

Middle-class Jewish women, like their non-Jewish peers, took advantage
of the opportunity to serve their communities, and Jewish life in the postwar suburbs depended on their efforts. Women's fundraising provided much
of the money for both local Jewish institutions and for international Jewish
causes, such as support for the survivors of the Holocaust. Within the synagogue, suburban Jewish women organized social and fundraising events, ran
libraries and gift shops, served on educational committees, and taught in religious schools. They were more than twice as likely as their male counterparts
to hold a leadership position in the local chapter of a Jewish organization and
to consider this work their most satisfying activity. "This is the one thing I
do that isn't for myself or for my children," explained one suburban Jewish
woman to sociologist Marshall Sklare as she described her work on behalf
of vocational programs for disadvantaged Jewish youth through her involvement in Women's ORT, the Organization of Rehabilitation through Training.
"In general, the women live a greater part of their life within the Jewish group,
and are more concerned with it and about it than the men," found sociologist
Herbert Gans in yet another study of the postwar Jewish suburbs.[5]

Jewish women such as Faye Harriton of Levittown, Long Island, felt quite
proud of the crucial role they played in building and sustaining the suburban
Jewish infrastructure. Harriton, who moved to in Levittown as a young mother
in the late 1940s, described the process by which she and her peers organized
and funded the Jewish institutions in their new communities. She and her
fellow suburban Jewish housewives asked their husbands "to be home early on
Sisterhood nights" during which they "nominated ... officers, ran card parties,
sold home-made Jewish delicacies, held a Community Seder ... solicited donations, ran dances, apple festivals, *Hanukkah* parties, and the like." Largely as
a result of their efforts, their congregation was soon able to erect a synagogue
building, construct a religious school, and hire a rabbi. Harriton noted that the
members of her community were "increasingly aware of the important role
women play in the modern synagogue and our necessary contribution toward
its financial and spiritual support."[6]

Not all leaders applauded the positions of authority held by Jewish
women in the suburban synagogues they had worked so hard to build.
Newton's Rabbi Albert Gordon, for instance, thought women lay leaders
lacked the qualifications to uphold a viable religious institution. "Judaism

requires that its lay leaders also possess specific and even detailed knowledge of the basic texts and rituals of Judaism. The Jewish woman is unfortunately not prepared as yet for this kind of leadership," he contended. But instead of recommending that the synagogues offer their female leaders the education that he deemed necessary for the roles they performed, Gordon instead suggested that Jewish women limit their involvement to social programming and leave the weightier tasks for the men.[7]

Other leaders begrudged Jewish women the time they spent outside of the home as they sustained Jewish life in the suburbs. These leaders embraced the dominant ideal of the male breadwinner and the female homemaker, describing middle-class gender norms newly adopted by upwardly mobile American Jews as a quintessentially Jewish way of organizing family life. In a 1955 manual distributed by the Reform movement to couples about to be wed, Rabbi Jerome Folkman went so far as to imprint these domestic ideals on the religious rituals practiced at the Sabbath table. "The role of the husband and father," explained Folkman, "includes the blessing of the bread . . . which represents the physical necessities of life." This ritual properly belonged to the Jewish husband, continued Folkman, because "he is the breadwinner."[8]

Similarly, in a 1959 guide for Jewish homemakers, authors Shonie B. Levi and Sylvia R. Kaplan insisted that Jewish culture had long depended on the work of Jewish housewives who devoted themselves entirely to domestic pursuits. Levi and Kaplan, both leaders in the National Women's League of Conservative Judaism, argued that traditional Judaism offered these female homemakers a kind of respect that they no longer enjoyed. The Yiddish language, they explained, referred to housewives by the word *balabosteh*, which "literally means 'mistress of the home.'" According to Levi and Kaplan, the term itself proved that Old World Jews had once thought of homemakers as "important executives." Knowing the significance of the housewife's role in traditional Judaism, they added, "should raise our status in our own eyes" and "offset the diffidence we sometimes feel when we fill out a form 'Occupation—Housewife.'"[9]

For the Reform movement's Albert Vorspan and Eugene Lipman, the upward mobility of American Jews threatened the integrity of the traditional Jewish family that they understood as being supported economically by a male earner and nurtured by a full-time mother. In *Justice and Judaism*, a 1956 volume otherwise aimed at bolstering American Jewish commitments to social justice and economic equality, they warned Jewish women against working for wages. The materialist society of postwar America, they argued, compelled even financially secure families to "keep up with the Joneses" and buy things that they could not easily afford. In this situation, they believed, "many middle-class wives who would prefer to concentrate on their homes and children feel themselves forced into the job market to supplement the earnings of their husbands in order to provide the expanded 'necessities' of the family." Mothers who spent a great deal of time away from their homes, they warned, destroyed their family's "cohesiveness" and compromised the "security" of the children. To combat these and other incursions upon what they viewed as the ideal Jewish family, Vorspan and Lipman suggested that synagogues educate their congregants about the "uniquely Jewish conception of marriage and the family" through sermons, lectures, religious school lessons, and adult education courses.[10]

Molly Forman, a Jewish mother and sisterhood member from Camden, New Jersey, echoed the idea that the money women could earn through wage work threatened to lure them from their proper place in the home. In an article that appeared in *Women's League Outlook*, a magazine distributed to the 200,000 members of the National Women's League of Conservative Judaism, she offered her own life story as a morality tale for other Jewish women. While Forman had originally "loved and lived for her work" and "shuddered" at the thought of living the "dull, drab and out-of-touch existence" of a housewife, she nonetheless felt compelled to become a full-time homemaker when her capable housekeeper quit. Upon noticing her daughter's joy at seeing her when she returned home from school, Forman finally recognized that "all the material things which my independent income could shower on her were not enough! It was me, my presence, my nearness she wanted most."[11]

For Forman, leaving the workforce allowed her to become not only "a mother in the fullest sense of the word" but also a better *Jewish* mother. No longer beset with workplace obligations, she joined her local synagogue and began to learn more about her "rich heritage." "I knew naught before," she explained, "I hadn't the time for such things." Within this article, acknowledged by the editors of *Outlook* as being "challenging," the salaries earned by women (but not men) distracted them from their more important and fulfilling roles as parents and active Jews.[12]

It was not only working mothers who were cautioned against neglecting their domestic responsibilities as they enjoyed the benefits of the postwar economic boom. The vilification of affluent Jewish housewives emerged as a pervasive theme in postwar Jewish discourse, as critics charged that these women damaged their families as they pursued unpaid communal involvements outside of the home. Trude Weiss-Rosmarin's *The Jewish Spectator* printed one of the most vitriolic rants targeting suburban Jewish homemakers in 1962. In an article entitled "The Organization Woman," psychologist

Samuel Kling attacked middle-class Jewish housewives for being "arrogant, spoiled and exceptionally aggressive" as they abandoned their families in favor of "clubs, organizations, luncheons, courses, book reviews and other 'cultural' activities." Taking his cues from Philip Wylie's *Generation of Vipers*, which had accused "idle" American mothers of using their organizational work not to improve society but to "compel an abject compliance of her environs to her personal desires," Kling too viewed Jewish women's unpaid labor as something destructive rather than admirable. Eventually, he insisted, those affluent Jewish mothers who pursued interests apart from the needs of their husbands and children would "destroy" the "family fabric" of American Jews.[13]

Similar thoughts came from Victor Geller, who supported Orthodox Jewish communities in suburbia through his position in the Community Service division of Yeshiva University. Geller, too, begrudged Jewish women their unpaid labor as communal leaders in the suburbs of postwar America. Suburban Jewish mothers, Geller noted, spent a great deal of time at meetings of the local religious school, the synagogue sisterhood, and Hadassah. While Geller conceded the worth of these activities, he nonetheless accused affluent Jewish women of being "over-involved" and neglecting to make family "togetherness" a priority. For Geller, the tendency of Jewish women to pursue interests outside of the care of husbands and children compromised both the integrity of the Jewish community and the health of the Jewish family.[14]

As Kling and Geller posited that middle-class Jewish housewives neglected their families as they pursued organizational work, Jewish sociologist Erich Rosenthal warned that affluent Jewish women proved less likely to bear children, eroding what he considered to be a "traditional" Jewish emphasis on fertility and child-rearing. In a 1961 study, Rosenthal found that American Jews did not participate in the postwar "baby boom" at the same rate as other religious groups. As of 1957, children under fourteen years of age represented 27.7 percent of the Catholic community, 26.7 percent of white Protestants, but only 22.2 percent of Jews. Rosenthal attributed the lower levels of Jewish fertility to the greater proportion of American Jews who had adopted middle-class lifestyle patterns. Not only did he discover that high-earning households tended to have fewer children; he also found that women with higher levels of education were less likely to have large families. This particularly affected middle-class Jewish women, who had been twice as likely to graduate from college as other white American women during the postwar years.[15] For Rosenthal and others concerned with Jewish natalism, the increasing financial and educational achievements of American Jewry seemed to impede their ability to reproduce and endangered the continuity of Jewish life in America.[16]

Debating Middle-Class Jewish Femininity

While newly affluent Jewish women certainly received their share of directives telling them to spend less time on work, education, and communal service and more time bearing children and nurturing their families, they also encountered just as much—if not more—of the opposite advice. Many Jewish leaders, both male and female, strongly encouraged women to reach outside of their homes and have an impact in the public sphere. Even Shonie Levi and Sylvia Kaplan, who had exhorted Jewish women to take pride in their status as homemakers, also felt strongly that Jewish housewives should volunteer their time in both Jewish and non-Jewish organizations. These affiliations not only enabled Jewish women "to perform the mitzvah [commandment] of service" but also provided them a "ready outlet" for their talents and skills.[17]

Indeed, some of these leaders even cautioned teenaged girls that a life entirely devoted to their own homes and families would lead to discontent. In *Blessed Is the Daughter*, a 1959 volume intended as a gift to girls celebrating their bat mitzvah milestone, Sulamith Ish-Kishor, a well-known author of Jewish children's literature, warned her young, female readers that a Jewish woman's "usefulness must extend beyond her own family." Jewish women, she insisted, had a responsibility to serve and educate their communities and to aid poor and suffering people around the world. Those who did not, she added, would certainly come to regret it, as "the really unhappy woman is the selfish woman."[18]

Many of the Jewish housewives who heeded this call to service and activism did so through the auspices of Hadassah, the Women's Zionist Organization of America. Founded by Henrietta Szold in 1912 in order to establish Jewish institutions in Palestine and to promote Zionism in America, the organization funded and built a system of health clinics, hospitals, and vocational programs throughout Israel. One of the main organizations to benefit from the unpaid labor of affluent Jewish women in the postwar years, Hadassah, in the opinion of writer Maurice Samuel, "rescued tens of thousands of Jewish women from the futilities and vacuities of the middle-class pattern of recent times."[19]

Much of Hadassah's promotional material built on the assumption that upwardly mobile, American Jewish women might welcome the opportunity to accomplish more than what might be expected of them within middle-class norms of domesticity. The "Hadassah Makes You Important" campaign of 1957, for instance, promised potential members that the organization would enable them to "*work* through the largest and most important organization of its kind *to defend* the American way of life," underlining active verbs like

"This Is Your Life in Hadassah" brochure cover, 1954.
Used with permission from American Jewish Historical Society, New York and Boston.

"work" and "defend" that the conventions of postwar America associated more with male soldiers and breadwinners than with feminine housewives.[20]

Another brochure from 1954, under the headline "This Is Your Life in Hadassah," displayed a picture of a carefully coiffed woman superimposed in front of photographs of female nurses, male surgeons, and male welders in Israel. If the well-off American Jewish housewife would not actually go to work as a nurse, surgeon, or welder herself, this campaign assured her that her support for those who performed these important tasks made her contribution just as crucial. "Your life has meaning for you because it is bringing meaning to the life of others," read the back cover of the brochure, promising middle-class Jewish homemakers that their involvement in Hadassah could help them build more significant lives that transcended, to some extent, the limits of postwar femininity.[21]

In addition to rhetorically linking the unpaid labor of American Jewish housewives with the ostensibly more important activities of the Israelis that they supported, the Hadassah organization also offered some of its younger members an opportunity to move to Israel and engage directly in the enterprise of state building. Beginning in 1946, Hadassah provided its junior members with an avenue to relinquish the comforts of the American middle class and join the movement to build the land of Israel through a *chalutziut*, or pioneering, program. This initiative supported young American Jews who wanted to live permanently in Israel and start their own kibbutz. In a 1948 brochure for Junior Hadassah, the organization promised that "the best of American youth" would embrace this chance to serve the Jewish state and that those who remained in America would "derive inspiration" from the ones who made the move. The photograph accompanying this description of the program portrayed a young woman wearing boots and trousers and working in a chicken coop, an image that contrasted quite sharply with popular notions of middle-class femininity. "This young American chose a life on the soil as her way of finding self-fulfillment" read the caption, insinuating that the affluent, domestic lifestyle that most of their constituency were poised to adopt might not prove quite as fulfilling.[22]

While it is impossible to know how most upwardly mobile Jewish women responded to Hadassah pamphlets that promised them avenues through which to circumvent middle-class gender expectations, we do know that Hadassah membership grew in the years in which they included these brochures in their arsenal of outreach materials. Other major American Zionist organizations, such as the Zionist Organization of America, lost members during the 1950s and 1960s as the thrill of Israel's independence in 1948 began to wane. Of all these organizations, only Hadassah maintained its membership and also managed to attract 25,000 new members to its ranks. Indeed, with its 287,854 members in 1956, Hadassah was the world's largest Zionist organization. While this particular advertising campaign may not have accounted for Hadassah's popularity among postwar Jewish women, these numbers testify, at the very least, that these women did not shy away from an organization that acknowledged the limitations of middle-class gender norms.[23]

As Hadassah brochures linked American Jewish housewives to the drama of building the new state of Israel, idealized images of Israeli women circulated among American Jews and introduced alternative models of Jewish femininity. While Israeli society had never been as committed to the ideal of women's equality as American Jews imagined it to be, romantic visions of female pioneers who devoted their lives to the Jewish state nonetheless provided a counterpoint to middle-class expectations of women's domesticity. Many postwar Jewish leaders, both male and female, understood these women to be heroes and applauded their exploits beyond the private sphere. Their admiration for these Israeli women revealed a measure of dissatisfaction with the limited opportunities available to the Jewish women who conformed to the mores of the American middle class.[24]

Using stock photographs reminiscent of the "Rosie the Riveter" images that proliferated throughout the United States during World War II, magazines and books circulating in the American Jewish community printed glowing reports of Israeli women succeeding in fields that the American context reserved for men. In December 1945, under the heading "Women of Valor," the *Hadassah Newsletter*—a magazine distributed to all Hadassah members—published a pictorial centerfold of some of the "women pioneers" laboring to build a Jewish state. None of these photographs showcased women tending to their homes and families; rather, they featured women driving tractors, fighting fires, working in metal factories, laying telephone wire, and, in one particularly arresting image, smiling brightly at the camera from the cockpit of a fighter jet. In celebrating the lives and choices of those women who worked and fought for a Jewish state, *Hadassah Newsletter* leveled an indirect challenge against those middle-class gender norms that kept women out of the workforce and public life.[25]

A similar message was offered to the bat mitzvah girls who received a copy of the aforementioned *Blessed Is the Daughter*. This volume also included a photographic spread of Israeli women performing labor normally associated with male workers. One featured a woman picking cotton in a wide-brimmed hat, another showed a steely-eyed young woman in full army regalia, and a final photograph focused on women bent over microscopes at the Technion Institute. The text introducing these images proclaimed these female soldiers, farmers, and scientists to be models for women everywhere: "Capable in peace, valiant in war, their devotion unmatched among modern womankind, they have written a glorious chapter in the history of Israel and of all humanity." Moreover, the editors of the volume presented the State of Israel as uniquely praiseworthy specifically because "in no other country do women play so important a role among their people." Unlike the middle-class, American milieu in which the young readers of *Blessed Is the Daughter* presumably found themselves, the editors of the volume praised a society that welcomed the involvement of women in "every sphere of human activity— science, agriculture, the arts, literature, government, even the military."[26]

In addition to romanticizing anonymous Israeli women who worked in fields marked as masculine, American Jews also celebrated individual, accomplished Israeli women who shunned middle-class comforts and conventions as they made their mark outside of the domestic sphere. The writings of Marie Syrkin, a well-known journalist and American Zionist, played a particularly significant role in publicizing images of strong, heroic Israeli women. Syrkin herself, much like the Israeli women she profiled, never left the workforce. The daughter of Nachman Syrkin, the socialist-Zionist theoretician, she began her illustrious career as a journalist in 1934 when she joined the staff of the Labor-Zionist newspaper *Jewish Frontier*. She gained prominence in her profession by reporting heavily on the Nazi genocide of Jews in Europe and used her influence to lobby for the open immigration of Jews to Palestine and the United States. After the war, she became a professor of English at Brandeis University—the institution's first female faculty hire—and published books about the war, Zionism, and the State of Israel.[27]

In 1947 the Jewish Publication Society of America published Syrkin's *Blessed Is the Match*, a work that profiled Jews who resisted the Nazi onslaught during World War II. The book highlighted the story of Hannah Senesh, the Hungarian-born Jewish woman who left her affluent family in 1939 to become a member of a kibbutz in Mandate Palestine. At the age of twenty-three, however, Senesh voluntarily left the relative safety of her kibbutz and joined the British army. Under the auspices of the British military, she parachuted back into her native Hungary, now occupied by the Nazis, in an attempt to rescue as many Jews as possible. Tragically, before she could complete her mission, the Gestapo captured her, tortured her, and turned her over to hostile Hungarian courts that executed her as a traitor and a spy.

Syrkin's profile of Senesh's military exploits certainly provided the American Jewish public with an image of a heroic Jewish woman whose life did not conform to middle-class expectations of femininity. But Syrkin went one step further in contrasting Senesh's life and choices to those of her well-off, American Jewish audience. *Blessed Is the Match* focused not only on Senesh's dramatic mission and eventual execution but also on her initial decision to leave her wealthy family in Hungary to join the kibbutz movement in Israel. Senesh, in Syrkin's rendering of the story, struggled with her resolve to abandon such middle-class concerns as developing her skills as a poet, wearing fashionable clothes, and attending lively parties, in favor of the backbreaking agricultural work of the kibbutz. Syrkin analyzed a play penned by Senesh for the members of her kibbutz, which centered on a gifted, middle-class violinist faced with the decision of continuing her musical career or moving to a Jewish agricultural collective. "The plot of the play is transparent," wrote Syrkin, "It is Hanna's problem and choice." She quotes from Senesh's diary: "My eyes surveyed my hands, sore from work. . . . I wondered if it was not simply romanticism which had driven me from a comfortable home to a life of physical work . . . but, no, I am right." Syrkin portrayed Senesh not as a natural-born hero, but rather as a woman who made the very difficult choice to give up her artistic aspirations and affluent lifestyle in order to devote her life to the Jewish people.[28]

Syrkin's lengthy interrogation of Senesh's decision to relinquish her middle-class world by moving to the Jewish settlements in Palestine represented a somewhat peculiar authorial choice. Certainly, Syrkin's postwar readers understood that Senesh's life on a kibbutz, no matter how austere, would still have proved infinitely more comfortable than the horrors she would have faced in Hungary had she remained there after the Nazi occupation. However, for Syrkin, an American Jew writing for an audience of affluent American Jews, Senesh's middle-class background seemed a very relevant piece of information to share. It accentuated the notion that Senesh did not differ fundamentally from the American Jewish women who would read her story and introduced the possibility that they, too, might one day give up their middle-class security in order to aid the Jewish state.

Syrkin continued to profile heroic women who contributed to the State of Israel with her biographies of Golda Meir. She published *Way of Valor: A Biography of Golda Myerson* in 1955 and updated the narrative in 1963 under the title *Golda Meir: Woman with a Cause*, after Meir had Hebraicized her last name and been appointed as the Israeli foreign minister. Syrkin traced Meir's life from her 1898 birth in Kiev, her migration to the United States in 1906, her move to Mandate Palestine in 1921, and her eventual rise to political prominence in the new state of Israel. By the early 1960s, wrote Syrkin, Meir's many admirers viewed her as "already a legend: the American girl who became one of the founders of Israel; the heroine of Jewish national independence."[29]

Syrkin painted Golda Meir as a woman who defied every stereotype associated with middle-class femininity, becoming a hero as she reached far beyond the private sphere. Throughout the biography, Syrkin celebrated and justified Meir's decision to cultivate her career as a stateswoman instead of limiting her activities to domestic pursuits. Meir's marriage failed, Syrkin argued, largely because she and her husband fundamentally disagreed about whether "a woman's place" lay in "the home and the hearth" or "the public arena." Indeed, according to Syrkin, the four years in which Meir retreated from public life in deference to her husband's wishes proved "the most wretched of her life." Meir despised being "swallowed up by her home to the exclusion of every other interest . . . neither childbearing nor the tough round of daily tasks had stilled her restlessness." In Syrkin's estimation, not only would Meir herself have suffered miserably had she continued to refrain from public service, but the budding state "was not rich enough in human material" to allow her that "extravagance." Syrkin's biography defended Meir's choices and, in doing so, indirectly contested the middle-class expectations that would prevent American Jewish women from participating in public life.[30]

Along with Hannah Senesh and Golda Meir, Henrietta Szold also emerged as an iconic figure among American Jews in the postwar years because of her contributions to the developing Israeli state. Born in Baltimore in 1860, Szold distinguished herself as a scholar early in her career by becoming the first woman to study at the Jewish Theological Seminary, as well as the first executive secretary of the Jewish Publication Society. But she achieved her greatest recognition for the work she accomplished on behalf of the Jewish settlements in Palestine. Szold created the Hadassah organization in 1912 before moving to the Middle East in 1920, at the age of sixty. There, she founded the Hadassah Medical Organization, served on the three-person executive of the World Zionist Organization, where she organized budgets for the education and medical systems of the Jewish settlements, and then, with the outbreak of World War II, organized the "Youth Aliyah" movement that rescued thousands of Jewish children from Nazi Europe and brought them to Palestine.[31]

Commentary writer Midge Decter assessed Szold's legacy in a 1960 article. Ironically, while Decter would become well known in the 1970s for savaging the women's liberation movement, her analysis of Szold extolled her decision to eschew the comforts of middle-class domesticity and become a prominent public figure in the new state of Israel. In spite of Szold's many accomplishments as an intellectual and activist even before she moved to the Middle East, Decter argued that Szold would never have become a hero had she remained in her affluent, American milieu. Although Szold had been "respected and valued and surrounding by loving friends" in the United States, wrote Decter, she nonetheless decided to move to "a wilderness, whose physical conditions were almost intolerable to people much younger and much less kindly treated by life than she." The twenty-four years she spent in the Jewish settlements of Palestine, Decter believed, "converted Henrietta Szold from an admirable woman of her day into a great woman."[32]

Though Szold, throughout her years in Palestine, had regularly written of her desire to return to the United States, Decter dismissed Szold's professed homesickness as empty sentimentality. Indeed, Decter argued that after living among the Jews of Palestine, Henrietta Szold "could no longer find being in America meaningful." According to Decter's portrayal, Szold became "discouraged and despondent" when she briefly returned to America in 1930 and did not find her continued work with the American women of Hadassah to be sufficiently rewarding. As proof of this claim, Decter made much of a small comment Szold had written about her activities in America making her "unfit" for "real things," though this theme turned up in Szold's writings far less often than her desire to return to the United States.

While it remains impossible to know how truthful Szold had been when she articulated her longing for America, or how serious when she described the work of the Hadassah women as less than "real," Decter made her own opinions abundantly clear. Certainly Decter, if not necessarily Szold herself, believed that Jewish women had more avenues for heroism when they escaped the privileged and protected world of the American middle class.[33]

Many other postwar American Jewish writers picked up on what Zionist leader Louis Lipsky termed Henrietta Szold's "curious" wish to return to Baltimore in her later years—a wish that she never had the chance to fulfill. Like Decter, they made the case that returning to the abundance of America would have been the choice of a lesser woman and that remaining in Palestine helped prove Szold's status as a hero and role model. "When Henrietta Szold was seventy-three years old, she wanted to return to America 'to be coddled by my sisters,' but her deep sense of responsibility" prevented her from doing so, wrote Naomi Ben-Asher and Hayim Leaf in *The Junior Jewish Encyclopedia*, the volume from which many Jewish youngsters would learn of Szold's achievements. Similarly, Jewish children's writer Elma Ehrlich Levinger, in a 1946 biography of Szold, rhetorically asked her young readers: "Hadn't [Szold] served her people longer and more faithfully in Palestine than any other Jewess of her day? Hadn't she earned the right to honorable retirement [in America]?" Levinger answered her questions in words attributed to Szold: "It would be easier to return to America . . . but one has a conscience."[34]

According to the Canadian-born "Jerusalem housewife" Molly Lyons Bar-David, even those Israeli women who were not particularly famous or accomplished were still more heroic than their middle-class, American Jewish counterparts. Born in Saskatchewan in 1910, Molly Lyons migrated to Mandate Palestine at the age of twenty-six. Soon after, she and her husband Jaap Bar-David settled in Jerusalem, where they remained through the 1948 War of Independence and the siege of the city. In addition to running a literary agency with her husband, throughout the postwar years Lyons Bar-David wrote a column entitled "Diary of a Jerusalem Housewife" for *Hadassah* magazine, later changed to "Diary of an Israel Housewife" after her family moved from Jerusalem to a suburb of Tel Aviv. Her success as a *Hadassah* columnist led her to become a well-known, beloved figure among American Jewish women. Lyons Bar David's American Jewish fans read *Women in Israel*, her overview of the status of women in the Jewish state published in 1950 through Hadassah's education department, as well as her 1953 memoir *My Promised Land*. They also bought the cookbooks she published in the early 1960s, such as *The Israeli Cookbook* (1964) and *Jewish Cooking for*

Pleasure (1965). Her writings often valorized the choices of women like herself, who could have remained in Western abundance but elected instead to adopt the relative austerity that characterized life in the Jewish state during the postwar decades.[35]

Running throughout Lyons Bar-David's columns and memoirs is the notion that quite ordinary women in Israel, by making the sacrifices necessary to live in the Jewish state, surpassed American Jewish women in their idealism and their sense of purpose. Unlike American Jewish women, she wrote in her introduction to *Women in Israel*, the "pioneer woman of Israel has committed herself to an ideal: the development of a better human being and a better future for him. She has deliberately turned her back on comfort and ease to struggle for this goal." According to Lyons Bar-David, relinquishing material abundance in order to live in the Jewish state had only positive consequences for the Jewish women who made this choice. "Women in Israel on the whole live more seriously than women do in the United States," she admitted, but "on the other hand their joys are deeper than mere pleasures, and they drink from the depths of life rather than from the light and frothy surface of fun." In her view, these deeply fulfilled women in Israel did not need to achieve prominence in order to live meaningful lives, as "their very presence in Israel" drew them into "the great forces of Jewish history."[36]

As she told the story of her own life in her *Hadassah* column and memoir, Lyons Bar-David emphasized her belief that she and other "ordinary" Israeli housewives were no less heroic than the male soldiers who fought for their country. During the siege of Jerusalem, she maintained, it was the "the hungry women and children" who "held Jerusalem's houses, home by home, while their men in the trenches gave answering fire." Her valiant sacrifices during the Jerusalem siege, she would later claim, justified her political engagements in the new Jewish state: "Your Jerusalem housewife is only a woman with a brood of kids, and she doesn't pretend to know much about politics and its tactics," she wrote in 1949. "But she does know that she didn't desert Jerusalem, and that she pitted her children against the enemy in a starving city for Israel's sake." She continued to valorize her own sacrifices as an Israeli housewife well into the 1950s, when she and other Israeli homemakers were compelled to feed their families on meager rations so as to ensure that Jewish refugees coming to the new state from Muslim lands would have enough to eat. These deprivations were something to be proud of, she wrote, as "it made the housewife feel that she was fighting on a kitchen front."[37]

At times, Lyon Bar-David gently berated her well-to-do, American Jewish fans for not making the same sort of material sacrifices that Israeli women made for their homeland and the Jewish people. Though she often praised the American women of Hadassah for their great financial contributions to Israel, she also did not shy away from comparing them, often unfavorably, to their heroic Israeli counterparts. When writing about her 1950 lecture tour in the United States and Canada, for instance, she discussed the shock of experiencing American plenty after coping with Israeli austerity for so long: "I cried a great deal the first few days. I could not bear to see so much abundance and the sin of so much waste about me, knowing how I left my little Israel." Eventually, she grew more acclimated to the wealth she saw around her, which made her "able to understand even if I couldn't forgive how it was possible for a woman in the USA to get a new fur coat when she knew that her sister in Israel hadn't a sweater."[38]

Lyons Bar-David was no easier on her former countrywomen in Canada when she compared their middle-class habits to her own life of scarcity. "Don't you hate us all? Whenever I come back home from a visit to Israel I hate everyone here for their splashy parties and their splashing," she quoted Sally Gotlieb, president of Canadian Hadassah, as asking her when she visited the land of her birth. Lyons Bar-David found the comment ironic, as Gotlieb had made this complaint at a "very splashy party" that she herself had hosted. "She was as caught in the net of this way of life as they," noted Lyons Bar-David, adding that she "felt a curious pity" for Canadian Jews, especially those who "had grown wealthy." It was only after they had achieved their ambition of becoming affluent, she maintained, that "the real poverty of their lives faced them." By the end of the trip, she could not wait to get back to the "harsh austerity of Israel."[39]

The notion that the deprivations experienced by Jewish women in Israel made their lives more heroic, authentic, and meaningful than those of American Jewish women also threaded through the work of novelist Zelda Popkin. Born in Brooklyn in 1898, Popkin (nee Feinberg) grew up in Eastern Pennsylvania and became the first female general assignment reporter of the *Wilkes-Barre Times-Leader* at the age of sixteen. In the late 1930s, she published a series of mystery novels featuring detective Mary Carner and then in 1945 went on to write her most popular novel, *The Journey Home*, which relayed a love story between a working woman and a soldier just returned from World War II.

Popkin began to introduce Jewish characters and subjects in her writing after the winter of 1945–46, when she went on a mission with the Red Cross to help Holocaust survivors languishing in displaced persons camps. That experience inspired her to write a series of novels with Jewish themes, including *Small Victory* (1947) which dealt with the hostile treatment of Holocaust survivors by American authorities, and *Quiet Street* (1951), the first American novel to center its drama around the newly independent state of Israel. Later, Popkin's 1956 memoir *Open Every Door* offered a nonfiction account of her time with the Red Cross as well as her travels to Jerusalem in the fall of 1948, where she went to visit her sister Helen, who had moved there in the 1930s. Though Popkin herself never chose to live in Israel permanently, her sympathy for the Jewish state and her admiration for its inhabitants come through clearly in her writing.[40]

Quiet Street follows the life of Edith Hirsch, an American-born doctor's wife living in Jerusalem, and the neighbors who live on her street. Set during the 1948 war that led to Israel's independence, the novel recounts Edith's struggle to provide as normal a life as possible for her husband and their ten-year-old son Teddy, and to cope with her fears for her eighteen-year-old daughter Dinah, who was fighting on the front lines of the Negev Desert. By the end of the novel, the characters celebrate the birth of an independent state of Israel even as they mourn the death of many of the inhabitants of their once "quiet street," including Edith's daughter Dinah.

Quiet Street focused on the bravery of everyday people who lived through the siege of Jerusalem rather than on the fierce warriors favored by Leon Uris in *Exodus*. As Zelda Popkin herself wrote in her memoir, she was determined to write the novel not about "exotic people" who lived in Jerusalem but about the "ordinary people who might have lived in Plainfield or Wilkes-Barre." Such people, she insisted, were "in a way immortal. Through the simple fact of staying here [in Jerusalem], by coming to work, taking the hunger, thirst and shelling, they had become heroes."[41]

Much like the work of Molly Lyons Bar-David, Popkin's novel also relayed the message that housewives in Israel displayed remarkable heroism by continuing to raise their families in the Jewish state in spite of the hardships. Popkin spilled a great deal of ink detailing the deprivations suffered by Edith Hirsch in her determination to remain in her home in Jerusalem, sacrifices made all the more poignant because she was raised in middle-class, American abundance. In one scene, Edith had to convince her ten-year-old son to eat oatmeal (*kvacker*, in Hebrew) infested with worms, as it was the only food they had left to consume. Popkin portrayed Edith's ingestion of the foul food as an act of valor, as it convinced her disgusted son to do likewise and get the nutrition he so desperately needed. Her son "saw her throat muscles ripple when the kvacker went down," wrote Popkin. "She didn't grimace; her face was serene. He was flabbergasted. His mother, that dainty lady from Boston . . . his mother, that fussy lady . . . was eating kvacker *with worms*."[42]

For Popkin, everyday moments like these, in which Edith found ways to conserve meager supplies of food and water in order to sustain her family's life in Israel, proved the mettle of her main character. She has Edith and her husband express this point of view quite explicitly when they explain to their visiting daughter what it was like to live through the siege of Jerusalem:

> "Jerusalem was saved . . . not by arms—we had none—not by an enemy's cowardice. . . . But by discipline and stubbornness. By the drivers of the food convoys, the bakers, the water carts . . . "
>
> "And the doctors," his wife put in.
>
> He smiled at her. "And the housewives."[43]

To be fair, Popkin's characters are complex, and Edith Hirsch does harbor doubts over whether the sacrifices she made on behalf of the Jewish state were worth it, particularly after the death of her daughter. And yet, these misgivings never compromise Edith's status as the moral center of the novel, whose kindness and stoic bravery make her a role model and whose life, however painful, was full of weight, meaning, and Jewish authenticity. "Here is a woman . . .," Popkin wrote from the perspective of Dinah's grieving love interest, who "by her very presence, here, in this spot, has made history."[44]

For Popkin, as for Lyons Bar-David, the self-denial of living in the Jewish state made heroes out of housewives, and their writings presented middle-class American Jewish women with an implicit, and sometimes explicit, critique of their life choices. Both writers sent their Jewish, female readers the message that a life of scarcity in Israel would have been far more meaningful and gallant than a life of abundance in America, because the sacrifices made by Israeli women helped bolster the Jewish state and the Jewish people.

While Popkin and Lyons-Bar David questioned middle-class ideals of femininity by idealizing the sacrifices of Israeli women, other writers popular among American Jews leveled similar challenges in their positive portrayals of American women who did not conform to middle-class gender expectations. Interrogating the benefits of middle-class affluence ran through the work of essayist, novelist, and short-story writer Sylvia Rothchild, and much of her writing dealt quite specifically with the fate of American Jewish women during a moment of upward mobility. In a 1952 short story entitled "My Mrs. Schnitzer," for instance, Rothchild offered a romanticized portrait of a strong, working-class, American Jewish woman who did not attempt to assimilate into middle-class culture. She told the story through the eyes of Rosalyn, an adolescent girl who had befriended a woman named Bella Schnitzer while growing up in a tenement apartment in Brooklyn. Rosalyn's

Debating Middle-Class Jewish Femininity

own family, who aspired to a respectable, middle-class life, disapproved of Mrs. Schnitzer for being loud and coarse. But Rosalyn loved Mrs. Schnitzer for the treats and praise that she lavished upon her and admired the outspokenness that made her seem so much more vital than her own upwardly mobile family.

Rothchild depicted Bella Schnitzer as the antithesis of middle-class femininity, a woman with little concern for respectability and few compunctions about making her private problems public. In one instance, the two women found themselves on a crowded city bus, when a drunken man made the mistake of pinching Mrs. Schnitzer's bottom. Rosalyn begged Mrs. Schnitzer not to make a scene, but the older woman refused: "I'm not a little girl that stands on one foot and then the other, making herself small. I don't make believe nothing is happening because I don't know what to do. I'm not afraid of anything, not of anyone, not even of myself." Mrs. Schnitzer proceeded to yell at the man and physically throw him off the bus, teaching Rosalyn the value of standing up for herself, even at the risk of flouting middle-class propriety. [45]

Rothchild's depiction of the impoverished, unmannered Bella Schnitzer as a strong and loving role model revealed not only a certain amount of affection for the working-class, American Jewish past but also admiration for those Jewish women who had never been limited by middle-class conventions. It underscored the suspicion that as Jewish women acquired middle-class respectability, they may simultaneously have given up their right to publicly confront abuse and demand self-respect.

Rothchild offered a more complicated view of Jewish women's upward mobility in her 1958 novel *Sunshine and Salt*. The narrative offered readers two contrasting models of Jewish femininity. Rothchild told the story from the perspective of Madeline, a dissatisfied, middle-class Jewish housewife. The central conflict of the story began when Madeline's newly widowed mother Celia, who had always lived in a close-knit, working-class, urban Jewish neighborhood, came to Madeline's wealthy suburb to live with her and her family. Indeed, the "sunshine" and "salt" of the title referred to the seemingly opposite values and lifestyles of these two women; Madeline considered her own life of permissiveness and material abundance as a world of "sunshine," and her mother's milieu of traditional Judaism, worry, and devotion to others as one of "salt."[46]

While Madeline had left her working-class parents in Brooklyn years before the novel began, her character is unable to find fulfillment in her life as a suburban housewife. Throughout the novel, Madeline complained that being a homemaker made her feel "empty and useless" and that she "wanted a reason for living that had nothing to do with . . . Susie's lost socks and Debby's skirts that needed lengthening, or David's scraped knees and Johnny's eggs." At one point, in a fit of tears, she wondered if she cried because her husband "spent his days at meetings with interesting people while I . . . talked only to children and sick neighbors" or whether she was upset "because Mama was coming to drag me back to my childhood and I was worn out with pretending that I was pleased."[47]

Though Madeline worried about how her mother would adapt to a middle-class lifestyle, Celia ended up surprising Madeline with her adaptability. While Celia initially complained about the lack of sidewalks and streetlights, the dangers of the wooded acres behind the house, and the way in which the non-Jewish neighbors neglected their children, Celia eventually found a place for herself within the suburban milieu. She began to bake cookies for the neighborhood children, even taking one troubled boy under her wing by letting him help her with household chores. She brought traditional Jewish foods and rituals into her daughter's house, which Madeline's husband and children enjoyed and cherished. To her atheist daughter's annoyance, Celia also became very involved in a nearby synagogue, often joining in their fundraising and philanthropic activities.

The novel ends with Celia's tragic death due to a heart attack as she tried to rescue some of the neighborhood children from a fire. But in the wake of this heartbreak, Madeline managed to find greater meaning in her own life because of her mother's legacy. She and her family become involved with the local synagogue, having been quite touched by the congregation's thoughtfulness after Celia's death. And Madeline found herself continuing many of the things that her mother had introduced into her household: "Her [Sabbath] candles were on my table. Her favorite foods simmered in my pot because Lou and the children liked them." In the end, she forged a balance between the "sunshine" of the carefree, middle-class suburbs and the "salt" of her mother's traditions.[48]

While Rothchild did not idealize the character of Celia in quite the same way that she romanticized Bella Schnitzer, *Sunshine and Salt* nonetheless relayed the message that upwardly mobile Jewish women had a lot to learn from their working-class mothers. Madeline's life certainly became more meaningful once she engaged with her local Jewish community and brought her mother's Jewish traditions into her home. More importantly, Celia taught her daughter how to truly care for others, a trait that the narrator associates with unassimilated Jews. In showing how Celia brought significance to her unhappy daughter's life as a suburban housewife, Rothchild leveled a critique against those upwardly mobile Jewish families who rejected even the positive aspects of their traditional, working-class backgrounds.

Novelist Herman Wouk also seemed to understand that, at times, middle-class gender expectations felt constraining to Jewish women. He dramatized the limitations of postwar Jewish femininity in his best-selling 1955 novel *Marjorie Morningstar*. The book focused on the young adulthood of Marjorie Morgenstern, whose mother entreated her to uphold a particularly Jewish version of the "feminine mystique" by marrying an affluent Jewish man and settling down to a life of domestic housewifery. Young Marjorie, however, resisted these expectations and, instead, nurtured ambitions of becoming an actress. In pursuit of this dream, she entered into a tumultuous, passionate, and—in her most dramatic break with middle-class conventions of femininity—sexual relationship with Noel Airman, a dashing songwriter and playwright who embodied the bohemian, artistic world to which she aspired.

Wouk reinforced the ideals of Jewish, middle-class respectability at the end of the novel, when a more mature Marjorie finally recognized both her relationship with Noel and her desire to become an actress as elements of a childish dream. A chastened Marjorie thus accepted her proper role in life and wed Milton Schwartz, a prosperous Jewish lawyer. The epilogue to the book finds her a happily married, gray-haired mother-of-four living in the New York suburb of Mamaroneck. She had, in the end, subscribed quite fully to middle-class ideals of Jewish femininity. And Wouk implied that, in spite of her initial hesitancy to be confined to a life of domesticity, this had been the only decision that could have offered her true satisfaction.[49]

While the final chapters of the book undercut the frustrations felt by Marjorie Morgenstern about the limited choices she was offered as a middle-class Jewish woman, most of the novel illustrated Marjorie's spirited quest for alternatives. Although Wouk may have intended the novel to be a morality tale for Jewish girls desiring to break free from the constraints of respectable femininity, *Marjorie Morningstar* nonetheless acknowledged, in a rather sympathetic way, that young Jewish women of the postwar era might have wanted more options than what middle-class America promised them.

Indeed, literary scholar Barbara Sicherman discovered that the Jewish women who read the novel during the postwar years did not necessarily accept the manner in which Wouk chose to end Marjorie's story. Wouk received letters from hundreds of postwar housewives, almost all of them with Jewish last names. Many chided him for allowing Marjorie to end up a middle-class matron. One went so far as to rewrite the ending of the novel, insisting that rather than becoming a dull homemaker, Marjorie instead grew into an artsy young wife, "sitting on the terrace, reading the Theater Arts Magazine in Bermuda shorts, drying her black hair in the sun." These postwar Jewish women refused to read *Marjorie Morningstar* as a cautionary tale and instead took both Marjorie's vexation with middle-class conventions and her ambitions to break out of those constraints quite seriously.[50]

As Wouk recognized, in a limited way, Jewish women's dissatisfaction with middle-class ideals of domesticity, another, less-well-known postwar author sensationalized the unsavory underside of the gender dynamics of Jewish upward mobility. *Everything but a Husband*, a steamy romance written by Jeanette Kamins, followed the adventures of five young Jewish women in search of marriage. Kamins portrayed unmarried Jewish women as quite desperate in their quest for a husband who would raise them out of financial uncertainty and into a middle-class world of economic security. She also painted married Jewish women as avaricious schemers who achieved their middle-class status through mercenary marriages. "She looked beauty-parlored, golfed and bridged. She also looked as if she had shopped for a sponsor for a mink coat and found him," wrote Kamins of one of the married housewives in her novel.

Though the unmarried main characters in Kamin's novel disapproved of most of the married women, they envied them their husbands. As one of the protagonists commented about the aforementioned unsavory wife, "The way she was holding court, you'd think she was Queen of the May. Well, she's got a husband, so I guess she is. She's Mrs. Somebody Somebody. In this world, a girl isn't much unless she's got a husband to prove it."[51]

Everything but a Husband offered a telling, angry comment on the politics of heterosexual courtship in an upwardly mobile community. After all, Jewish men had far more opportunities than Jewish women to take advantage of the postwar economic boom. This created a situation, exaggerated for purposes of titillation by Kamins, in which Jewish women who sought to enter the middle class depended on the income of male spouses to catapult them there. In addition to the romance, the novel explored the tensions surrounding women's limited avenues to join the middle class without the help of a male partner.

As Jewish women moved into the middle class and were expected to take charge of the middle-class family, they received various, and often contradictory instructions on how to negotiate new gender norms. Clearly, American Jewish leaders, thinkers, and writers had different conceptions as to what represented an "authentic" or "ideal" Jewish family, and divergent understandings of what constituted the proper roles of women within these families. They offered mixed messages to Jewish women, who were simultaneously encouraged to engage outside of the domestic sphere and also cautioned that these outside interests would damage their families.

Debating Middle-Class Jewish Femininity

In the end, all of these thinkers, writers, and leaders agreed that affluence posed a threat to Jewish women. Although they did not interpret the situation in the same way, and indeed counseled Jewish women differently, they understood that a middle-class milieu placed new demands on American Jews in terms of how they divided up gendered tasks and organized their families. These leaders, for all of their different points of view, aimed to preserve what they perceived as the authentic Jewish family. That the new, middle-class Jewish family might fail to uphold Jewish traditions or transmit Jewish values to the next generation seemed to them an unthinkable tragedy.

What became of the children who grew up in Jewish families that had been so transformed by postwar affluence? Did they maintain Jewish traditions, as their rabbis and teachers hoped they would? Or did they realize the worst fears of their leaders by abandoning their Jewish distinctiveness in favor of middle-class security and comfort?

There is no singular answer to the question of what happened to the generation of American Jews who had been raised in postwar suburbia, and a full report on their fates falls beyond the scope of this project. The next chapter, however, follows one group of young Jews who adamantly, and with considerably more vitriol than the rabbis who educated them, railed against the prospect of adapting Jewish life to fit the norms of middle-class American culture.

This cadre of Jewish youth grew up surrounded by the ambivalence over upward mobility that their elders continuously expressed. They, too, felt the tension between the history of Jewish poverty and the new realities of Jewish privilege. Moreover, they heard, and internalized, their parents' and rabbis' concerns that the Jewish culture being forged in postwar suburbia lacked authenticity. As they reached young adulthood in the tumultuous years of the late 1960s, they began their own search for the genuine Jewish life that they believed the older generation had given up in their quest for middle-class security. We will now focus our attention on these Jewish children of suburbia once they grew into young adults and examine their searing critiques of upward mobility in the late 1960s and 1970s.

SIX

From Generation to Generation

The Jewish Counterculture's Critique of Affluence

In 1971 the Baltimore-Washington Union of Jewish Students published the following scathing assessment of Jewish life in America: "To be a Jew on America's terms is to go to temple on the High Holy Days for $50 a seat. . . . To be a Jew on America's terms is to trade in historical and religious ethics of social justice for a $60,000 house in Silver Spring or Stevenson. . . . To be a Jew on America's terms is to forget 2000 years of oppression because of 20 years of prosperity." The final words of this advertisement, printed in all capital letters to emphasize its importance, summed up their perspective: "TO BE A JEW ON AMERICA'S TERMS IS NOT TO BE A JEW AT ALL."[1]

The Baltimore-Washington Union of Jewish students represented one of the many Jewish youth collectives that began to crop up in North America beginning in the late 1960s. Largely the products of middle-class, suburban, Jewish neighborhoods, these young Jews tried to reinvent American Jewish life in the spirit of the global youth revolt of the late 1960s. Referring to themselves as "Jewish Radicals," the "New Jewish Left," the "Jewish movement," and the "Jewish counterculture," they rejected the culture of affluence in which they had been raised and denied the possibility that a middle-class lifestyle could be compatible with an authentically Jewish one.[2]

The many, loosely organized collectives inspired by the Jewish counterculture included a myriad of residential communes, alternative prayer communities, and political action groups. They advanced a variety of causes, some of which overlapped, and some that actually contradicted one another.[3] The common denominator linking together all of these disparate undertakings, however, was a pointed critique of the middle-class Jewish culture that had been instituted by the older generation of American Jews. Indeed, the "New

Jews" often cited the corrosive impact of American prosperity as a primary justification for their activism and engagement.[4]

Within much of the rhetoric of the Jewish counterculture, even causes that did not seem to be connected to the class position of American Jewry became intertwined with the presumed dangers of affluence, underscoring the centrality of this critique to their activism and worldview. This chapter examines the ways in which members of the Jewish counterculture articulated their investments in key issues, including the plight of Soviet Jewry; the inclusion of women, gays, and lesbians in American Jewish life; Zionism; and the restructuring of the Jewish religion. On the surface, none of these issues pertained directly to affluence or its effects. But when the members of the Jewish counterculture created narratives and interpreted histories to explain their participation in these causes, they often cited the wealth of American Jewry as not only relevant but often fundamental to the problems they were trying solve.[5]

The Jewish counterculture's ubiquitous critique of affluence points to the complicated relationship that these young Jews had with their relative position of privilege in American society. The middle-class environment in which so many of them had been raised, and that hinged on their acceptance as racial whites, placed them on a rather high rung of the American social hierarchy. The last vestiges of the structural antisemitism that had plagued their parents' generation had largely disappeared by the late 1960s, and this generation of American Jews did not face educational quotas restricting their admissions to elite universities or employers who openly refused to hire Jews.

Even so, many of these young Jews did not necessarily, or at least did not always, feel like part of the elite. They shared a religious and cultural heritage that the wider American culture rarely seemed to value. Moreover, much like their parents and teachers of the older generation, they were keenly aware of the history of antisemitism in the United States and the recent genocide of Jews in Europe; indeed, a minority of American Jews in their age cohort were the children of Holocaust survivors, and some had been born in displaced person's camps. Aviva Cantor Zuckoff, an outspoken leader of the Jewish Liberation Project and herself the child of immigrants from Eastern Europe, represented the point of view of many Jewish counterculturalists when she insisted that Jews in America continue to feel marginalized in spite of "the fact that they happen to be, by and large, economically well-off and not subject to the kind of physical oppression faced by blacks, Indians, and Chicanos." Much of these young Jews' unease regarding Jewish affluence emerged out of the conflict between being middle-class, white, and privileged and yet identifying with a history of poverty and oppression and a lived culture that often felt quite different from that of the American majority.[6]

Being part of a wider, youthful counterculture that derided middle-class America as sterile, conformist, and immoral heightened the eagerness of these "New Jews" to dissociate themselves from the culture of prosperity in which they had been raised. Influenced in part by black power advocates who publicly embraced their alienation from a dominant American society they had come to characterize as oppressive and corrupt, these young Jews likewise celebrated the ways in which they were different from other middle-class Americans. By denying the possibility that an authentic Jewish lifestyle could flourish alongside middle-class norms and customs, they registered their discomfort with their status as "insiders" in American society and highlighted the ways in which they continued to feel like "outsiders."[7]

While inspired by the youthful counterculture of the late 1960s and 1970s, the complaints of these young Jewish radicals also echoed the ambivalence expressed by their parents' generation as they climbed into the middle class in the two decades following World War II. During the immediate postwar era, the leaders of American Jewry had often voiced the opinion that the new, consumer-laden Jewish culture being forged in postwar America lacked the authenticity and vitality of earlier, impoverished Jewish communities. They, too, agreed that affluence had corrupted the political, religious, and gender identities of American Jews. And they also romanticized earlier generations of indigent and working-class Jews, as well as Jews in Israel, as representatives of a more genuine Jewish life less imbricated in middle-class culture and values. The Jewish counterculture's expressed disdain for money and materialism, therefore, linked it not only to peers in the New Left but also to an earlier generation of Jewish leaders who had long-expressed misgivings over the middle-class lifestyle of American Jews.

The Jewish counterculture emerged as a distinct movement when changes within the New Left encouraged some Jewish activists to develop a program specific to their own interests. By the late 1960s, the philosophy of black power had gained prominence within the civil rights coalition, prompting participants to question the efficacy and suitability of white activists within the struggle for African American liberation. In 1966, for instance, the Student Non-Violent Coordinating Committee, the powerful organization that had once embraced an interracial cadre of young, radical activists, became a black power organization and expelled all of its white participants. This fragmentation of the New Left along racial lines became apparent at

The Jewish Counterculture's Critique of Affluence

Chicago's Conference on New Politics in August of 1967, when black power activists directed their white counterparts to stop working on behalf of African Americans and "organize among your own." Some Jewish activists took this message to heart and decided to devote their energies toward mobilizing the Jewish community.

For certain Jewish attendees, however, the most stinging moment of the Conference on New Politics did not revolve around the rift between black and white activists but rather arose when the black caucus called for a resolution against Zionist imperialism. To be sure, a majority of the young Jews active in the New Left did not challenge this resolution and, indeed, may not have been bothered by it. Many New Left Jews understood the Jewish history of oppression in universal terms and viewed it as their duty, as Jews or simply as human beings, to support the struggles of those whom they saw as most victimized in the context of the late 1960 and 1970s, such as African Americans, the Vietnamese, and other people of color. The particular concerns of Jews may not have been on their radar or may not have seemed dire enough to merit as much attention.

However, for those Jewish activists who felt less sanguine about the security and safety of Jews, and for those who held stronger Zionist convictions, the anti-Zionist resolution of the Conference on New Politics seemed insensitive and unfair. After Israel's victory during the 1967 war and the subsequent occupation of the West Bank and Gaza, many New Leftists condemned the Israeli government's policy toward Palestinians and began to view Israel as the colonialist oppressor of a Third World population. This stance infuriated those Zionist activists in the New Left who understood Zionism as the national self-determination of an oppressed people, and they objected when their fellow leftists lumped Israel together with imperialist Western powers. Although this would soon change, as of the late 1960s most young, radical American Zionists could not conceive of the possibility that a Jewish state could become an occupying power or that it could persecute Palestinians.[8]

This growing tension surrounding the Middle East convinced some Jewish members of the New Left that they needed to build an independent, radical, and particularistic Jewish movement that would support Zionism and rebuke the New Left when it failed, in their view, to advance the liberation of Jews along with the liberation of other subjugated groups. "I shall join no movement that does not accept and support my people's struggle," announced M. Jay Rosenberg, a student at State University of New York at Albany who had considered himself part of the New Left before shifting his allegiance to the "Radical Zionists." "If I must choose between the Jewish cause and a 'progressive' anti-Israel SDS, I shall choose the Jewish cause," he declared.[9]

Jewish radicals were not the only group to splinter from the New Left in the late 1960s. Taking their cues from the black power activists who would no longer work in coalition with whites, other groups based on common ethnic, gender, sexual, and religious affiliations began to organize their own social movements. The late 1960s saw, as one observer put it, the ascendance of "Catholic and Protestant radical theologians and rebels like Father James Groppi, the Berrigan brothers, and Bishop Pike; 'Jesus Freaks,' 'Polish Power,' . . . 'Indian Power.'"[10] Even Tom Hayden, the former president of Students for a Democratic Society (SDS), the flagship organization of the New Left, flirted with ethnic identity politics in 1971 when he changed his name to Emmett Garity and attempted to visit Dublin, only to have the Irish government reject him as an undesirable alien.[11]

Events in the late 1960s signaled the beginning of a distinctly Jewish counterculture. Washington, D.C.'s Jews for Urban Justice, a political action group that worked for racial and economic equality in the United States, began its activities on Yom Kippur of 1967. On the evening of the holiday, members of the group gathered in front of the Washington Hebrew Congregation to protest Jewish apartment owners who, they charged, had restricted their buildings to white tenants. The founding members of the group, which included Sharon Rose and Arthur Waskow, had been New Left activists and prominent members of ACCESS, an organization aimed at desegregating housing in the Washington, D.C., area. Their Yom Kippur demonstration marked the first time they employed their Jewishness as a tool in tackling desegregation and used their connections within the Jewish community to further their activist aims. Also in 1967, Yale undergraduate James Sleeper and Columbia student Alan Mintz published the first issue of *Response*, which became the intellectual journal of the Jewish countercultural community. Soon after, in 1968, Rabbi Arthur Green founded the first alternative Jewish rabbinical seminary, which quickly evolved into an experimental prayer community called *Havurat Shalom* (the fellowship of peace), and catered to the spiritual needs of this cohort of countercultural Jews.[12]

Young Jews participated in this movement in different ways and with various levels of commitment. The newspapers produced by young, radical Jews reached the largest population by far, with a 1971 *New York Times* report counting thirty-six individual publications with a combined circulation of 300,000.[13] Those more invested in the movement had the option of praying, or even living, with like-minded Jewish counterculturalists. An estimated sixty *havurot* (fellowships), alternative prayer communities that challenged the scale and opulence of synagogues, and *batim* (houses), campus cooperatives made up of Jewish students living communally, flourished by the mid-1970s and involved

The Jewish Counterculture's Critique of Affluence

roughly 1,200 members.[14] Although this Jewish countercultural impulse did not include most American Jewish youth, the movement dominated American Jewish discourse. By the late 1960s, discussions of the Jewish radicals, their politics, and their critiques of Jewish life proliferated not only within the "radical" and "student" Jewish newspapers but also the mainstream Jewish press.[15]

In many ways, the critique of affluence that emerged among the Jewish countercultural groups that struggled against the oppression of Soviet Jewry seems particularly surprising. After all, as the 1959 "kitchen debates" between Soviet Premier Nikita Khrushchev and then Vice President Richard Nixon revealed, Cold War rhetoric commonly touted the relative wealth of postwar Americans as proof of the superiority of the United States over the Soviet Union. One might imagine that the campaign for Soviet Jewry would have built on this logic and point to the upward mobility of American Jews as further proof that the United States represented a greater friend to the Jews than the Soviet Union. The campaign for Soviet Jewry would hardly seem a likely platform from which to condemn the affluence that American society offered its Jews, and yet, some of the New Jews involved in this cause did just that.

The organized American Jewish community had worried about the Jews living in the Soviet Union since the end of World War II. They responded in horror to reports that Stalin's government repressed Jewish cultural institutions and had purged, imprisoned, and murdered prominent Soviet Jews. Throughout the 1950s and early 1960s, American Jewish organizations condemned Soviet antisemitism and called upon the Soviet government to allow its Jewish citizens to emigrate to Israel if they so desired. However, during these years, they failed to develop a single, coherent strategy for alleviating the plight of Soviet Jewry, with some groups, such as the left-wing Jewish Labor Committee, organizing grassroots protest rallies, and others, like the American Jewish Committee, preferring quiet diplomatic meetings with American and Soviet officials. The establishment of the American Jewish Conference for Soviet Jewry in 1964 represented an attempt to rationalize and systematize actions on behalf of Soviet Jews.

When younger Jews formed the Student Struggle for Soviet Jewry, also in 1964, they advanced new, more militant approaches to the issue. This group, one of the earliest forerunners of the Jewish counterculture, used the confrontational tactics of the student New Left to aid Soviet Jews. Their demonstrations, vigils, and marches proved highly successful in drawing national and international attention to the plight of Soviet Jewry. And as the Jewish counterculture grew in the late 1960s, the struggle for Soviet Jewry became a popular cause among quite disparate organizations.[16]

The members of the Jewish counterculture faced a certain amount of tension in their attempts to formulate a leftist response to the plight of Soviet Jewry. They knew that the movement on behalf of Soviet Jews could easily be co-opted by Cold Warriors interested more in exposing the perceived evils of Communism and dismantling the American social welfare programs that they associated with Communism than in aiding the Jews who lived behind the Iron Curtain. "There is a danger that anti-Communist appeals will rally people to the Soviet Jewry cause—perhaps at the expense of enlightened domestic policies," noted Jack Nusan Porter and Peter Dreier, editors of *Jewish Radicalism*. "The Jewish left has had to walk this tightrope and combat these Cold War sentiments while developing an alternative strategy to save Soviet Jews."[17]

One of the "alternative strategies" adopted by some members of the Jewish counterculture as they engaged in the struggle for Soviet Jewry hinged on a critique of American Jews' middle-class prosperity. Even as they marched on behalf of Jews in the Soviet Union, some of these young Jewish activists denied that American Jews were much better off than their Soviet coreligionists, since the wealth enjoyed by American Jews alienated them from an authentic Jewish culture. "Those of us who believe that here in America *we* are free are deceived more brutally than our Sisters and Brothers in the Soviet Union," declared one member of Brooklyn Bridge, a radical Jewish collective, in 1971. Soviet Jews, he argued, understood that their government would "annihilate" them if they did not give up their Jewish identity. But American Jews, on the other hand, had been convinced to betray their ethical heritage because their government had thrown them the "crumbs" of comfort and affluence. The possibility that their social and financial acceptance would be taken away from them, continued the author, made them incapable of making the changes necessary to reclaim an authentically Jewish life.[18]

Some also argued that American and Soviet Jews endured similar experiences of cultural loss. Gerald Serrota, then a rabbinical student at Hebrew University, articulated this idea in a 1971 poem titled "blood brother of Kiev":

no cause for wonder that repression finds us
    both clinging to the shreds
of identity our alien cultures suffer us to grasp
    ... yours, vile representative
of the fear of freedom, of learning, and of love
    ... mine, the strangling glut
of material superabundance ...[19]

Serrota and others developed an interpretation of the struggle for Soviet Jewry quite unique to the Jewish counterculture. Unlike mainstream Jewish liberals, they did not see themselves as the Jews of "freedom" coming to save the Jews besieged by Communism. Rather, as radical opponents of an American capitalist system that, they believed, had coerced American Jews to relinquish their culture in exchange for the promise of economic security, they understood Soviet and American Jews to be partners in suffering. American wealth and Soviet repression, they felt, stifled authentic Jewish life in quite similar ways.

Much like the "New Jews" who organized on behalf of Soviet Jewry, Jewish feminists represented another powerful contingent within the Jewish counterculture that viewed upward mobility as a catalyst of oppression. In fact, the emergence of the women's liberation movement had its roots in the same 1967 Chicago Conference on New Politics that spawned the Jewish counterculture. At that fateful gathering, a conference leader patted feminist Shulamith Firestone on the head, telling her to "cool it, little girl, we have more important things to discuss than women's liberation," an infuriating moment that helped convince Firestone and other female activists of the need to mobilize a radical women's movement. This women's movement, which developed simultaneously alongside the Jewish counterculture, exacted a tremendous influence among the Jewish group, and many of the female Jewish counterculturalists became equally invested in both causes.[20]

More sympathetic to feminist concerns than most, if not all, Jewish institutions at the time, Jewish countercultural groups served as incubators for women's leadership. In the late 1960s, Radical Zionists found a powerful leader in Aviva Cantor Zuckoff, editor of the *Jewish Liberation Journal*, while Sharon Rose served as the Executive Director of Jews for Urban Justice. By the 1970s, feminists within the Jewish counterculture such as Paula Hyman and Martha Ackelsberg began to apply the lessons of the women's movement to Jewish religion and culture. The Jewish counterculture offered them a relatively supportive infrastructure from which they advanced feminist change throughout the Jewish world.[21]

Their attempts to change the status of women both within the Jewish community and in the larger society certainly reflected the strong influence of the larger feminist movement on these young women. In a less dramatic way, however, their activism also hearkened back to the tensions surrounding Jewish gender ideals in the 1950s. Young American Jewish women witnessed their mothers capably taking on new leadership roles in their synagogues and their communities throughout the immediate postwar years, and being simultaneously thanked and criticized by their leaders for doing so. Understandably, some Jewish daughters turned to the feminist movement to make sense of the confusing messages regarding gender that they had encountered in their childhoods and to challenge the communal attitudes that did not adequately support and reward women for their service.

The first activist collective in what became a specifically Jewish feminist movement began in 1972 when *Ezrat Nashim* (the name given to the women's section of the ancient temple in Jerusalem, which translates literally to "help for women") publicly challenged women's roles in Judaism. *Ezrat Nashim* started as a women's study group within the New York Havurah, one of the most vibrant experimental prayer communities to emerge out of the Jewish counterculture. They had been analyzing religious texts pertaining to women when they decided to take practical steps to change the religious status of women within Judaism. At the March 1972 meeting of the Conservative movement's Rabbinical Assembly, the ten young women of *Ezrat Nashim*, the oldest of whom was twenty-seven, presented attendees with their "Call for Change." Though the Rabbinical Assembly denied Ezrat Nashim a place on the formal program, the rabbis received a copy of their call in their conference packets, and the women of Ezrat Nashim arranged separate meetings with interested rabbis and their wives. Their manifesto called upon the Conservative movement, the denomination that had educated Paula Hyman, Martha Ackelsberg, and most of its members, to count women in its prayer quorums, to train women as rabbis and cantors, to promote women's leadership roles in the synagogue and in the wider community, and to allow women to initiate religious divorces.[22]

It is unsurprising that Ezrat Nashim grew out of the New York Havurah, one of the collectives aimed at revamping the religious life of American Jews according to countercultural principles. Havurot offered women opportunities for religious leadership and ritual participation not available to them in the synagogue. Even in the Reform and Reconstructionist movements, the only American denominations that did not formally restrict women's religious participation in some way, male rabbis led services during these years as Sally Priesand, America's first woman rabbi, did not receive ordination until 1972. In contrast, in most havurot, male and female members shared equal status. As time went on and the influence of the feminist movement grew, female members often took the opportunity to lead services. Some young Jews reported joining Havurot largely out of frustration with the lack of gender egalitarianism in established synagogues.[23]

While the inclusion of women in Jewish ritual and prayer became a key goal for feminists within the Jewish counterculture, they did not limit their concerns to the realm of religion. Held in 1973, the first Jewish Women's Conference represented another milestone for Jewish feminism as it brought together five hundred activists to discuss the purpose and future of their movement. The wide range of topics covered at the conference, which included sessions and workshops on education, communal leadership, sexuality, and class, revealed the expansive interests of Jewish feminists during these years. As these Jewish feminists critically analyzed their position within their community, many of them, too, began to view the influence of middle-class culture as fundamental to their subjugation as Jewish women.[24]

Some of these Jewish feminists argued that upward mobility had led directly to their social oppression. They reinterpreted the history of Jewish immigration to reflect this belief and ascribed the particular plight of Jewish women to the change in socioeconomic patterns that marked their move from the impoverished, European shtetl to the American middle class. Charlotte Baum, a feminist activist and literary agent, argued in *Response* that Jewish norms in Eastern Europe encouraged Jewish women to support the household economically, sometimes as the sole provider in cases where a husband would spend most of his time studying religious texts. But when Jews moved to America and began to achieve financial success, they adopted middle-class norms of women's domesticity. This shift, Baum believed, caused the status of women within the Jewish community to deteriorate, and changed their role "from that of provider to that of housewife and from that of partner to that of dependent."[25]

Baum's gendered interpretation of Jewish history painted the world of the shtetl as a "proto-feminist" society that anticipated the feminist concern for women's financial and emotional independence. The political weight of this theory depended on the long-term tendency among postwar Jews to view the impoverished shtetl as the locus of authentic Jewish habits and values. The "authentic" life of the Jewish poor, Baum implied, had offered Jewish women satisfaction and respect. With the Jewish move to the middle class and the breakdown of traditional Jewish gender norms, Baum concluded, Jewish women lost their advantages and were forced into subjugation. By framing Jewish history in this manner, Baum presented Jewish feminism not as an alien innovation within Jewish life but as an essential component of the more genuine Jewish existence that had thrived in the impoverished Jewish towns of Eastern Europe.

Other Jewish feminists echoed Baum's idea that joining the middle class had constrained the opportunities and freedoms available to Jewish women. Aviva Cantor Zuckoff, who by the 1970s had expanded her role as a leader of the Jewish Liberation Project to become a prominent Jewish feminist, agreed with Baum that Jewish gender patterns worsened as Jews moved to America and joined the middle class. In Eastern Europe, she claimed, where women often supported the family economically, "women were not seen as sex objects . . . what was admired in a woman was her ability to manage well, to be strong and realistic." This system, she insisted, had a salubrious effect on relationships between men and women: "If you want to marry a strong, realistic woman who will support the family while you study, you can't expect her to be passive and docile at home."

Cantor also believed that the "proto-feminist" environment of the Jewish poor broke down once American Jews moved to America and became middle class. Upwardly mobile Jewish men, she explained, "looked at the bourgeois non-Jewish women into whose class they wanted to assimilate," and recognized them as "passive, unassertive, and fearful, existing just for the family. They asked themselves, "Why aren't our wives like that?" Cantor felt that this history left American Jewish women in a "nerve-wracking double bind," stuck between a traditional Jewish culture that expected them to be competent and resourceful, and middle-class gender norms that demanded helplessness and submission. The situation caused tension between Jewish women and Jewish men, as Jewish men, she argued, "want women who are both useful and independent like their mothers and, at the same time, helpless and dependent as they perceive middle-class, non-Jewish women to be . . . Jewish women have gotten enough double messages to cause anyone to be neurotic, which is, of course, a common criticism of Jewish women," she concluded.[26]

Similarly, feminists within the Brooklyn Bridge collective contended that before immigration to America, Jewish women who had provided economically for their families had developed the fortitude to protect their husbands and families from the oppression of the outside world. When Jews moved to the United States, however, the demands of upward mobility dictated that Jewish women relinquish "their strength, their intelligence, their self-sufficiency, and their demand for respect," as these qualities "were in complete contradiction with the image of the American woman that Jewish men needed in order to legitimate their new [middle-class] status." This left Jewish women caught in a cultural conflict, they argued, between the middle-class ideal of passive femininity and the demand that Jewish women be strong bulwarks against the destruction of Jewish culture. "These contradictions take curious forms," they mused. "Jewish men now demand that their women be intellectual sex objects."[27]

Jewish feminists not only saw the impoverished Jewish women of the shtetl as worthy of emulation but also admired the working-class Jewish women of the immigrant generation, many of whom had participated in rallies and labor strikes. On March 8, 1974, for instance, in coalition with the Chicago Women's Liberation Union, a Jewish countercultural collective called Chutzpah organized a Jewish contingent within the International Women's Day march. The collective distributed leaflets among the local Jewish community, informing them of the role that immigrant Jewish women played in establishing the first International Women's Day in 1908, when tens of thousands of shirtwaist makers in New York City, most of them young Jewish women, left their factories to march for better working conditions.

The young Jewish feminists who participated in the International Women's Day event enthusiastically embraced the opportunity to march alongside the elderly Jewish women of the Emma Lazarus Clubs. Known as the "Emmas," this group of elderly, left-wing Jewish women had been striking on behalf of worker's rights for decades. Young Jewish feminists proudly reported that the elderly Jewish women who had demonstrated alongside them "informed us that they were marching and going to rallies before many of us were even born." In their monthly journal, the Chutzpah collective printed photographs of these younger and older Jewish activists marching side-by-side. For the younger Jewish feminists, most of whom had been raised in a middle-class environment, meeting these elderly activists proved something of a revelation. These women seemed living reminders of a working-class Jewish history that they felt supported their activist and feminist ideals far better than the affluent Jewish communities in which they had grown up.[28]

Indeed, the many Jewish feminists who had come to view their affluent backgrounds as stifling and oppressive took pains to ensure that their own, burgeoning movement did not reflect the middle-class values they perceived in the Jewish world at large. One woman feared that her newly formed Jewish women's consciousness-raising group would be too redolent of the middle-class milieu that she had long since rejected. "Talking about 'The Jewish Woman' was for Hadassah meetings and we certainly weren't going to get stuck into that," she recalled. Instead, thrashing out issues of class became a primary focus of the group. Members raised in families of modest means recounted "the insecurity, the shame, and the privations of growing up in a Jewish working-class family" and "the implication (often perpetrated by more successful relatives) that their class somehow denied them their Jewishness."

Chutzpah's coverage of International Women's Day, 1971.
Used with permission from American Jewish Historical Society, New York and Boston.

Jewish women from wealthier backgrounds, on the other hand, decried "the emptiness, the pressure and the pomposity of upper-middle-class life."[29]

Class conflict also erupted at the first Jewish Women's Conference in February 1973, when some attendees accused the conference organizers of catering only to affluent Jewish feminists. In the middle of a Saturday afternoon panel, a group of women from a self-described "working-class, lesbian collective" interrupted a speaker and demanded the podium. By charging forty dollars to attend the conference, the protesters alleged, the organizers had excluded working-class Jews from the event. Additionally, they faulted

The Jewish Counterculture's Critique of Affluence

the organizers for emphasizing topics that appealed to their middle-class sensibilities. Issues relating to Sephardic and black Jewish women, gay Jewish women, unmarried Jewish mothers, and working-class Jewish women, they argued, received only scant coverage within the conference program. Many conference attendees shared the protesters' concern that a Jewish women's conference not mirror the middle-class biases of mainstream Jewish organizations.[30]

With the growth of the gay liberation movement in late 1960s and 1970s, gay and lesbian Jews also grew vocal within the Jewish counterculture and directed their own critique against the middle-class pressures of American Jewish life. Gay Jewish activist Robbie Skeist, for instance, railed against American Jewish norms of masculinity, which demanded that "we all be heterosexual, get and stay married, have smart kids, become professionals, and achieve a certain kind of 'success.' We don't fit into that pattern and we're still Jews, and we can make the contribution of challenging other people's ways of living."[31]

While an earlier generation of Jewish leaders had also voiced concerns over Jewish masculinity, Skeist's analysis of this issue, rooted in the lessons of gay liberation, articulated a crucial aspect of middle-class ideals of masculinity that had gone unspoken in the immediate postwar years. The postwar Jewish leaders who had complained about middle-class masculinity had noted, correctly, that these norms pushed men toward lucrative, professional careers to the exclusion of other pursuits. Skeist, however, also recognized that this masculine ideal included the assumption that middle-class men would provide financial support for a heteronormative family. The reason it was "hard to be a queer kike," Skeist argued, lay specifically in the American Jewish tendency to organize family lives according to heterosexual, middle-class gender norms. Skeist understood that his sexuality disrupted his ability to conform to this expectation and forced Jews to confront new models of what a Jewish man could be. For the members of the Jewish counterculture, this represented an extremely powerful activist position.[32]

Batya Bauman, who cofounded both the Jewish feminist magazine *Lilith* and the Gay Women's Alternative, a Washington, D.C.–based social and educational group for lesbians, contended that gays and Jews shared parallel experiences of rejection as they sought acceptance in the American middle class. "Many Jews have been in the closet, concealing their Jewishness (often behind changed names and noses) for business, social and personal reasons," she wrote in the winter 1976–77 issue of *Lilith* magazine, while "many lesbians and male homosexuals have been hiding their true identity in the closet for similar reasons." Middle-class American culture, in Bauman's assessment, compelled its members to conform to a white, heteronormative Protestant standard and to suppress the elements of their identity that marked them as other. Those who opted for acceptance by remaining "in the closet," she believed, paid for their choice with feelings of humiliation and self-loathing.

Significantly, Bauman extended the metaphor of "the closet" to the history of American Jewish upward mobility. For Bauman, the terminology of "the closet," popular among gays and lesbians, applied just as much to those American Jews who felt pressured to play down their Jewishness as they advanced into the middle class as it did to those gays and lesbians who hid their sexual orientation as they sought economic and social acceptance. In framing the history of American Jews in these terms, she not only leveled her own critique against Jewish affluence but also articulated an important rationale for an American Jewish community that would understand, embrace, and support the lesbians and gays in its midst.[33]

Criticism of the upward mobility of American Jews also played an important role for those members of the Jewish counterculture who placed the State of Israel at the center of their activist agenda. Like American Jewish leaders in the years just after the Second World War, the radical Zionists of the late 1960s and 1970s also romanticized Israel as a place where Jews sacrificed their economic security in order to serve the Jewish people. Indeed, many of these radical Zionists believed that American abundance had so corrupted the culture of American Jews that they turned to Israel as the only possible solution to the continued survival of the Jewish people. "Judaism in the United States is decadent. . . . The whole Jewish community and its institutions have grown to resemble the American society to a very dangerous degree," declared Michael Rosenberg in 1971. American materialism, Rosenberg argued, had corrupted Jewish life to such a great extent that it could not be salvaged or reformed. The only solution, he believed, lay in moving "to an intensely Jewish cultural setting—Israel."[34]

Countercultural Zionists like Rosenberg insisted that American Jews who did not move to Israel valued American affluence over living a viable, authentic and sustainable Jewish life. Remaining in the United States, Rosenberg contended, proved their preference for the "'comforts' of materialistic America and its fleshpots" over the "survival of a healthy Jewish culture and people." The organizers of the "Student Mobilization for Israel Aliya Corps," a group established with the cooperation of the Jewish

The Jewish Counterculture's Critique of Affluence

Agency for Israel, harnessed this idea during its 1976 campaign to encourage young American Jews to move to Israel during the American bicentennial. "We believe that American Jewry is living a lie when it attempts to rationalize its immobility," read the advertisements the group printed in movement newspapers. "All the arguments we have heard boil down, with few exceptions, to the reluctance to abandon the material comforts of Galut [exile]."[35]

Countercultural Zionists often painted the experience of migrating to Israel as a heroic rejection of their middle-class backgrounds in exchange for a more authentically Jewish one. David Breakstone, a Boston-based student who would move to Israel in 1974, offered the following glowing assessment of the eight thousand American Jews who had moved to Israel in 1971: "These Jews, had they chosen to remain in the United States, would have been able to lead comfortable and secure lives," he wrote. "But then, they feel, their lives would not have been Jewish ones. Only in Israel . . . can they feel satisfaction with themselves and with their Jewishness." The choice, according to Breakstone, was a stark one: young Jews could live a prosperous life in America but remain spiritually and culturally unfulfilled, or they could choose a financially insecure, yet meaningful life in Israel. Within this framework, the prosperity of American Jews was linked not only to their diasporic condition but also to their presumed lack of satisfaction, authenticity, and fulfillment.[36]

According to Gabriel Ende, a member of the American Jewish counterculture who moved to Israel in 1969, the experience of living in Israel finally rid him of his middle-class biases and changed his assumptions of whom he considered to be an "ideal Jew." Still writing for the newspapers of the American Jewish counterculture, he recounted meeting up with an older couple who had recently moved to Israel from the United States. Their children, who remained in the United States, had lived out "a veritable success story in conventional American Jewish terms" by becoming physicians, professors, and lawyers. Ende realized that he had exchanged his "entire value system" from one built on American standards of middle-class success to one based on cross-class ethnic solidarity once he understood that these "bright young American professionals . . . paled into inanity" when compared with "Moshe," the young, "modestly educated" Israeli who performed handyman chores for the couple. Working with what he understood to be a more authentically Jewish point of view, he argued that his affluent friends could not "hold a candle" to a working-class Israeli "whose lot is thrown in with that of his people."[37]

In addition to the political goals expressed by the Zionists, feminists, and Soviet Jewry activists, restructuring the religious practices of American Jews became a primary objective for many members of the Jewish counterculture. In the harshest terms, these religiously oriented members of the Jewish counterculture accused their parent's generation of transforming the Jewish religion into a tool to bolster their upward mobility, and mangling it in the process. "The second generation was interested in 'making it,' financially and socially, and wanted their Judaism reduced to a sparseness that would be parallel to their lifestyle," argued Jack Nusan Porter, a leading intellectual of the Jewish left.[38] Upwardly mobile American Jews had created "uniquely sterile and empty Jewish institutions which would allow them to ameliorate their own Jewish consciences, and yet still gain success in America," complained a student from the University of Michigan. For these young Jews, American Judaism had been reduced to a utilitarian phenomenon in the service of personal financial gain. It no longer felt like an authentic channel for rich, spiritual experiences.[39]

The suburban synagogue emerged as a popular target of scorn for the Jewish counterculture, much as it had been for an earlier generation of upwardly mobile Jews. For these young radicals, suburban synagogues had become "soured, gold-leafed shells" that served as showcases for wealth and grandeur rather than sanctuaries for meditation and prayer. Instead of fostering a sense of community and authentic spiritual feeling, members of the Jewish counterculture believed that American synagogues had come to mirror the alienating, money-driven culture of American capitalism. In the words of Rabbi Arthur Green, founder of Havurat Shalom, these synagogues had become "the ally of the most dreaded aspects of the American Dream: bigness, superficiality, self-deception and perhaps, worst of all, the financial yardstick as the ultimate measure of success." The authentic synagogue and the "American Dream," in Green's estimation, had proved irreconcilable, and he referred to the young Jews who rejected that institution as "refugees from the suburban synagogue."[40]

In 1969 and 1970, some Jewish countercultural newspapers posthumously printed a poem by d. a. levy that expressed his disillusionment with the middle-class synagogue. Levy, a poet, publisher, and free-speech advocate who had a following in countercultural circles, had committed suicide in 1968. For members of the Jewish counterculture, levy's tragic suicide heightened the poignancy of his alienation from Jewish spiritual institutions:

my father and i
went to a temple to hear
the services . . .
when someone told us we had to stand in the
back—we had chosen 'reserved seats'
seats that had been paid for
we left & it was thus i completed
my external jewish education . . .
we never visited another temple
& now i wonder how many jews are
destroyed in this country each year
my father with his lonely eyes
trying to return home
only to have the american god of money
slapped in his face
when we left it was as if
he passed the message on to me
"there are no jews left in this place"[41]

Although the custom of "selling" synagogue seats and other religious honors long predated the Jewish move into the American middle class, levy understood this practice as a metaphor for a middle-class Judaism that made only the wealthy feel welcome. As he saw it, the materialism that had become part of American Judaic practice not only "destroyed" his father when he sought out the comfort of his religion but also destroyed the essence of Judaism itself. For the troubled poet, there were "no [authentic] Jews left" in the middle-class synagogue.

Levy was not the only "New Jew" who believed that American synagogues upheld values antithetical to what they understood as authentic Jewish ideals. Much like the leaders of the immediate postwar period who questioned the morality of building large synagogues during a time when Holocaust survivors depended on the philanthropy of American Jews, members of the Jewish counterculture also believed that Jews should not be renovating synagogue buildings in a world plagued with so much poverty. "Any institution which claims to be deeply concerned about 'civil rights,' peace, and poverty and then spends several million dollars on an architectural facelift needs to have its priorities rearranged," railed a young member of Miami Beach's Temple Israel who wrote to his home congregation as he worked with impoverished communities in Appalachia.[42]

Echoing the concerns that plagued the midcentury members of Congregation Solel, Jewish counterculturalists took particular delight in mocking the multitude of plaques typically installed in large synagogues that publicly honored the donors who paid for the various pews, vestibules, educational wings, and other elements of the building. To the "New Jews," these plaques represented the ultimate symbol of a culture that conferred status according to what one could purchase. "This page has been made possible through the generosity of Abraham and Mildred Goldenputz,"[43] read a satirical text box at the bottom of a 1972 issue of *Doreinu*, a newspaper written by Jewish students in the Washington, D.C., area.[44] Danny Siegel, a prominent poet of the Jewish counterculture, ridiculed these fixtures by pondering the absurd possibility of having the following plaque affixed to the sky: "This sky contributed by the Lord (or is it endowed by the Lord) to the Jews of all the world."[45]

The "New Jews" did not simply complain about middle-class Judaism and the modern synagogue. Unlike the rabbis and leaders of the 1950s, whose frustrations they often echoed, these Jewish counterculturalists attempted to reinvent a Judaism freed of the pernicious influence of American consumerism. They built alternatives that, they believed, would better reflect what they understood as authentic Jewish values and fashioned a web of religious experiments that enabled them to reject "the prevailing Jewish life-style without rejecting Judaism and Jewish culture."[46]

In 1973 Richard Siegel, Michael Strassfeld, and Sharon Strassfeld published *The Jewish Catalogue* to serve as a guide to the innovations of countercultural Judaism. Modeled after the countercultural handbook *The Whole Earth Catalogue*, the volume included essays, resources, and detailed instructions on how to create rituals, celebrations, and artifacts that reflected the anticonsumerist and anti-institutional ethos of the "New Jews." *The Jewish Catalogue* proved successful, becoming one of the best-selling Jewish books of the era. A second and third *Jewish Catalogue* followed the initial volume, and the series sold more than 200,000 copies by the early 1980s. The enormous popularity of these catalogues signaled the strong influence that the Jewish counterculture had upon the Jewish community at large, as well as the self-critical attitude that pervaded American Jewry.[47]

A rejection of middle-class culture lay at the heart of *The Jewish Catalogue*. In the words of the originators of the catalogue project, the volume aimed to serve those who felt the need to "transcend supermarket challah and factory-made Talleisim [prayer shawls]" and other "impersonal, commercializing trends in Jewish life." Instead, *The Jewish Catalogue* showcased the handmade Judaica, intimate prayer groups, and informal celebrations that characterized the Jewish counterculture. The volume offered instructions on how to ferment kosher wine, knot prayer-shawls, bake challah, and carve *mezuzot* (sacred documents traditionally posted on doorposts) to people who, by and large, could easily afford to purchase such items from a store but preferred the feeling of authenticity derived from the handmade.

The Jewish Catalogue also instructed readers on how to form *havurot*, the small-scale collectives in which members of the Jewish counterculture gathered for study, prayer, communal meals, and holiday celebrations. In fact, of all the religious innovations created by the "New Jews," the havurah became the most widespread and successful. During these years, havurot functioned independently of denominational affiliations, large synagogue buildings, and, often, rabbis. Instead, the groups met in one another's homes or apartments, or, in those havurot in which members also lived together, in the shared spaces of their communal houses. They fostered intimate communities of like-minded Jewish counterculturalists and provided them with an alternative to the large, showpiece synagogues and Jewish community centers they detested.[48]

The first of these experimental groups, Havurat Shalom, began in Somerville, Massachusetts, in the fall of 1968. Founder Rabbi Arthur Green, inspired both by the anti-institutional, "underground church" advanced by radical priest Daniel Berrigan and by the small study groups promoted by the Reconstructionist movement in publications like Jacob Neusner's 1960 "The Havurah Idea," initially conceived of Havurat Shalom as a countercultural rabbinical seminary. The group soon decided to concentrate on the formation of a religious community rather than the training of new rabbis. Havurat Shalom served as a model for other small and independent prayer and study collectives around the country, including the New York Havurah on Manhattan's Upper West Side, and Fabrangen, a Washington, D.C.–based "Jewish free culture center" that splintered off from the political-action group Jews for Urban Justice.[49]

These havurot positioned themselves in opposition to synagogues and Jewish cultural centers that, in their view, had been tainted by the sterility and conformity of affluent, middle-class culture. After all, according to a guide for starting havurot penned by Havurat Shalom's Burt Jacobson, members had to "begin with a shared dissent from existing Jewish institutions and their modes of participation" and be prepared to "initiate an alternative model."[50]

Havurot positioned themselves in opposition to synagogues not only in their small scale and institutional independence but also in their approach to finances. They prided themselves on their skeleton budgets, their lack of a

salaried rabbi, and minimal need for formal fundraising—qualities that differentiated them from the many American synagogues that depended on hefty
membership fees and donations to maintain their staff and buildings. As one
1971 flyer for the Fabrangen group advertised:

> There is no organization to join. No "membership." No fees. . . . We
> have no "grant" from any foundation. We have no big money givers
> (you won't find any plaques around our building). Individuals send
> in monthly contributions ranging from $5 to $35—whatever they
> can afford each month. The rent on our building comes to $375 per
> month and our total monthly costs amount to $500. So think of mak-
> ing a contribution (we are tax deductible) some time.[51]

Fabrangen's claim to function without large donations proved somewhat dis-
ingenuous, as the collective had accepted a $15,000 grant from the United
Jewish Appeal in February 1971. But whatever the reality of the situation,
this flyer clearly illustrated the group's attitude toward finances. Fabrangen,
like most countercultural havurot, viewed itself as a small-scale collective
supported by sporadic, grassroots donations. It deemphasized, and sometimes even denied, its ability to access larger grants from established Jewish
organizations. This contrasted sharply with the practice of most American
synagogues, which tended to conspicuously reward and encourage large donations through commemorative plaques and honorary dinners. Members of
the Jewish counterculture rejected the synagogues' celebration of large donations and the validation of wealth that they felt this represented. They advertised their havurot as a counterpoint to the synagogue's culture of affluence.[52]

Havurah participants and other enthusiasts of countercultural Judaism
developed ways of celebrating Jewish holidays and life-cycle events that reflected their rejection of middle-class values. Sounding much like the leaders
of an earlier generation of American Jews, members of the Jewish counterculture derided typical American bar and bat mitzvah celebrations as "opportunities for parents to pay off their dinner invitations among wealthier Jews. . . .
Not only is the Jewish content of the event glossed over, the form of the celebration that takes place goes against Jewish values."[53] The Second Jewish Catalogue's response to this complaint, however, reflected the particular aesthetics
of the Jewish counterculture. In order to make the celebrations feel more
personal and less formal, they suggested holding the ceremony outside or in
a tent rather than in "sterile" banquet halls, designing simple invitations by
silk-screen or woodcut, and preparing "the loving labor of the meal" instead
of hiring a caterer. Under the heading of "some things you might think you

need but don't," they advised parents planning bar and bat mitzvah celebrations that they did not need to have a bar, hired musicians, or even a rabbi at their event. The catalogue assured readers that a simple celebration arranged by the family would be more beautiful and meaningful than a lavish, expensive party managed by professional caterers, bartenders, and even clergy.[54]

The Jewish counterculture's attempts to overhaul bar mitzvah parties inspired the 1971 experimental film *Thirteen Years*. The piece began as a classroom project that filmmaker Bernard Timberg brought to a class of twelve- and thirteen-year-old students that he taught in a synagogue religious school. The resulting fifteen-minute film, which circulated among the Jewish counterculture through the New Jewish Media Project distribution collective, featured a bar mitzvah boy by the name of Horace Schlub[55] suffering through a bar mitzvah at a large, gilded synagogue. In this filmic depiction of a "standard" bar mitzvah, guests in formal dress surrounded Horace and stuffed presents and envelopes full of money into his suit pockets. The film intermittently cut away from Horace's reception to another bar mitzvah taking place in a park. At this modest event, a circle of long-haired celebrants, simply dressed in the jeans and peasant blouses favored by countercultural youth, sang songs, solemnly blessed and then shared an apple, and discussed biblical passages. Following each scene, the film cut to black-and-white photographs of bearded, male, Eastern European Jews who sit in judgment over both styles of celebration. "*A shonda*" (An embarrassment!), they exclaimed in Yiddish after clips of the formal affair, while declaring "*Dos iz gut, dos iz toyre*" (This is good, this is Torah) after scenes of the bar mitzvah in the park. Through this device, the film made the claim that the modest, anticonsumerist celebrations advocated by the Jewish counterculture were more authentic and in tune with the Jewish past than the more lavish receptions adopted by the bulk of the American Jewish population.[56]

The Jewish counterculture also created alternatives to the celebration of Jewish holidays in America. On April 4, 1969, Jews for Urban Justice organized the first "Freedom Seder." The event, which took place at the Lincoln Temple, an African American church in Washington D.C., drew a diverse group of eight hundred celebrants, including Jewish countercultural activists, Jewish families from the suburbs, black militants and other members of the African American community, non-Jewish members of the New Left, and even a small group of Yeshiva students. They read from a haggadah penned by Arthur Waskow, which updated the traditional liturgy with non-Jewish figures such as "the rabbi Thoreau," the "prophet Ghandi," and "the *shofet* [judge] Eldridge Cleaver."[57]

While some critics, many of whom even came from the ranks of the Jewish counterculture, accused the orchestrators of the Freedom Seder of obscuring Jewish traditions in their enthusiasm for images and quotes from non-Jewish revolutionary leaders, others thrilled to the Freedom Seder's spirited fusion of Jewish customs and radical politics. Celebrating a Jewish holiday in a space built by African Americans and along with African Americans represented the ultimate rejection of a Jewish middle-class identity that depended on their acceptance as racial whites. For the members of Jews for Urban Justice and those who agreed with them, celebrating Passover in a black church, and lionizing black militants and other radical figures within the Passover liturgy, did not detract from the Jewishness of the event. Rather, it expressed a vision that felt more in tune with where they felt the Jewish community would have been positioning itself, both socially and politically, had it not made the mistake of aligning itself with the white middle class. Arthur Waskow, for instance, specifically intended for his haggadah to "assert a unity . . . between the historic imperatives of Jewish liberation and the urgency of today's black rebellion."[58] For many radical Jews, celebrating Passover in this way felt more authentically Jewish than commemorating the holiday through a traditional seder in an affluent Jewish home or synagogue. In the words of activist Mike Tabor, "All the meaningless, drab, dull, synthetic, assimilationist veneer was, for an evening it seemed, wiped away."[59]

The Freedom Seder became the stuff of legend among members of the Jewish counterculture. It garnered a good deal of media publicity, attracting journalists from the *Washington Post* and the *Village Voice*, while the influential New Left journal *Ramparts* published the text of Waskow's haggadah in its entirety. WBAI, the New York Pacifica Radio station, broadcast the Freedom Seder live, and the Canadian Broadcasting Company televised a documentary about it soon after. In the wake of Waskow's revamped haggadah, revising the haggadah to reflect countercultural beliefs evolved into a common practice within the Jewish movement. Many Jewish countercultural groups crafted their own versions of the text, including *The Jewish Liberation Hagada* of the Jewish Liberation Project, which gave the liturgy a Zionist bent, and *The Fourth World Haggadah* of the World Union of Jewish Students, which emphasized religion and spirituality. And when feminism took hold among the Jewish counterculture in the 1970s, Jewish feminists published *The Women's Haggadah,* which drew a parallel between the liberation of the Jews from Egypt and their own struggle for liberation as Jewish women.[60]

In addition to creating countercultural alternatives to the holiday of Passover, the "New Jews" put their stamp on a variety of holiday celebrations.

In December 1971, for instance, Chicago's Chutzpah collective organized an "anti-imperialist" Chanukah party. Instead of changing the holiday's rituals or liturgy, the group's members concentrated their efforts on ridding Chanukah of the commercialism they associated with Christmas and American consumer culture. "America has corrupted Chanukah as it has corrupted so many other things," lamented a member of the collective. They charged American Jews with treating the holiday as a "pale imitation of the *goyish* [non-Jewish] holiday of Christmas" by incorporating "Chanukah bushes, light displays . . . [and] gift giving" into the celebration. Instead, revelers at the Chutzpah Chanukah party commemorated the event by preparing their own *latkes* [potato pancakes] and applesauce, the traditional foods of the holiday, and lighting the Chanukah menorah together.

For members of the Jewish counterculture, creating a Chanukah celebration free of gift giving and other commercial aspects adopted by American Jews felt like a crucial step toward reclaiming a more authentic holiday. "The way my parents had done Chanukah mostly turned me off," wrote a young mother who had attended the Chutzpah collective's party. Although she recalled that her immigrant grandmother had celebrated the holiday in a modest way, her parents' observance of the holiday had included glittery decorations and a present for each of the eight nights. In her view, her affluent, middle-class parents had degraded the holiday to the point that the traditional ritual of "lighting the candles was something to get through in order to get to the presents."

In contrast to her parent's commercialized celebration of the holiday, this young mother felt that the countercultural party she had attended, though "peopled by radicals, freaks, gays, etc., reminded me of my grandmother's!" Comparing this Chanukah celebration to those she had known at her grandmother's home underscored the impulse of these New Jews to connect their religious practices to those of earlier generations of working-class Jews. Rhetorically linking their countercultural celebrations to the Jewish history of poverty simultaneously inculcated their innovations with a sense of authenticity and justified their rejection of middle-class Jewish culture.[61]

Whether they were advocating for Zionism, Jewish feminism, the inclusion of gay and lesbian Jews into the Jewish community, the cause of Soviet Jewry, or a reinvented religious Judaism, the members of the Jewish counterculture pointed to the wealth of American Jews as an obstacle to a genuine Jewish life. A condemnation of middle-class affluence played a key role in the way that these young American Jews narrated and justified their political and cultural engagements, even when their stated goals seemed to have little to do with class or upward mobility. Depicting middle-class affluence as being incompatible, and even destructive, to an authentic Jewish culture became a crucial way in which these young Jews expressed their unease at being "insiders" within American society in terms of their relative prosperity, and yet nonetheless feeling like cultural "outsiders."

Both scholarly and popular assessments of the Jewish counterculture tend to attribute this anticonsumerist, anti-middle-class message to the influence of the New Left of the 1960s. And indeed, the values, rhetoric, and political style of the New Left had a crucial impact on these young activists and helped shape their critique of Jewish life in North America. The "New Jews" clearly identified with the leaders of the New Left, who, in the Port Huron Statement of 1962, had described themselves as a generation "bred in at least modest comfort... looking uncomfortably to the world we inherit." Like many others in the New Left, they, too, viewed middle-class culture as stifling and immoral and lambasted their parents' generation for embracing it.[62]

While the influence of the New Left was certainly important to the growth of the Jewish counterculture, the tendency to concentrate solely on the ways in which the "New Jews" drew from the New Left has obscured how their critique also echoed those of the rabbis and Jewish intellectuals of the postwar years. Although they adopted the rhetoric of revolt, the class critiques of the Jewish counterculture also mirrored those of Jewish leaders who expressed their own ambivalence about upward mobility in the two decades after World War II. While the criticisms of Jewish youth often targeted these same leaders as part of the "establishment" that, they felt, had damaged American Judaism so badly, this rebellious younger generation often sounded much like its rabbis and teachers as it took American Jews to task for their attachment to middle-class affluence. The members of the Jewish counterculture, much like their parents, rabbis, and teachers, understood that middle-class wealth had transformed American Jewish life and worried that these changes strayed too far from what they understood as an authentic Jewishness.

The continuities between postwar leaders' ambivalence over affluence and their children's revolt against middle-class Judaism should not strike us as surprising. After all, the children raised during the postwar decades had a great deal of exposure to the anxieties of their religious leaders. More children attended religious school during the postwar years than at any previous time in American Jewish history, with some communities boasting enrollment rate of as high as 80 percent.[63] These years also witnessed important expansions in Jewish summer camping, with the Conservative

The Jewish Counterculture's Critique of Affluence

movement founding the first Camp Ramah in 1947 and the Reform movement's establishment of its first camp, the Union Institute (which later became the Olin-Sang-Ruby Union Institute) in 1952.[64] Jewish youth in the postwar years had ample access to both formal and informal Jewish education, and many countercultural leaders had been highly involved in the "established" world of Jewish denominationalism before they began their countercultural rebellion.[65]

But even if they had not had so much exposure to the ambivalence of their parents, the circumstances experienced by the Jewish youth of the late 1960s may have accounted for their very similar anxieties. These two generations shared the same tendency to identify with the history of Jewish marginalization, even as they found themselves living relatively privileged lives among the American middle class. Both midcentury American Jews and their countercultural children felt the tensions of this contradiction.

At times, both the members of the Jewish counterculture and the Jewish leaders who educated them acknowledged their shared, longstanding misgivings over the effects of Jewish upward mobility. At a Hadassah conference in 1969, for instance, Albert Vorspan, the director of the Commission on Social Action of Reform Judaism who had long been an abiding critic of the Jewish middle class, dubbed these young Jewish radicals the "most moral" generation of Jewish youth. "Although they would not admit it," he stated, "they are carrying out their Jewish ethical values and rebelling against the fact that their parents have not taken action to correct problems, but confined themselves to words."[66]

Contrary to Vorspan's belief that the young upstarts of the Jewish counterculture would never "admit" that their activism stemmed from concerns often expressed by their parents, at times these "New Jews" did articulate their deep sense of connection with the values of the older generation. "We are your children and affirm this," declared Hillel Levine, a prominent activist of the Jewish counterculture, in his 1969 speech to the Council of Jewish Federations and Welfare Funds. These deeply felt connections, he continued, accounted for their disappointment in "the reality of American Jewish life which we cannot reconcile with what you have taught us to cherish."[67]

Dismissing the commonalities between the concerns over affluence expressed by the "New Jews" and those that had long been articulated by the teachers, parents, and rabbis who educated them misses a key factor in the development of the Jewish counterculture. Highlighting these continuities, on the other hand, provides insight not only into why these young Jews behaved the way that they did but also into the reactions of their elders. It explains why the established Jewish community often provided these young upstarts with financial and moral support and why so many members of the Jewish counterculture ended up becoming leaders within the established Jewish community after the flush of their rebellion cooled. In the end, it may make more sense to view the activists of the Jewish counterculture not as rebels or iconoclasts but rather as the inheritors of an enduring Jewish ambivalence over the effects of American prosperity.[68]

Conclusion

The new middle-class American Jews of the late 1940s, 1950s, and early 1960s did not climb the economic ladder to a chorus of accolades and applause. On the contrary, they stood accused of pursuing crass assimilationism and of being too concerned about their own economic and social status to nurture an authentic Jewish life in the United States. They bore the criticism of the very rabbis, novelists, and intellectuals they supported financially through their synagogue dues and magazine subscriptions. Later, they endured similar condemnations from the children they raised in an environment of comfort and security they themselves had not known in their own youth. Indeed, much truth lay in Canadian writer Mordecai Richler's 1965 claim that the "most fired-at class of American Jews" may well be "this generation between, this unlovely spiky bunch that climbed with the rest of middle-class America out of the Depression into the pot of prosperity." One might wonder along with Richler if there has ever been a group of Jews "so plagued by moralists" or "so blamed for making money."[1]

The Jewish anxieties over upward mobility that peaked in the years after World War II and continued through the countercultural moment that followed it emerged out of the incongruity between Jews' self-image as outsiders and their newfound status as white, middle-class, even privileged insiders. These acerbic reactions to the new Jewish middle class, therefore, were shaped as much by Jewish achievement and success as by deeply felt histories of Jewish poverty and oppression.

During the postwar years, though internal critiques of the Jewish middle class abounded, little effort was made to meaningfully alter their lifestyle. The leaders who condemned the expense of middle-class suburban synagogues, for instance, also helped to build and maintain them. And while a small minority of middle-class Jews tried to challenge conventions by building self-consciously nonconformist institutions like Congregation Solel, these synagogues did not differ significantly from their mainstream counterparts. By and large, Jewish resistance to middle-class norms took the form of verbal and written warnings that did not translate to concrete change.

The gap between this widespread denigration of middle-class Jewish life and the minimal attempts to create alternatives to it represents more than just a quirk of postwar American Jewish history. Instead, these critiques of Jewish upward mobility comprised, in and of themselves, a crucial means by which American Jews adapted to prosperity and social acceptance. Looking toward impoverished and isolated Jewish communities as paragons of Jewish authenticity, and condemning the influence of upward mobility on Jewish religion, politics, and gendered behavior, became important ways through which Jews, and especially their leaders, articulated their difference from other middle-class Americans. Significantly, this manner of asserting their Jewishness did not jeopardize the social and economic security that their new status afforded them. It enabled them to honor their history as outsiders without risking the chance of reliving it.

Analyzing the content of these critiques also offers insight into how post-war Jews, following the leaders they sponsored, understood themselves in relation to the middle class they sought to join. They framed their upward mobility through the lens of Jewish history. The general critique of affluence that permeated through American culture in the years after World War II did not satisfy them; they imbued these conversations with Jewish symbols and experiences and developed a particularly Jewish language through which to interrogate the promise of postwar America. This rhetorical move does not match the reigning image of a postwar Jewish community striving to melt into an undifferentiated middle class. Rather, it points to their quite reasonable desire to remain distinctive without endangering their new social and economic status.

This discourse also reveals the complex landscape upon which upwardly mobile American Jews charted their shifting identities in the postwar period. Though they certainly acknowledged their connections to the other white, middle-class Americans among whom they now made their homes, as American Jewish leaders expressed their anxieties over affluence they also emphasized their transnational ties to the Jews of Israel and the victimized Jews of Eastern Europe, as well as their historical and emotional affinities with America's working-class and racial outsiders. Without risking their new advantages, they continued to express their connections with those who did not share them. This, too, demonstrated their ambivalent relationship to their upward mobility, even as they embraced it.

Looking at the ways that midcentury Jews critiqued their own communities also tempers our assessment of their radical children, many of whom joined the New Left or helped to develop a distinctly Jewish counterculture. Previous scholars have noted the significant continuities between the young revolutionaries of the late 1960s and the generation that preceded them. Maurice Isserman, for instance, has documented the political connections between the Old and the New Left; Doug Rossinow traced the existential Christianity that infused both the New Left and an earlier generation of liberal Christian activists; and Alan Petigny spoke to the liberalization of American attitudes toward sexuality and domestic life that began in the 1950s, well before the start of the late-1960s counterculture.[2]

In a similar vein, rather than viewing the late 1960s as a drastic rupture, this study also finds much continuity between postwar Jews and the next generation that condemned them so harshly. Much like their parents, the countercultural Jews of the late 1960s also responded to the dissonance between Jewish histories of oppression and their own middle-class standing. What differentiated them from their parents was not their suspicion of Jewish upward mobility but rather their success at creating religious and political collectives that, at least for a time, provided meaningful alternatives to what they viewed as the problems of middle-class Jewish life. Immersed in a nonconformist youth culture and more secure in their social status, they were in a better position than their parents to act on concerns that both generations shared. The long history of Jewish anxieties over upward mobility, therefore, compels us to view the postwar generation of Jews as less complacent, and the countercultural generation as less rebellious, than we have previously assumed.

Since the 1970s, many American Jews continue to foreground their history of exclusion and poverty while enjoying a high social and economic status. This has left a complicated legacy. On the one hand, American Jews' long-standing propensity to identify with their history of oppression has, in some cases, inspired them toward critical political stances aimed at extending their advantages to those who do not (yet) share them. A 2012 survey sponsored by the Public Religion Research Institute, for instance, found that strong majorities of American Jews believe that the government unfairly favors the wealthy and that it ought to raise the taxes of citizens who earn more than $1 million per year and do more to close the gap between rich and poor. When asked about the factors that fed into these political attitudes, 70 percent cited communal histories of poverty and prejudice such as the Jewish immigrant experience, while another 87 percent mentioned the Holocaust.[3]

While most contemporary Jewish social justice organizations cite religious principles as the primary inspiration for their work, some also point to Jewish histories of subjugation as another motivating factor. The website of the American Jewish World Service, a Jewish organization aimed at fighting for human rights around the globe, notes that many of its supporters see the organization's human rights mission as a direct response to "persecution and genocide perpetrated against Jews in the past." Bend the Arc, an American Jewish organization involved in civil rights, civil liberties, and antipoverty work, is driven by "the stories of ancestors both ancient and recent," a nod to both the religious prophets of the ancient world and modern Jewish experiences of poverty and oppression.[4]

American Jews' propensity to identify with a history of exclusion also helps to explain what pundits have long considered to be the paradox of Jewish voting patterns. Contrary to long-standing predictions that Jews would cease to vote for left-of-center candidates as they grew more secure in their middle-class rank, this shift toward the right has yet to occur for the bulk of the American Jewish population. In 1973 sociologist Milton Himmelfarb introduced the uncomfortable quip that Jews "earn like Episcopalians but vote like Puerto Ricans," reflecting the remarkable consistency of Jews' liberal voting records from the early twentieth century through the Trump-Clinton campaign of 2016, when 71 percent of Jewish voters, as opposed to 48 percent of the general population, voted for the Democratic candidate.[5] While Jews' preoccupation with their history of oppression cannot fully explain the persistence of Jewish liberalism—a liberalism which, as many scholars have demonstrated, has long had its limits—it also cannot be discounted as a significant factor within the political leanings of many American Jews.[6]

On the other hand, American Jews' continued identification with family histories of oppression have also led some of them to underplay or even discount the ways that structural inequalities continue to offer them opportunities that are not shared by all Americans. To wit, a problematic but telling joke that has circulated among American Jews since at least the 1980s featured an African American man who accused a white interlocutor of having ancestors who enslaved his own forebears. "Where did this happen, in Vilna?" countered his white conversation partner, in a punchline meant not only to reveal his Jewishness but also his lack of responsibility for the legacy of American racism. And yet, even as this joke tries to find humor in the notion that Jews, burdened with their own histories of suffering, could ever have had enough power to oppress anyone else, there is also an uncertainty evident in the joke's very premise. After all, what does it say about the social position of American Jews if the Jewish figure in this joke could have been so easily confused with the descendants of elite, white, slave owners?

Recent discussions on social media over whether the descendants of Eastern European Jews ought to be considered "privileged" further illustrate the social blindness that can result from identifying with Jewish histories of oppression without also fully acknowledging most Jews' postwar advantages. Take, as just one example, the 2014 brouhaha over the insistence of Jewish Princeton student Tal Fortgang that his grandparents' suffering under the Nazis proved that it was his own hard work that earned him a spot in the Ivy League rather than "'power systems' or other conspiratorial imaginary institutions." His selective retelling of his family history did not include his own experiences of being educated in schools that prepared students for college, of having teachers who assumed that he was destined to succeed, and of not having to worry about food, shelter, clothing, or violence. These were not privileges shared by his ancestors, certainly, and there is no inherent problem in closely identifying with their legacy. But Fortgang was justifiably criticized for using his family history to discount the advantages that he did benefit from and the challenges faced by those who do not share them.[7]

Seventy years after their forebears began their ascent into the middle class, American Jews continue to leverage their communal histories of poverty and subjugation as a way of asserting their difference from other middle-class Americans. This trend has sometimes sparked creative engagement with Jewish culture, social justice activism, and critical assessments of how power and privilege continue to create injustice. At other times, Jews have used their own historical marginality as a way of downplaying their current advantages and mitigating their own responsibility in helping others make that upward climb. But whatever the political ramifications, American Jews' tendency to identify with legacies of poverty and exclusion as they live lives of prosperity and relative acceptance was not limited to the decades just after World War II. On the contrary, this has proved a persistent means through which Jews understand their social position in the United States and maintain a distinctive niche within the American middle class.

Notes

INTRODUCTION

1. Rothchild (writing as Evelyn Rossman), "The Community and I," 398.

2. Kates, "Sylvia Rosner Rothchild."

3. Previous articles examining the uncomfortable middle-class identity of postwar American Jews include Berman, "American Jews and the Ambivalence of Middle-Classness"; Glenn, "The Vogue of Jewish Self-Hatred in Postwar World War II America"; Prell, "Community and the Discourse of Elegy."

4. On how fears of Jewish power influenced these conversations, see Berman, "American Jews and the Ambivalence of Middle-Classness," 410–11; on the tendency of an earlier generation of upwardly mobile Jews to identify with their history of marginality and poverty, see Alexander, *Jazz Age Jews*.

5. On how these developments played out in Los Angeles and Miami, see Moore, *To the Golden Cities*.

6. Kramer and Leventman, *Children of the Gilded Ghetto*, 53–54; Gordon, *Jews in Suburbia*, 170; E. Goldstein, *The Price of Whiteness*.

7. "Fiddler on the Roof," sermon, January 15, 1965 (4/1), Rabbi Harold Saperstein Papers, mss. 718, American Jewish Archives.

8. On the perception that suburban Jewish life lacked authenticity, and on the tendency to link Jewish authenticity and urban space, see Prell, "Community and the Discourse of Elegy," 70–73; Diner, *Lower East Side Memories*; Kirshenblatt-Gimblett, "Imagining Europe"; Zipperstein, *Imagining Russian Jewry*; Prell, "Triumph," 116.

9. Taylor, *The Ethics of Authenticity*, 25–29; Appiah, *The Ethics of Identity*, 17–21; Lindholm, *Culture and Authenticity*, 100–101.

10. On how postwar Americans understood the concept of authenticity, see Hale, *A Nation of Outsiders*; and Rossinow, *The Politics of Authenticity*. On postwar Jews and authenticity, see Prell, "Community and the Discourse of Elegy," 70–73.

11. MacCannell, *The Tourist*; Hobsbawm and Ranger, *The Invention of Tradition*; Anderson, *Imagined Communities*. Scholars who adapt these principles to notions of

cultural authenticity include Grazian, *Blue Chicago*; Peterson, *Creating Country Music*; Kirshenblatt-Gimblett, *Destination Culture*.

12. Penslar, *Shylock's Children*; Diner, *A Time for Gathering*, 185–200; Dinnerstein, *Antisemitism in America*; Berman, "American Jews and the Ambivalence of Middle-Classness," 410–11.

13. Learsi, *The Jews in America*, 312; Diner, *We Remember with Reverence and Love*; Moore, *To the Golden Cities*, 2; Prell, "Triumph," 117.

14. Moore, *At Home in America*.

15. Diner, *Jews of the United States*, 228–32; Wenger, *Uncertain Promise*; Wechsler, "The Rationale for Restriction."

16. Cahan, *The Rise of David Levinsky*; Yezierka, *Salome of the Tenements*; Ornitz, *Haunch, Paunch, and Jowl*; Weidman, *I Can Get It for You Wholesale*.

17. In a related point, Mark Shechner drew the distinction between the Marxist bent that filtered through American Jewish literature in the early twentieth century and the shift to psychoanalytic concerns in the years after World War II. See Shechner, *After the Revolution*.

18. Brodkin, *How Jews Became White Folks and What That Says about Race in America*, 38–44; Katznelson, *When Affirmative Action Was White*. On the need to explain Jewish success through sociohistorical measures, see Hollinger, "Rich, Powerful and Smart."

19. National Opinion Research Center Study, cited in Bogue, *The Population of the United States*, 706; Glazer, "The Attainment of Middle-Class Rank," 141.

20. Berman, "American Jews and the Ambivalence of Middle-Classness," 413–14; Bledstein and Johnston, *The Middling Sorts*; Ortner, "Reading America"; Ortner, *New Jersey Dreaming*; Rottenberg, *Performing Americanness*; Walkowitz, *Working with Class*, 6–7.

21. Hochschild, *Facing Up to the American Dream*; Rottenberg, *Performing Americanness*, 53–69.

22. Riesman, Glazer, and Denney, *The Lonely Crowd*; Whyte, *The Organization Man*; Galbraith, *The Affluent Society*; Friedan, *The Feminine Mystique*. See also Horowitz, *The Anxieties of Affluence*.

23. If I had intended here to follow David Hollinger's call for more "dispersionist" studies of American Jewish history, I might have ventured to guess why so many of these best-selling critics of American, middle-class culture were Jews. However, my goals in this study are unabashedly "communalist" in that I trace what is primarily an intracommunal conversation. Hollinger, "Communalist and Dispersionist Approaches to American Jewish History in an Increasingly Post-Jewish Era."

24. This is not to say that the general conversation regarding affluence never overlapped with the more specifically Jewish one. William Whyte, for instance, included a discussion of suburban Jews drawn from Herbert Gans's 1951 study of Jews in suburban Park Forest, Illinois (*The Organization Man*, 414–17). On the impact of Jewishness on these social critics, see Horowitz, "Jewish Women Remaking American Feminism," 235–56; Fermaglich, *American Dreams and Nazi Nightmares*, 58–82; Berman, "American Jews and the Ambivalence of Middle-Classness," 421–22.

25. Berger, *The Noise of Solemn Assemblies*; Winter, *The Suburban Captivity of the Churches*; Greeley, *The Church and the Suburbs*; Hudnut-Beumler, *Looking for God in the Suburbs*.

26. Frazier, *Black Bourgeoisie*.

27. Ralph E. Samuel, "A Message from the Chairman," *300*, no. 19 (September 1954), cited in Goldman, "'Along with all Other Americans,'" 8; Berman, "American Jews and the Ambivalence of Middle-Classness," 415–16; Goldman, "The View from 1954"; Goren, *The Politics and Public Culture of American Jews*, 195–200.

28. Wenger, *History Lessons: The Creation of American Jewish Heritage*; Sarna, "The Cult of Synthesis in American Jewish Culture." On how Jews explained their difference to the American public, see Berman, *Speaking of Jews*.

29. On the tendency of American Jewish historians to posit a triumphant synthesis between America and Jewish culture, see Michels, *A Fire in Their Hearts*, 18. Scholars who explore Jews' successful adaptation to prosperity include Moore, *To the Golden Cities*; Diamond, *And I Will Dwell in Their Midst*; Heinze, *Adapting to Abundance*; Joselit, *The Wonders of America*.

30. Shapiro, *A Time for Healing*, 257; Brodkin, *How Jews Became White Folks and What That Says about Race in America*; Lederhendler, *New York Jews and the Decline of Urban Ethnicity*. Also see the historiographical notes in Berman, "American Jews and the Ambivalence of Middle-Classness," 411–12; and Prell, "Community and the Discourse of Elegy," 83.

31. My thoughts here draw in part from conversations I shared with Lila Corwin Berman over Sacvan Bercovitch's discussion in *The American Jeremiad*. In this classic work, Bercovitch argued that dissent in American history has often been limited by a tendency to couch exhortations for social change within a language that ultimately supports American ideals. On how postwar American Jews did not always act on political convictions that threatened their upward mobility, see Dollinger, *Quest for Inclusion*; Berman, *Metropolitan Jews*, 11.

CHAPTER 1

1. Pilch, "Old Values and New Purposes," 6–11.

2. On the way that 1920s-era urban Jewish neighborhoods also played into discussions of Jewish authenticity, see Prell, "Community and the Discourse of Elegy," 70–73.

3. Shandler, *Shtetl*, 1–3; "shtetl, n.," OED Online. http://www.oed.com/view/Entry/178977?redirectedFrom=shtetl, accessed May 14, 2012; Ain, "Swislocz: Portrait of a Jewish Community in Eastern Europe." While in the Yiddish vernacular, the term *shtetl* can refer to a town inhabited by any group of people in any place in the world (*shtot* in Yiddish means city, while *shtetl*, the diminutive form of *shtot*, can literally be translated to "little city"), when brought into English parlance the term specifically refers to the largely Jewish market villages of Eastern Europe. As Jeffrey Shandler points out, the postvernacular life of the word *shtetl* imbues the word with a cultural and geographic specificity that it never had in its original language.

4. Duker, "Patterns that Preserve," 1; Howe and Greenberg, *A Treasury of Yiddish Stories*, 4.

5. Diner, *We Remember with Reverence and Love*; Kirshenblatt-Gimblett, "Imagining Europe."

6. Diner, *We Remember with Reverence and Love*, 160.

7. Heschel, *The Earth Is the Lord's*, 43–44.

8. Ibid., 47–48.

9. Ibid., 77–79.

10. Ibid., 25–26.

11. Ibid., 10, 105.

12. Vishniac, *Polish Jews, 11*; Vishniac's work did not achieve its current iconic status until years later, after his photographs were featured in a Jewish Museum exhibit in 1971 and Farrar, Straus and Giroux published *A Vanished World* in 1983. Heschel's introductory essay was first delivered in Yiddish at the nineteenth annual YIVO Conference in New York, and then was printed in both Yiddish and English in various contexts before appearing in Vishniac's *Polish Jews*. For a full history of the development of *The Earth Is the Lord's*, see Shandler, "Heschel and Yiddish"; For the history of Heschel's speech at YIVO, see Moore, *East European Jews in Two Worlds*, viii.

13. Benton, *Roman Vishniac Rediscovered*; Newhouse, "A Closer Reading of Roman Vishniac," 36.

14. Kirshenblatt-Gimblett, introduction to *Life Is with People*, ix–xlvii.

15. C. Rosenthal, "Social Stratification"; C. Rosenthal, "Deviation and Social Change in the Jewish Community of a Small Polish Town"; C. Rosenthal, "How the Polish Jew Saw His World"; Joffe, "The Dynamics of Benefice among East European Jews"; Landes and Zborowski, "Hypotheses concerning the Eastern European Jewish Family."

16. Zborowski and Herzog, *Life Is with People*, 74; Joffe, "The Dynamics of Benefice among East European Jews," 242; C. Rosenthal, "Social Stratification," 6–7.

17. Zborowski and Herzog, *Life Is with People*, 239, 265; C. Rosenthal, "Social Stratification," 5.

18. Stein, Harnick and Block, *Fiddler on the Roof*, original production 1964; Solomon, *Wonder of Wonders*; Whitfield, "Fiddling with Sholem Aleichem"; Dauber, *The Worlds of Sholem Aleichem*, 353–63; Zipperstein, *Imagining Russian Jewry*, 33–35; Diner, *Jews of the United States*, 286–87.

19. Shandler, "Religion, Democracy, and the Radio Waves," 130–32.

20. "The World of Sholem Aleichem," *The Eternal Light*, 1–11.

21. Perl, *The World of Sholom Aleichem*, 21.

22. Segal, "Hot Rolls and Cream," 42.

23. Atkinson, "Three Short Plays,"","," X1; Decter, "Belittling Sholom Aleichem's Jews"; Dauber, *The Worlds of Sholem Aleichem*, 347–49.

24. Decter, "Belittling Sholom Aleichem's Jews"; Dauber, *The Worlds of Sholem Aleichem*, 348–49; Fermaglich, "Midge Decter."

25. Diner, *Jews of the United States*, 290; Sarna, *American Judaism*, 279–80.

26. Gamoran, *The New Jewish History, Book Three*; Klaperman and Klaperman, *The Story of the Jewish People*, vol. 3; Levinger, Levinger, and Gersh, *The Story of the Jew*; Pessin, *The Jewish People Book III*; Lehman, "Mamie Gamoran; "Libby Klaperman, Dead at 60," June 22, 1982, Jewish Telegraphic Agency, http://www.jta.org/1982/06/22/archive/libby-klaperman-dead-at-60, accessed June 3, 2015.

27. Pessin, *The Jewish People Book III*, 60; Gamoran, *The New Jewish History, Book III*, 159.

28. Klaperman and Klaperman, *The Story of the Jewish People*, 3:159; Levinger, Levinger and Gersh, *The Story of the Jew*, 186.

29. Pessin *The Jewish People Book III*, 69; Gamoran, *The New Jewish History, Book III*, 162; Klaperman and Klaperman, *The Story of the Jewish People*, 3:159; Levinger, Levinger, and Gersh, *The Story of the Jew*, 186.

30. Gamoran, *The New Jewish History, Book III*, 168; Levinger, Levinger, Gersh, *The Story of the Jew*, 185.

31. Pessin, *The Jewish People Book III*, 74–75.

32. Ibid., 75–77.

33. Diner, *Lower East Side Memories*, 35.

34. Wasserman, "Re-creating Recreations on the Lower East Side" Diner, *Lower East Side Memories*, 175–76.

35. Glazer and Moynihan, *Beyond the Melting Pot*, 180.

36. Postal and Koppman, *A Jewish Tourist's Guide to the United States*, 381.

37. Simon, *New York: Places and Pleasures*, 58, 63–64.

38. Weales, "Make Mine Manhattan," 344–45.

39. "New York City," in Ben-Asher and Leaf, *The Junior Jewish Encyclopedia*; Klaperman and Klaperman, *The Story of the Jewish People*, 4:149–51; Pessin, *The Jewish People III*, 243–45.

40. "The Press: The Victim of Success"; Wakefield, "New York's Lower East Side Today."

41. Menes, "The East Side—Matrix of the Jewish Labor Movement."

42. Grinstein, "Flight from the Slums"; Salo Baron first spoke out against the "lachrymose conception of Jewish history" in "Ghetto and Emancipation."

43. Gold, "The East Side I Knew," 25–27.

44. Chotzinoff, *A Lost Paradise*, 69, 70, 91; Chotzinoff, "East Side Boyhood."

45. Taylor, *All-of-a-Kind Family*, 12, 57–62, 64–77, 96–103, 156, discussed in Diner, *Lower East Side Memories*, 59–66.

46. S. Rosenthal, "Long-Distance Nationalism: American Jews, Zionism, and Israel"; Sarna, *American Judaism*, 335–36; Silver, *Our Exodus*; Katz, *Bringing Zion Home*.

47. Wouk, "For the Flavor of this Wonderful Land You Must Go There Yourself," 7.

48. Diner, *We Remember with Reverence and Love*, 311–20; Gamoran, *The New Jewish History, Book III*, 311; Levinger, Levinger and Gersh, *The Story of the Jew*, 264.

49. "Notes for Hadassah Tithes Dinner, 1/6/46," Rabbi Charles Shulman Papers, mss. 124, box 5, folder 4, American Jewish Archives.

50. "An American Jew Dreamed," sermon, Yom Kippur Eve, October 4, 1946, Rabbi Charles Shulman Papers, mss. 124, box 2, folder 15, American Jewish Archives.

51. Seaman, "Ruth Gruber."

52. Gruber, *Israel without Tears*, 40.

53. Ibid., 13–14, 36; Gruber, *Israel Today*, 41.

54. Gruber, *Israel Today*, 5, 12.

55. Klaperman and Klaperman, *The Story of the Jewish People IV*, 259.

56. Silverman, *Habibi's Adventures in the Land of Israel*, 73.

57. Ibid., 115.

58. Kubie, *The First Book of Israel*, 10.

59. Ibid., 32–34.

60. Diner, *We Remember with Reverence and Love*, 311–20; "Do you Live According to Your Means?," sermon, January 20, 1956, Edgar Siskin Papers, mss. 64, folder 2, box 2, American Jewish Archives.

61. "Ronald Sanders Papers: Biographical/Historical Information," http://archives
.nypl.org/mss/3617, accessed July 29, 15; Sanders, "Settling in Israel?," 39.

62. Pekarsky, "Shopping, Swapping, *Shepping Nahas* in Israel," 6; Jane Fineberg-Kaplan,
"Nell Ziff Pekarsky: Hadassah Leader," http://jwa.org/weremember/pekarsky-nell,
accessed July 29, 2015.

63. Hirsch, *An American Housewife in Israel*, 43–44, 46, 77, 108.

64. Sanders, "Settling in Israel?," 41; Gruber, *Israel Today*, 49, 67; Spiro, *Kibbutz:
Venture in Utopia*.

65. Weingarten, *Life on a Kibbutz*, 57, 123–39.

66. Ibid., 179–83.

CHAPTER 2

1. "Shall We Conform?," sermon, March 2, 1956, Rabbi Harold Saperstein Papers, mss.
718, box 3, folder 1, American Jewish Archives. Findings like these anticipated Milton
Himmelfarb's later, oft-quoted quip that "Jews earn like Episcopalians but vote like
Puerto Ricans," a paraphrase of what he wrote in "The Jewish Vote—Again." Barry Popik
uncovered the published history of this sound-bite here: http://www.barrypopik.com/
index.php/new_york_city/entry/jews_earn_like_episcopalians_and_vote_like_
puerto_ricans, accessed March 13, 14.

2. Sherman, "Harvey and Sheila."

3. Svonkin, *Jews against Prejudice*; Zeitz, *White Ethnic New York*. On the liberal agenda
of postwar Jewish women's organizations, see Brautbar, *From Fashion to Politics*, 49–67;
Boim-Wolf, "Its Good Americanism to Join Hadassah,"; Laughlin, "'Our Defense against
Despair.'" Poll cited in C. Sherman, *The Jew within American Society*, and Diner, *Jews of the
United States*, 277.

4. Dollinger, *Quest for Inclusion*, 183–90; Staub, *Torn at the Roots*; Berman, *Metropolitan
Jews*, 10–11; C. Greenberg, "Liberal NIMBY."

5. Sinkoff, "The Polishness of Lucy S. Dawidowicz's Jewish Cold War"; Podhoretz,
"My Negro Problem—And Ours"; Staub, *Torn at the Roots*; On the history of Jewish
neoconservatism, see Bloom, *Prodigal Sons*; Wald, *The New York Intellectuals*; Jumonville,
Critical Crossings; Friedman, *The Neoconservative Revolution*.

6. Dollinger, *Quest for Inclusion*, 186–87; Rieder, *Canarsie*; Berman, *Metropolitan Jews*,
10–11.

7. Melvin Tumin, "Conservative Trends in American Jewish Life," 136–39, cited in
Staub, *Torn at the Roots*, 83; Glazer and Moynihan, *Beyond the Melting Pot*, 176–79.

8. "Two Thirds of America's Jews Now Live in Suburbs, Expert Estimates," Jewish
Telegraphic Agency, October 16, 1959, http://archive.jta.org, accessed May 3, 2011;
Gordon, *Jews in Suburbia*, xvii, 34; A. Fishman, "Keeping Up with the Goldbergs," 27;
Prell, "Community and the Discourse of Elegy" 68; Diner, Kohn, and Kranson, *A Jewish
Feminine Mystique*, 1–12.

9. Wood, *Suburbia*. On the belief that suburbia compelled its residents toward
conformity and conservativism, see Nicolaides and Wiese, *The Suburb Reader*, 291–92;
Louis Harris, *Is There a Republican Majority?* (New York, 1954), cited in Wood, 137.

10. Murray, *The Progressive Housewife*, 63–64; Rothchild (writing as Evelyn Rossman), "Judaism in Northrup," 384.

11. *American Jewish Yearbook* 62 (1961): 26, 34; Lazerwitz, "Suburban Voting Trends, 1948–1956," 34.

12. Gordon, *Jews in Suburbia*, 217.

13. "Our Greatest Dangers," sermon, Rosh Hashanah, 1964, Rabbi Harold Saperstein Papers, mss. 718, box 6, folder 3, American Jewish Archives.

14. Gersh, "The New Suburbanites of the 50s" 221.

15. Rothchild (writing as Evelyn Rossman), "The Community and I," 404, 397.

16. Pawel, *From the Dark Tower*; Dempsey, "Conformity, Inc."; Ribalow, "From *Hungry Hearts* to *Marjorie Morningstar*," 47.

17. "Judaism in Suburbia," sermon, January 10, 1958, Rabbi Harold Saperstein Papers, mss. 718, box 3, folder 2, American Jewish Archives.

18. Vorspan and Lipman, *A Tale of Ten Cities*, 231–52. For more examples of the activism of the Jewish women of suburban Queens, see Murray, *The Progressive Housewife*.

19. Boris Smolar, "Chanukah-Christmas Issue," *Between You and Me*, November 17, 1961, Boris Smolar Papers, P-588, 2–3, American Jewish Historical Society (hereafter AJHS).

20. Ivers, *To Build a Wall*, 66–145; "To Our Jewish Friends," *America*, September 1, 1962, cited in Ivers, 139–40.

21. Ivers, *To Build a Wall*, 116, 124–40; "The Engel Case," .

22. Cited in C. Greenberg, *Troubling the Waters*, 120.

23. M. Bauman and Kalin, *The Quiet Voices*; Webb, *Fight against Fear*; Diner, *Jews of the United States*, 270–74; Sarna, *American Judaism*, 309–10.

24. The literature on Jewish involvement in the civil rights movement, and on the relationship between blacks and Jews, is enormous. Significant works include Diner, *In an Almost Promised Land*; Schultz, *Going South*; C. Greenberg, *Troubling the Waters*; Friedman, *What Went Wrong?*; Kaufman, *Broken Alliances*; Forman, *Blacks in the Jewish Mind*; Webb, *Fight against Fear*.

25. C. Greenberg, *Troubling the Waters*, 124, 135.

26. Ibid., 153–58.

27. *American Jewish Yearbook* 62 (1961): 134, cited in Diner, *Jews of the United States*, 270; also "Suburban Trend Blasted."

28. Gamm, *Urban Exodus*, 229–37; H. Levine and Harmon, *The Death of an American Jewish Community*, 44–65; Hyman, "From City to Suburb." On how gendered concerns played into a family's decision to migrate, see Berman, "Gendered Journeys."

29. Various synagogues in Chicago, Cleveland, Washington, D.C., Cincinnati, Buffalo, and Los Angeles also maintained their urban presence as their constituents migrated to the suburbs. Stanger-Ross, "Neither Fight nor Flight"; Berman, *Metropolitan Jews*, 152–61.

30. "Young Married Group," *Brooklyn Jewish Center Review* 34, no. 12 (November 1952): 21, Brooklyn Jewish Center Collection, 42/5, Ratner Center.

31. Rabbi Israel H. Levinthal, "A Frank Statement on a Sensitive Issue," *Brooklyn Jewish Center Review* 34, no. 21 (January 1953), 4, Brooklyn Jewish Center Collection, 42/6, Ratner Center.

32. "Charge that Jews 'Escape' Non-white City Neighbors Held Unwarranted," Jewish Telegraphic Agency, December 4, 1959, http://archive.jta.org, accessed May 3, 2011.

33. Vorspan, "The Negro Victory and the Jewish Failure."

34. Rabbi Arnold Jacob Wolf, "From the Rabbi," *Solel Pathfinder* 3, no. 10 (December 29, 1959), Publication H653, Jewish Newspapers and Periodicals on Microfilm, Klau Library. Sklare published his findings in 1967 in *Jewish Identity on the Suburban Frontier*. Interestingly, the findings regarding race relations quoted by Wolf did not make it into the final text.

35. Rabbi Arnold Jacob Wolf, "From the Rabbi," *Solel Pathfinder* 5, no. 15 (February 20, 1962), Publication H653, Jewish Newspapers and Periodicals on Microfilm, Klau Library.

36. Rabbi Earl S. Starr, "Rabbi's Column," *Congregation Rodeph Shalom Bulletin* 34, no. 9 (November 11, 1957), Publication P54R, Jewish Newspapers and Periodicals on Microfilm, Klau Library; Gordon, *Jews in Suburbia*, 219–20.

37. Rabbi Arnold Jacob Wolf, "From the Rabbi," *Solel Pathfinder* 7, no. 4 (October 16, 1963), Publication H653, Jewish Newspapers and Periodicals on Microfilm, Klau Library.

38. Dollinger, *Quest for Inclusion*, 173; Vorspan, "In St. Augustine."

39. "Jewish Young Freedom Fighters and the Role of the Jewish Community," 7.

40. On the history of the Jewish left, see Michels, *A Fire in their Hearts*; Sorin, *The Prophetic Minority*.

41. Svonkin, *Jews against Prejudice*, 166–67.

42. J. Pilch, *A History of Jewish Education in the United States*, 130, cited in Sarna, *American Judaism*, 282.

43. "Jewish Life/Jewish Currents."

44. Svonkin, *Jews against Prejudice*, 113–48, Diner, *Jews of the United States*, 277–79. Moore, "Reconsidering the Rosenbergs"; *American Jewish Yearbook* 52 (1951): 62–63, 535; Staub, *Torn from the Roots*, 26–44. For an eyewitness account of the Peekskill riots, see Fast, *Peekskill USA*.

45. Svonkin, *Jews against Prejudice*, 117–34; Markowitz, *My Daughter the Teacher*, 169; Epstein, "The Other Rosenbergs."

46. Svonkin, *Jews against Prejudice*, 161–77.

47. Glazer, *American Judaism*, 125.

48. *Jewish Life* changed its name to *Jewish Currents* in 1956, when its editors disaffiliated with the Communist Party.

49. Perel and Perel, "Jews in a Mill Town."

50. Perlo, "Outlook for White Collar, Trade, and the Professions."

51. "Letters from Readers"; Schappes, "Thirty Years of Jewish Life"; Harap, "Is American Jewry Prepared?"

52. Khoury, "William A Stern, 90, Advocate for Jewish and Socialist Causes; W. Stern, "Tipping the Scales," *The Call*, February 1955, 10; W. Stern, "Tipping the Scales," *The Call*, March 1957, 7.

53. W. Stern, "Tipping the Scales," *The Call*, March 1957, 7. Michigan-area Jewish labor activist Frances Cousens offered a similar perspective, "The Forward Look for Workmen's Circle."

54. "Our Readers Respond."

CHAPTER 3

1. Rabbi Arnold Jacob Wolf, "From the Rabbi," *Solel Pathfinder* 6, no. 6 (Wednesday, October 31, 1962): 1, Publication H653, Jewish Newspapers and Periodicals on Microfilm, Klau Library.

2. Wolf, "Experimental Synagogue in Suburbia"; "Rabbi Arnold Jacob Wolf, Statement of Program," box 1: Congregation Solel Early History, 1957 folder, and "Statement from Board of Directors, June 10, 1958," box 3: Board of Directors Meetings and Minutes 1957–1968 folder, 1957–1959 folder, all in Congregation Solel Archives.

3. Dawidowicz, "Middle-Class Judaism: A Case Study," 494

4. Hudnut-Beumler, *Looking for God in the Suburbs*, 33; Statement by the President upon Signing Bill to Include the Worlds "Under God" in the Pledge to the Flag, June 14, 1954, and Address at the Freedoms Foundation, Waldorf-Astoria, New York City, December 12, 1952, http://www.eisenhower.archives.gov/all_about_ike/quotes.html, accessed February 21, 2012; Whitfield, *The Culture of the Cold War*, 88–91.

5. *American Jewish Year Book* 59 (1958): 114–18; Sklare, *Jewish Identity on the Suburban Frontier*, 60–64; Diner, *Jews of the United States*, 288.

6. Griefer, "Suburbia and Jewish Conformity," 15; Berger, *The Noise of Solemn Assemblies*; Winter, *The Suburban Captivity of the Churches*; Marty, *The New Shape of American Religion*; Greeley, *The Church and the Suburbs*; Prell, "Community and the Discourse of Elegy," 70; Hudnut-Beumler, *Looking for God in the Suburbs*, 109–74.

7. Herberg, *Protestant, Catholic, Jew*. For a convincing counterargument to Herberg's assertion that religious differences replaced and superseded ethnic particularities, see Zeitz, *White Ethnic New York*, 3–5.

8. Kramer and Leventman, *Children of the Gilded Ghetto*, 16–17, cited in Berman, "American Jews and the Ambivalence of Middle-Classness," 428.

9. Shulman, "It's Hard to Be a Jew"; "Self-Commitment," sermon, Rosh Hashanah, September 29, 1962, Papers of Rabbi Philip Lipis, box 1, folder 4, Ratner Center.

10. "Statement: June 10, 1958," box 3: Board of Directors Meetings and Minutes 1957–1968, 1957–1959 folder, Congregation Solel Archives; Wolf, "Experimental Synagogue in Suburbia," 15.

11. Diner, *Jews of the United States*, 299; Sarna, *American Judaism*, 279; Sussman, "The Suburbanization of American Judaism"; "Judaism and Suburbia," 2.

12. Alfred Werner, "Synagogues of America," *Brooklyn Jewish Center Review* 37, no. 21 (January 26), 6–9, Brooklyn Jewish Center Collection, Ratner Center; Blake, *An American Synagogue for Today and Tomorrow*; Mendelsohn, "In the Spirit of Our Age," 541, cited in Berman, *Metropolitan Jews*, 154–55.

13. Freedman, "New Jewish Community in Formation," 36; Griefer, "Suburbia and Jewish Conformity," 15; Rabbi Benjamin Kreitman, "Introduction to Synagogues of America and Israel," *Brooklyn Jewish Center Review* 37, no. 21 (January 26): 5, Brooklyn Jewish Center Collection, Ratner Center.

14. Alfred Werner, "Synagogues of America," *Brooklyn Jewish Center Review* 37, no. 21 (January 26): 7, Brooklyn Jewish Center Collection, Ratner Center; American Seating advertisement, *American Judaism* 6, no. 2 (November 1956): 4; Freedman, "New Jewish Community in Formation," 39.

15. Freedman, "New Jewish Community in Formation," 40–41; Werner, "Synagogues of America," 6.

16. "Country Club Judaism" coined by Morton Sterne, echoed in Albert Gordon, *Jews in Suburbia*, 126, 202, cited in Prell, "Community and the Discourse of Elegy," 69.

17. Gay, "Nostalgia Is Not Enough," 39; Glazer, *American Judaism*, 126.

18. Weiss-Rosmarin, "The Three Days Season," 4; Rabbi Israel Levinthal, "Crowded Synagogues on High Holy Days Only," *Brooklyn Jewish Center Review*, 31, no. 3 (August–September 1949): 4, Brooklyn Jewish Center Collection, Ratner Center.

19. "Judaism and Suburbia,"2.

20. Sinkoff, "The Polishness of Lucy S. Dawidowicz' Postwar Jewish Cold War," 43; Dawidowicz, *From that Place and Time.*

21. Dawidowicz, "Middle-Class Judaism: A Case Study" 495; Heschel, "Spirit of Jewish Prayer," 151.

22. Schafler, "The Yom Kippur Service", Yiddish translation is my own.

23. Sklare's *Jewish Identity on the Suburban Frontier,* a study of Highland Park, Illinois, based on records from 1958, revealed that only 3 percent of the male Jews who resided there and only 1 percent of the women were age sixty or above. Herbert Gans noted in his 1951 study of the Jews of Park Forest, Illinois, that "anyone over 40 is considered old." See "Park Forest: Birth of a Jewish Community," 330.

24. http://macaulay.cuny.edu/eportfolios/qcpony11/judaism/the-temple/, accessed March 14, 2014.

25. Gruenwald [Gruenewald], "Building Drive."

26. Website of Congregation Bnai Israel, http://cbi-nj.org/about-us/our-history/, accessed June 6, 2016.

27. Rothchild (writing as Evelyn Rossman), "A Fund-Raiser Comes to Northrup," 222–25.

28. "Letter to the Editor," *American Judaism*, November 1957, 2. I converted 1957 to 2015 dollars through the U.S. Bureau of Labor Statistic's consumer price index inflation calendar: http://www.bls.gov/data/inflation_calculator.htm, accessed August 16, 2015.

29. Lipman and Schoen, "A Reply to the Call for 'Help,'" 8; "The Cost of Belonging to a Temple (continued)."

30. Sklare, *Jewish Identity on the Suburban Frontier*, 151–53.

31. Wolf, "Experimental Synagogue in Suburbia," 15; "Congregation Solel Early History," "Report of the Selection Committee, July 15th, 1957," and "Letter from Board of Directors to Congregation, June 27, 1957," all in box 1: Congregation Solel Early History, 1957 folder, Congregation Solel Archives; Sklare, *Jewish Identity on the Suburban Frontier*, 151–53; Fox, "Arnold Jacob Wolf, a Leading Reform Rabbi, Is Dead at 84."

32. "Board of Directors Meeting, November 23rd, 1959," "Board of Directors Meeting, October 27, 1960," and "Special Meeting of the Board of Directors, May 4th 1961," box 3: Board of Directors Meetings and Minutes 1957–1968, 1957-1959, 1959–1961 folders; and "Letter from Holland Flahavan, Lawyer for Winnetka Masonic Lodge, no. 1078, October 9, 1957," box 1: Congregation Solel Early History, 1957 folder, all in Congregation Solel Archives.

33. "Special Meeting of the Board of Directors, May 4th, 1961," box 3: Board of Directors Meetings and Minutes 1957–1968, 1959–1961 folder; "Report of the Committee

on Building Plans, Submitted to the Board of Directors," May 4, 1961, box 58: Building and Building Fund, Building Fund Campaign 1961 folder, both in Congregation Solel Archives.

34. "Board of Directors Meeting, January 18th, 1962," box 3: Board of Directors Meetings and Minutes, 1957–1968, 1959–1961 folder; "Board of Directors Meeting, July 19, 1962," box 3: Board of Directors Meetings and Minutes, 1957–1968, 1962–1963 folder; "Report of the Committee on Building Plans, Submitted to the Board of Directors," May 4, 1961, box 58: Building and Building Fund, Building Fund Campaign, 1961 folder; "From the Rabbi," box 16: Arnold Jacob Wolf, Misc. Correspondence, 1961–1964 folder; all in Congregation Solel Archives.

35. "Report of the Committee on Building Plans, Submitted to the Board of Directors," May 4, 1961, box 58: Building and Building Fund, Building Fund Campaign, 1961 folder; "From the Rabbi," box 16: Arnold Jacob Wolf, Misc. Correspondence, 1961–1964 folder; all in Congregation Solel Archives.

36. "Memo September 5th, 1961," box 58: Building and Building Fund, Building Fund Campaign, 1961 folder; "From the Rabbi," box 16: Arnold Jacob Wolf, Misc. Correspondence, 1961–1964 folder; all in Congregation Solel Archives.

37. "Memo, September 5th, 1961"; "A Possible Approach for Kick-off Meetings, September 7, 1961"; "Memo, General Solicitation Division, September 14th, 1961"; and "Note to General Solicitation Division, October 17th, 1961," all in box 58: Building and Building Fund, Building Fund Campaign 1961 folder, Congregation Solel Archives.

38. "Confidential: Preliminary evaluation of gift potential of Temple Solel Membership," box 58: Building and Building Fund, Building Fund Campaign 1961 folder, and "Board of Directors Meeting, February 22, 1962," box 3: Board of Directors Meetings and Minutes 1957–1968, 1959–1961 folder, both in Congregation Solel Archives. Conversions to 2015 dollars determined by the U.S. Bureau of Labor Statistics inflation calculator: http://www.bls.gov/data/inflation_calculator.htm, accessed August 27, 2015.

39. "Board of Directors Meeting, September 14th, 1961," box 3: Board of Directors Meetings and Minutes 1957–1968, 1959–1961 folder; "Letter from Building Campaign Manager Howard Landau to Executive Committee, August 24th, 1961," box 58: Building and Building Fund, Building Fund Campaign 1961 folder; "Board of Directors Meeting, May 21st, 1964," box 3: Board of Directors Meetings and Minutes 1957–1968, 1963–1964 folder; and "Board of Directors Meeting, February 24th, 1963," box 3: Board of Directors Meetings and Minutes 1957–1968, 1962–1963 folder, all in Congregation Solel Archives.

40. Wolf, "Experimental Synagogue in Suburbia," 16; "Letter from Wolf to Invitees of Building Fund Luncheon, September 1963," box 16: Arnold Jacob Wolf, Misc. Correspondence, 1961–1964 folder; "Board of Directors Meeting, September 14, 1961," box 3: Board of Directors Meetings and Minutes 1957–1968, 1969–1961 folder; "Report of President Howard M. Landau, Annual Meeting, May 22 1963," box 7: Annual Meetings and Annual Reports, Annual Meeting 1963 folder; and "From the Rabbi," box 16: Arnold Jacob Wolf, Misc. Correspondence, 1961–1964 folder, all in Congregation Solel Archives.

41. "Board of Directors Meeting, October 17th, 1963," box 3: Board of Directors Meetings and Minutes 1957–1968, 1963–1964 folder; "Note from Donald Abrahams," box 58: Building and Building Fund, Building Fund Campaign 1961 folder; and "Note from solicitor Howard Flanzer regarding member Richard Mandel, November 22 1961," box 58:

Building and Building Fund, Building Fund Campaign 1961 folder, all in Congregation Solel Archives.

42. "Annual Meeting Program 1963" and "Musical Program at Annual Meeting, Wednesday, May 22nd, 1963," box 7: Annual Meetings and Annual Reports, Annual Meeting 1963 folder, Congregation Solel Archives.

43. Hal Barkun, "Reflections . . . on a Temple," *Solel Pathfinder* 6, no. 5 (Tuesday, October 16, 1962), Publication H6S3, Jewish Newspapers and Periodicals on Microfilm, Klau Library.

44. Marcus, *The Jewish Life Cycle*, 82–105.

45. Joselit, *The Wonders of America*, 90–94.

46. Rabbi Erwin L. Herman's "Bar Mitzvah a la Carte," describes several particularly fanciful Bar Mitzvah receptions that he attended, including a party with a three-ring circus (complete with a live elephant) as well as a party in which the caterer released a slew of parakeets.

47. Joselit, *The Wonders of America*, 130–31; Stein, "The Road to Bat Mitzvah in America."

48. Meisler, "Big Bar Mitzvah."

49. "*Life* Goes to a Bar Mitzvah," 170–72.

50. Wouk, *Marjorie Morningstar*, 93–95, cited in Joselit, *The Wonders of America*, 98.

51. Wouk, *This Is My God*, 142–43.

52. Eisendrath, "Paean of Praise, Wouk Style," 6.

53. "Schindler v. Deeves," *New York Law Journal*, September 19, 1957, quoted in "Bar Mitzvah and the Courts," *Bulletin: Temple Beth El of Northern Westchester* 10, no. 4 (December 1957–January 1958), Temple Beth El of Northern Westchester Collection, mss. 728, box 5, folder 1, American Jewish Archives; also discussed in Gordon, *Jews in Suburbia*, 205.

54. D. Philipson, *The Reform Movement in Judaism*, cited in A. Goldstein, "Lets Bar Bar Mitzvah," 19; Gittelsohn, "Bar Mitzvah in Reform Judaism."

55. "How Much Religious Education"; Efron and Rubin, "The Reality of Bar Mitzvah"; "Rabbi's Report."

56. Charry, "Ben Torah: Bar Mitzvah at Sixteen"; Gewirtz, *The Authentic Jew and His Judaism*, 83.

57. "United Synagogue of America Standards for Synagogue Practice."

58. "Report of Committee on Guide for Synagogue Decorum," 60.

59. "New Approaches to Judaism," sermon, May 31, 1957 (3/1), and "What Is Jewish Tradition?," sermon, Sukkos 1963 (3/4), Rabbi Harold Saperstein Papers, mss. 718, American Jewish Archives.

60. "The Need for Jewish Dignity," sermon, January 4, 1963, Rabbi Harold Saperstein Papers, mss. 718 (3/4), American Jewish Archives.

61. Herman, "Bar Mitzvah a la Carte," 4–5.

62. Gordon, *Jews in Suburbia*, 205.

63. "Fathers and Sons," sermon, Rosh Hashanah, September 19 1963, Rabbi Edgar Siskin Papers, mss. 64, box 2, folder 4, American Jewish Archives.

64. "Bar Mitzvah for My Son?," sermon, March 14, 1950, Rabbi Roland Gittelsohn Papers, mss. 704, folder 35 box 5, American Jewish Archives.

65. Milstone, "Bar Mitzvah—A New Approach," 4.

66. Listing in *American Jewish Yearbook* directory, 65 (1964): 372.

67. "A Pattern for Jewish Boys Everywhere," 4–5.

68. "Board Meeting: March 25, 1959," box 3: Board of Directors Meetings and Minutes 1957–1968, 1957–1959 folder, Congregation Solel Archives.

69. Ibid.

70. Ibid.

71. "Report of the Bar Mitzvah Editorial Committee," Submitted to the Board of Directors, May 17, 1962, box 7: Annual Meetings and Annual Reports, Annual Meeting 1963 folder, Congregation Solel Archives.

72. Wolf, "Experimental Synagogue in Suburbia," 16.

CHAPTER 4

1. B. Rosenberg and Shapiro, "Marginality and Jewish Humor," 74.

2. On how the pressures on postwar Jewish men to become middle-class earners caused tension between Jewish men and women, see Prell, *Fighting to Become Americans*, 142–76.

3. Riesman, Glazer, and Denney, *The Lonely Crowd*; Whyte, *The Organization Man*; Ehrenreich, *The Hearts of Men*; Arthur Schlesinger Jr., "The Crisis of Masculinity," 63–65, cited in Berrett, "Feeding the Organization Man," 805; Berman, "American Jews and the Ambivalence of Middle-Classness," 425.

4. Glenn, *Daughters of the Shtetl*; Hyman, "Gender and the Immigrant Experience in the United States"; Hyman, "Culture and Gender," ; Weinberg, *World of our Mothers*; Wenger, *Uncertain Promise*, 34–39.

5. Lederhendler, *Jewish Immigrants and American Capitalism*; Cohen and Soyer, *My Future Is in America*, 11, 233–87.

6. Chiswick, "The Postwar Economy of American Jews"; Prell, "Triumph," 126–27.

7. Ibid., 92–96.

8. Kramer and Leventman, *Children of the Gilded Ghetto*, 130; Attwood, "The Position of Jews in America Today."

9. Roth, "Writing about Jews," 446; "National Jewish Book Award Winners," http://www.jewishbookcouncil.org/awards/njba-list, accessed November 24, 2014. On how the discourse of "Jewish self-hatred" affected Roth, see Glenn "The Vogue of Jewish Self-Hatred in Post World War II America." 116–20

10. Roth, *Goodbye, Columbus*, 88.

11. Ibid., 92.

12. Ibid., 136.

13. Freedman, "The Jewish College Student, 1951 Model," 305.

14. Ibid., 305–6.

15. *The Eternal Light*, "A Dreamer's Journey."

16. *The Eternal Light*, "Sweet Hemlock."

17. "Are We Different?," sermon, Rosh Hashono Morning, September 20, 1952, Rabbi Edgar Siskin Papers, mss. 64, box 1, folder 2, American Jewish Archives.

18. Eisendrath, "The Authority of the Rabbi," 3.

19. S. Greenberg, "Dissatisfied but Not Unhappy," 74.

20. Almog, *The Sabra*; Biale, *Eros and the Jews*; Mayer, "From Zero to Hero"; Mosse, *Confronting the Nation*; Presner, *Muscular Judaism*.

21. *American Hebrew*, May 11, 1917, cited in P. Levine, *Ellis Island to Ebbet's Field*, 17, and Wenger, "Constructing Manhood in American Jewish Culture," 353; Moore, *GI Jews*.

22. Playscript: Ben Hecht, *A Flag Is Born* (1946), 47, American League for a Free Palestine Papers, I-278, box 1, folder 4, AJHS.

23. Ibid., 20, cited in Goren, "Celebrating Zion in America," 53.

24. "A Message from Ben Hecht," pamphlet distributed to the audience of *A Flag Is Born* (1946), American League for a Free Palestine Papers, I-278, box 1 folder 2, AJHS.

25. Pamphlet, "Letter to the Terrorists of Palestine from Ben Hecht" (1946–47), American League for a Free Palestine Papers, I-278, box 1, folder 2, AJHS.

26. Advertisement for the American League for a Free Palestine printed in *PM Magazine*, Wednesday, March 12, 1947, 9, clipping found in American League for a Free Palestine Papers, I-278, OS1 folder 1, AJHS.

27. Levin, "After All I Did for Israel," 61.

28. Uris, *Exodus*; Mart, *Eye on Israel*, 169–75; Silver, *Our Exodus*; Moore, *To the Golden Cities*, 248–60.

29. Uris, *Exodus*, 614; Hertzberg, *The Jews in America*, 319, cited in Mart, *Eye on Israel*, 173.

30. Uris, *Exodus*, 283, 350, 406, 603; Mart, *Eye on Israel, 70*; Breines, *Tough Jews*.

31. Uris, *Exodus*, 55.

32. Ibid., 99–100.

33. Sklare, *Jewish Identity on the Suburban Frontier*, 224.

CHAPTER 5

1. Brochure (1957): "Hadassah Makes You Important!," Hadassah Archives, I-578, RG17, box 9, AJHS.

2. Chafe, *The American Woman*; Chiswick, "The Postwar Economy of American Jews," 92; Diner, Kohn, and Kranson, *A Jewish Feminine Mystique*, 1–12.

3. Chiswick, "The Postwar Economy of American Jews," 92; Diner, Kohn, and Kranson, *A Jewish Feminine Mystique*, 1–12; Prell, "Triumph," 126–27.

4. Diner, Kohn, and Kranson, *A Jewish Feminine Mystique*, 1–12; Baxandall and Ewen, *Picture Windows*, 152–57; Murray, *The Suburban Housewife*.

5. Diner, *Jews of the United States*, 301–3; Sklare, *Jewish Identity on the Suburban Frontier*, 258; Gans, "Park Forest: Birth of a Jewish Community," 339.

6. Harriton, "Twentieth Century Pioneers," 17.

7. Gordon, *Jews in Suburbia*, 63; Prell, *Fighting to Become Americans*, 153–54.

8. Folkman, *Design for Jewish Living*, 24; Brickner, "Education for Marriage," speech originally given in 1946, reprinted in Brav, *Marriage and the Jewish Tradition*, 179–80; Vorspan and Lipman, *Justice and Judaism*, 59.

9. Levi and Kaplan, *Across the Threshold: A Guide for the Jewish Homemaker*, 27.

10. Vorspan and Lipman, *Justice and Judaism*, 59–69.

11. Forman, "Career Woman versus Housewife: A Happy Choice," 8.

12. Ibid., 9.

13. Wylie, *Generation of Vipers*; Kling, "The Organization Woman," 22–23.

14. Geller, "How Jewish Is Jewish Suburbia?," 325.

15. Diner, Kohn and Kranson, *A Jewish Feminine Mystique*, 1–12.

16. E. Rosenthal, "Jewish Fertility in the United States."

17. Levi and Kaplan, *Across the Threshold*, 181.

18. Waxman, Ish-Kishor, and Sloan, *Blessed Is the Daughter*, 48.

19. Simmons, *Hadassah and the Zionist Project*; Brautbar, *From Fashion to Politics*; Boim-Wolf, "Its Good Americanism to Join Hadassah," 65–86; Samuel, "Why Israel Misunderstands American Jewry," 306–7.

20. "Hadassah Makes You Important!," brochure (1957), Hadassah Archives, I-578, RG17 box 9, AJHS (emphasis in original).

21. "This Is Your Life in Hadassah," brochure (1954), Hadassah Archives, I-578, RG17, box 9, AJHS.

22. "This Is Junior Hadassah," brochure (1948), Hadassah Archives, I-578, RG 17, box 9, AJHS.

23. Moore, "Hadassah in the United States"; Boim-Wolf, "'Its Good Americanism to Join Hadassah'" 65–86.

24. Bernstein, "Daughters of the Nation."

25. "Women of Valor."

26. Waxman, Ish-Kishor, and Sloan, *Blessed Is the Daughter*, 136–38.

27. Kessner, "Marie Syrkin."

28. Syrkin, *Blessed Is the Match*, 13–32.

29. Syrkin, *Way of Valor*; Syrkin, *Golda Meir*, 11. Meir would be elected Israeli prime minister in 1969.

30. Syrkin, *Golda Meir*, 50, 85–86; Syrkin, *Way of Valor*, 64–67.

31. Dash, *Summoned to Jerusalem*; Rubin-Schwartz, "Henrietta Szold."

32. Decter, "The Legacy of Henrietta Szold," 483. Decter's later works lambasting feminism include *The Liberated Woman and Other Americans* and *The New Chastity and Other Arguments against Women's Liberation.*

33. Decter, "The Legacy of Henrietta Szold," 485.

34. Levinger, *Fighting Angel*, 161; Lipsky, *A Gallery of Zionist Profiles*, 142; Ben-Asher and Leaf, "Henrietta Szold," in *The Junior Jewish Encyclopedia*, 303–5.

35. Bar-David, *Women in Israel*; Bar-David, *My Promised Land*; Bar-David, *The Israeli Cookbook*; Bar-David, *Jewish Cooking for Pleasure.*

36. Bar-David, *Women in Israel*, 1–2.

37. Bar-David, "Diary of a Jerusalem Housewife" (1948); Bar-David, "Diary of Jerusalem Housewife" (1949); Bar-David, *My Promised Land*, 253; Katz, *Bringing Zion Home* 35–37.

38. Bar-David, *My Promised Land*, 292. She made a similar point in "Diary of a Jerusalem Housewife" (1951).

39. Bar-David, *My Promised Land*, 296–97.

40. J. Popkin, introduction to *Quiet Street*; Popkin, *The Journey Home*; Popkin, *Small Victory*; Z. Popkin, *Quiet Street*; Z. Popkin, *Open Every Door.*

41. J. Popkin, introduction to *Quiet Street*, vii–xii; Z. Popkin, *Open Every Door*, 343.

42. J. Popkin, introduction to *Quiet Street*," x; Z. Popkin, *Quiet Street*, 187.

43. Z. Popkin, *Quiet Street*, 346.

44. Ibid., 370.

45. Rothchild, "My Mrs. Schnitzer."467

46. Rothchild, *Sunshine and Salt*, 174–75.

47. Ibid., 65, 86.

48. Ibid., 236.

49. Wouk, *Marjorie Morningstar*.

50. Letters to Herman Wouk from Jean Levy Collat (October 13, 1955) and Paula Shirley Farber (December 7, 1955), cited in Sicherman, "Reading *Marjorie Morningstar* in the Age of the Feminine Mystique," 200–201.

51. Kamins, *Everything but a Husband*, 123–25.

CHAPTER 6

1. Advertisement for the Baltimore-Washington Union of Jewish Students, *Doreinu* 2, no. 7 (April 1971): 11, Jewish Student Organization Collections, I-61, box 56, folder 32, AJHS.

2. Prell, *Prayer and Community*, 78–79.

3. This begs the question of which late 1960s–1970s Jewish youth collectives I consider to be part of "The Jewish Counterculture." I follow the lead of the self-proclaimed leaders of the "New Jews," who counted only left-wing collectives as bona-fide members of the movement. This characterization excluded, for instance, the Jewish Defense League, a collective that, like much of the Jewish counterculture, was youthful, militant, and quite class conscious. However, members of the Jewish Defense League differed from the Jewish counterculture in that they espoused right-wing politics and adopted racist rhetoric. In spite of these commonalities, members from both groups insisted that the Jewish Defense League differed from the "Jewish movement" in fundamental ways, and they did not understand themselves to be participating the same project. See Staub, *Torn at the Roots*, 220–31.

4. Previous studies of the American Jewish counterculture can be found in Prell, *Prayer and Community*; Staub, *Torn at the Roots*; Oppenheimer, *Knocking on Heaven's Door*; Jacobson, *Roots Too*.

5. The "New Jews" did engage in issues that related quite directly to the class position of American Jews, such as the programs they established to connect with poor elderly Jews, and their protests against the Jewish federations that controlled the funds raised by Jewish philanthropy. In this chapter, however, I am more interested in examining how Jewish counterculturalists talked about affluence even when referring to issues that did not seem directly related to money. It is in these instances, I believe, that we can see just how central the rejection of middle-class affluence and identity was to American Jewish youth during this period.

6. Zuckoff, "The Oppression of America's Jews," 30.

7. On insider-outsider tensions in contemporary discussions over multiculturalism, see Biale, Galchinsky, and Heschel, *Insider/Outsider*. In *Roots Too*, Jacobson argued that the

impulse among white ethnics to dissociate themselves from the white power structure during this time paved the way for a conservative racial politics in which (some of) the descendants of poor immigrants from Eastern and Southern Europe rejected the notion of their culpability in American racism. Without denying the truth of this assessment, the intention of these Jewish counterculturalists was only to interrogate the benefits that middle-class culture offered American Jews. They may, indeed, have been guilty of not fully acknowledging their privilege as whites; nevertheless, they never attempted to use the history of American anti-Semitism to deny the history and legacy of American racism.

8. Porter and Drier, *Jewish Radicalism*, xiv–xxix; Jacobson, *Roots Too*, 221–25; Prell, *Prayer and Community*, 85–87. The first radical Jewish group to systematically critique the ways in which Israel dealt with Palestinians was the short-lived Breira, which operated between 1973 and 1977. See Staub, *Torn at the Roots*, 280–308.

9. M. J. Rosenberg, "To Uncle Tom and Other Jews," 10, cited in Staub, *Torn at the Roots*, 208, and Prell, *Prayer and Community*, 86.

10. Porter and Dreier, *Jewish Radicalism*, xii.

11. Jacobson, *Roots Too*, 46; Miller, *Democracy is in the Streets*, 318.

12. Porter and Drier, *Jewish Radicalism*, xxx; Staub, *Torn at the Roots*, 155–60.

13. McCandlish Phillips, "Jewish Student Press Seeing Swift Growth," *New York Times*, March 13, 1971, 31, cited in Oppenheimer, *Knocking on Heaven's Door*, 106.

14. Oppenheimer, *Knocking on Heaven's Door*, 117.

15. Stern, "My Jewish Problem—and Ours: Israel, the Left, and the Jewish Establishment," originally printed in *Ramparts*, August 1971; reprinted in Porter and Dreier, *Jewish Radicalism*, and *Hayom* 2, no. 1 (September 1971): 4–5, Jewish Student Organization Collections, I-61, box 63, folder 96, AJHS; and distributed as a pamphlet by the Radical Zionist Alliance, Jewish Student Organization Collections, I-61, box 47, folder 18, AJHS.

16. Feingold, *Silent No More*, 37–108. Beckerman, *When They Come for Us, We'll Be Gone*.

17. Porter and Dreier, *Jewish Radicalism*, 232.

18. "The Promised Land," *Brooklyn Bridge*, no. 1 (February 1971), Jewish Student Organization Collections, I-61, box 54 folder 13, AJHS.

19. Gerald Serotta, "Blood Brother of Kiev," *In Touch* 4, no. 2 (April 1971): 11, Jewish Student Organization Collections, I-61 box 13, folder 4, AJHS.

20. Freeman, "On the Origins of the Women's Liberation Movement from a Strictly Personal Perspective," 180.

21. Staub, *Torn at the Roots*, 205–7, 156, 180, 186–87; Oppenheimer, *Knocking on Heaven's Door*, 122–23.

22. Hyman, "Ezrat Nashim and the Emergence of a New Jewish Feminism"; "The Feminist Revolution: Paula Hyman"; "Jewish Women in the United States"; Lipstadt, "Feminism and American Judaism"; Nadell, "Women and American Judaism."

23. Anne Lapidus Lerner, "Who Hast Not Made Me a Man," 7.

24. Martha Ackelsberg, introduction, *Response* 7, no. 2 (Summer 1973): 7–9, special issue on Jewish women, Jewish Student Organization Collections, I-61, box 22, folder 2, AJHS; Lipstadt, "Feminism and American Judaism"; Hyman, "Ezrat Nashim and the Emergence of a New Jewish Feminism."

25. Charlotte Baum, "What Made Yetta Work: The Economic Role of Eastern European Jewish Women in the Family," *Response* 7, no. 2 (Summer 1973): 38, special issue on Jewish women, Jewish Student Organization Collections, I-61 box 22, folder 2,AJHS. In 1976 Charlotte Baum would cowrite *The Jewish Woman in America* with Paula Hyman and Sonia Michel.

26. Aviva Cantor Zuckoff, "The Oppression of the Jewish Woman," *Response* 7, no. 2 (Summer 1973), special issue on Jewish women, Jewish Student Organization Collections, I-61, box 22, folder 2, AJHS.

27. "Jewish Women: Life Force of a Culture?," *Brooklyn Bridge*, no. 1 (February 1971): 14, Jewish Student Organization Collections, I-61, box 54, folder 13, AJHS.

28. "International Women's Day," *Chutzpah*, no. 7 (Summer–Fall 1974): 9, box 55, folder 21, and "1908 and 1974—Jewish Women March," *Lilith's Rib*, no. 3 (June 1974): 4–5, box 18, folder 17, both in Jewish Student Organization Collections, I-61, AJHS; Antler, "Between Culture and Politics."

29. "The 5000 Year Old Woman," *Brooklyn Bridge*, no. 1 (February 1971): 3, Jewish Student Organization Collections, I-61, box 54, folder 13, AJHS.

30. Debbie Asher, "National Conference of Jewish Women: Four Days of Challenge and Response," *Hayom* 3, no. 4 (March 28–April 11, 1973): 6–7, box 63, folder 96; Fayla Schwartz, "Jewish Women: Closeness and Conflicts," *Jewish Radical* 5, no. 2 (Winter 1973): 2, box 65, folder 155; Maralee Gordon, "A Beginning," *Chutzpah*, no 5 (Summer 1973), box 2, folder 16, all in Jewish Student Organization Collections, I-61, AJHS.

31. Robbie Skeist, "Coming Out Jewish," originally printed in *Chicago Seed* (1971) and reprinted in Porter and Drier, *Jewish Radicalism*, 321.

32. Robbie Skeist, "From a Gay Jew," *Chutzpah*, no. 1 (February 1972): 5, Jewish Student Organization Collections, I-61, box 2, folder 16, AJHS. For a similar point of view, see "Gay and Jewish," *Ari* 3, no. 4 (December 1973): 9, box 1 folder 13, Jewish Student Organization Collections, I-61, AJHS.

33. Batya Bauman, untitled, 9–10.

34. Michael Rosenberg, "The Self-Destruction of Judaism in the American 'Jewish' Community," *Doreinu* 2, no. 5 (January 1971): 11, Jewish Student Organization Collections, I-61, box 56, folder 32, AJHS.

35. Ibid., 11; "A Farewell Message to the Jewish Community," advertisement for the Student Mobilization for Israel Aliya Corps, printed in *Achdut/Unity* 1, no. 1 (December 1975), Jewish Student Organization Collections, I-61, box 1, folder 3, AJHS.

36. David Breakstone, "Israeli Seeds Turn on Jewish Youth," *Genesis 2* 2, no. 5 (January 1971): 6, Jewish Student Organization Collections, I-61, box 57, folder 49, AJHS.

37. Gabriel Ende, "To Those who Really Care," *Davka* 4, no. 4 (Fall 1974): 40, Jewish Student Organization Collections, I-61, box 4, folder 1, AJHS.

38. Reprint of Jack Nusan Porter, "Jewish Student Activism," *Jewish Currents*, May 1970, 3, distributed by the Jewish Student Movement of Northwestern University, Jewish Student Organization Collections, I-61, box 43 folder 8, AJHS.

39. Joel Cordish, "Open Letter to Jewish Students," *Hevra* 1, no. 2 (March 15, 1972): 4, Jewish Student Organization Collections, I-61, box 73, folder 212, AJHS.

40. Brad Burston, "Is Nothing Sacred?," *Ari* 4, no. 2 (March 1975): 6, Jewish Student Organization Collections, I-61, box 1, folder 13, AJHS; Porter and Dreier, *Jewish*

Radicalism, 225; "Art Green of Havurat Shalom Speaking in Israel," *Network,* August 1969, 7, Jewish Student Organization Collections, I-61, box 20, folder 7, AJHS.

41. d. a. levy, "New Year," first printed in *Connections,* an underground newspaper from Wisconsin. In the Jewish press, it was printed first in the September 1969 issue of *Jewish Currents.* It was later printed in *Response* 4, no. 3 (Fall 1970): 33–36 and *Davka* 1, no. 1 (November–December 1970): 12–16, box 21, folder 21, AJHS. Raphael, "d. a. levy."

42. Jim Axelrod, "Second Response," *In Touch: Voice of the College Students of Temple Israel, Miami Beach* 2, no. 1 (December 1968): 11, Jewish Student Organization Collections, I-61, folder 13, box 14, AJHS.

43. *Putz,* a Yiddish term that has been folded into English slang, denotes a fool or an idiot but literally translates to penis.

44. *Doreinu* 3, no. 3 (February 7, 1972): 6, Jewish Student Organization Collections, I-61, box 56, folder 32, AJHS.

45. Danny Siegel, "Maybe," originally printed in Siegal, *Soulstoned,* reprinted in Porter and Drier, *Jewish Radicalism,* 136–37.

46. Introduction to Porter and Dreier, *Jewish Radicalism,* xli.

47. Richard Siegal and George Savran, "The Jewish Whole Earth Catalogue," *Response* 5, no. 3 (Winter 1971–72): 12, box 22, folder 1, and Richard Siegal and George Savran, "The Jewish Whole Earth Catalogue," *Genesis 2* 3, no. 5 (February 17, 1972): 2, box 57, folder 50, both in Jewish Student Organization Collections, I-61, AJHS; R. Siegel, Strassfeld, and Strassfeld, *The Jewish Catalogue;* Strassfeld and Strassfeld, *The Second Jewish Catalogue;* Strassfeld and Strassfeld, *The Third Jewish Catalogue.*

48. Prell, *Prayer and Community,* 16. By the late 1970s, synagogues started sponsoring their own Havurot in order to foster smaller, intimate communities within their membership.

49. Oppenheimer, *Knocking on Heaven's Door,* 96–129; Prell, *Prayer and Community,* 92–93; Staub, *Torn at the Roots,* 184–90.

50. B. Jacobson, "Blueprint for a Havurah."

51. Flyer for Fabrangen, circa 1971, printed in Staub, *Torn at the Roots,* 189.

52. On the grant accepted by Fabrangen, see ibid., 184–90.

53. Maralee Gordon, "Money and Jewish Education," *Chutzpah,* no. 2 (Summer 1972): 11, Jewish Student Organization Collections, I-61, box 55, folder 21, AJHS.

54. Strassfeld and Strassfeld, *The Second Jewish Catalogue,* 68–75.

55. A Yiddish word that has been incorporated into English slang, a *Schlub* refers to a coarse, clumsy, or stupid person.

56. Timberg, *Thirteen Years;* "The Celluloid Bar Mitzvah," *Jewish Radical* 4, no. 2 (January 1972): 2, box 65, folder 155, and 1974 Catalogue of the New Jewish Media Project, box 46, folder 8, both in Jewish Student Organization Collections, I-61, AJHS.

57. Waskow, *The Freedom Seder;* Balfour Brickner, "Notes on a Freedom Seder," originally printed in *The Reconstructionist,* June 13, 1969, and reprinted in Staub, *The Jewish 1960s,* 276–81; Staub, *Torn at the Roots,* 163–67.

58. Waskow, *The Freedom Seder,* cited in Staub, *Torn at the Roots,* 167.

59. Mike Tabor, "Jews for Urban Justice and Fabrangen," unpublished ms. (1972) 23, cited in Staub, *Torn at the Roots,* 167.

60. Zuckoff, Epstein, and Kirschen, *Jewish Liberation Hagada;* World Union of Jewish Students, *Fourth World Haggadah;* Staub, *Torn at the Roots,* 164; Goldberg, "Seasons

of Reinterpretation—Transforming Passover"; Zuckoff, "Jewish Women's Haggadah," 77–88.

61. Joan [No Last Name Given], "Ch(ristmas)anukah," *Chutzpah*, no. 1 (February 1972): 8, Jewish Student Organization Collections, I-61, box 55, folder 21, AJHS.

62. Prell, *Prayer and Community*; Oppenheimer *Knocking on Heaven's Door*; Staub, *Torn at the Roots*; Jacobson, *Roots Too*. The full text of the Port Huron Statement is available through the Sixties Project: http://www2.iath.virginia.edu/sixties/HTML_docs/Resources/Primary/Manifestos/SDS_Port_Huron.html, accessed October 9, 2009.

63. *American Jewish Yearbook* 59 (1958): 116, cited in Diner, *Jews of the United States*, 260.

64. Sarna, "The Crucial Decade in Jewish Camping."

65. Members of the New York Havurah such as Martha Ackelsberg, Jim Sleeper, Paula Hyman, and Alan Mintz all had strong Jewish backgrounds in camps, youth groups, and religious schools. Among the Fabrangen group, Rob Agus was the son of a rabbi, while Chava Weissler attended Camp Ramah. See Oppenheimer, *Knocking on Heaven's Door*, 111, 108, 121; Mandelkorn, "The Jewish Counterculture."

66. Presentation by Albert Vorspan, Hadassah National Board Minutes, Midwinter conference, February 2, 1969, Hadassah Archives, I-578, RG12, AJHS.

67. H. Levine, "To Share a Vision," 184.

68. Other scholars who examine the connections between the immediate postwar years and the late 1960s–1970s include Hunt, "How New Was the New Left?"; Isserman, *If I Had a Hammer*; Jamison and Eyerman, *Seeds of the Sixties*; Rossinow, *The Politics of Authenticity*; Petigny, *The Permissive Society*; Prell, "America, Mordecai Kaplan, and the Postwar Jewish Youth Revolt"; Prell, "Triumph"; Pollack, "'Where Have all the Cohens Gone?"

CONCLUSION

1. Richler, "Land of Milk and Money," 58.

2. Hunt, "How New Was the New Left?"; Isserman, *If I Had a Hammer*; Jamison and Eyerman, *Seeds of the Sixties*; Rossinow, *The Politics of Authenticity*; Petigny, *The Permissive Society*; Prell, "America, Mordecai Kaplan, and the Postwar Jewish Youth Revolt"; Prell, "Triumph"; Pollack, "'Where Have all the Cohens Gone?"

3. Jones and Cox, *Chosen for What? Jewish Values in 2012*.

4. "What Inspires Us," American Jewish World Service, https://ajws.org/who-we-are/resources/what-inspires-us/, accessed May 31, 2016; "About Us," Bend the Arc, http://www.bendthearc.us/about-us, accessed May 31, 2016.

5. "Election 2016: Exit Polls," http://www.nytimes.com/interactive/2016/11/08/us/politics/election-exit-polls.html, accessed November 11, 2016.

6. On the history of Milton Himmelfarb's quip, see http://www.barrypopik.com/index.php/new_york_city/entry/jews_earn_like_episcopalians_and_vote_like_puerto_ricans, accessed May 31, 2016.

7. Fortgang, "Why I'll Never Apologize for My White Male Privilege," *Time*, May 2, 2014, originally printed in *Princeton Tory*, April 2, 2014, http://time.com/85933/why-ill-never-apologize-for-my-white-male-privilege/, accessed May 31, 2016.

Bibliography

PRIMARY SOURCES

Manuscript and Archival Collections

Cincinnati, OH

  American Jewish Archives

    Rabbi Roland Gittelsohn Papers, MSS 704

    Rabbi Harold Saperstein Papers, MSS 718

    Rabbi Charles Shulman Papers, MSS 124

    Rabbi Edgar Siskin Papers, MSS 64

    Temple Beth El of Northern Westchester Collection, MSS 728

    Temple Bulletin Collection, MSS 882D

  Klau Library, Hebrew Union College

    Jewish Newspapers and Periodicals on Microfilm

Highland Park, IL

  Congregation Solel Archives

New York, NY

  American Jewish Historical Society (Note: archivists at the American Jewish Historical Society reorganized their Jewish student materials and their Hadassah materials in the years since I conducted my research. My citations refer to the older configuration of these records.)

    American League for a Free Palestine Papers, I-278

    The Eternal Light Radio Broadcast Scripts

    Hadassah Archives, I-578,

    Jewish Student Organization Collections, I-61,

    Boris Smolar Papers, P-588

  Ratner Center for the Study of Conservative Judaism

    Brooklyn Jewish Center Collection

    Papers of Rabbi Philip Lipis

Synagogue Bulletins

Brooklyn Jewish Center Review (Brooklyn, NY)
Bulletin: Temple Beth El of Northern Westchester (Chappaqua, NY)
Congregation Rodeph Shalom Bulletin (Philadelphia)
Solel Pathfinder (Highland Park, IL)

Jewish Countercultural/Feminist Publications and Organizations

Achdut/Unity (Metropolitan Union of Jewish Students, NY)
Ari (State University of New York at Buffalo)
Brooklyn Bridge (Brooklyn, NY)
Catalogue of the New Jewish Media Project (Waltham, MA)
Chutzpah (Chicago)
Davka (University of California, Los Angeles)
Doreinu (Union of Jewish Students, Baltimore-Washington)
Genesis 2 (Boston Student Jewish Community)
Hayom (Philadelphia Union of Jewish Students)
Hevra (Montreal, Canada)
In Touch (College Students of Temple Israel, Miami)
Jewish Radical (University of California, Berkeley)
Lilith (Jewish Feminist Magazine, New York)
Lilith's Rib (North American Jewish Feminist Organization, Chicago)
Network (Newark, NJ)
Radical Zionist Alliance (New York)
Response (New York

Newspapers, Magazines, Journals, and Periodicals

American Jewish Yearbook (American Jewish Committee)
American Judaism (Reform)
The Call (Workmen's Circle)
Central Conference of American Rabbis Journal (Reform)
Commentary (American Jewish Committee)
Congress Weekly/Bi-Weekly (American Jewish Congress)
Conservative Judaism (Conservative)
Hadassah Newsletter (Hadassah)
Jewish Exponent (Philadelphia, PA)
Jewish Life/Jewish Currents (Communist/Independent Left)
Jewish Spectator (New York)
Jewish Telegraphic Agency
Judaism (American Jewish Congress)
Midstream (Theodore Herzl Foundation)
The Reconstructionist (Reconstructionist)
Tradition: A Journal of Orthodox Jewish Thought (Modern Orthodox)
Women's League Outlook (Women's League for Conservative Judaism)

Published Primary Sources

Ain, Abraham. "Swislocz: Portrait of a Jewish Community in Eastern Europe." *YIVO Annual of Jewish Social Science* 4 (1949): 86–114.

Atkinson, Brooks. "Three Short Plays: The World of Sholom Aleichem Makes Art out of Simple Things about People." *New York Times*, September 20, 1953, X1.

Attwood, William. "The Position of Jews in America Today." *Look* 19, no. 24 (November 29, 1955): 27–35.

Bar-David, Molly Lyons. "Diary of a Jerusalem Housewife." *Hadassah Newsletter* (September 1948): 5.

———. "Diary of Jerusalem Housewife." *Hadassah Newsletter* (September 1949): 16.

———. "Diary of a Jerusalem Housewife." *Hadassah Newsletter* (December 1951):16.

———. *My Promised Land*. New York: G. P. Putman's Sons, 1953.

———. *The Israeli Cookbook*. New York: Crown Publishers, 1964.

———. *Jewish Cooking for Pleasure*. London: Paul Hamlyn, 1965.

———. *Women in Israel*. New York: Hadassah Education Department, 1950.

Baum, Charlotte, Paula Hyman, and Sonia Michel. *The Jewish Woman in America*. New York: Dial Press, 1976.

Bauman, Batya. [Untitled]. *Lilith* (Winter 1976–77): 9–10.

Baron, Salo. "Ghetto and Emancipation." *Menorah Journal* 14 (1928): 515–26.

Ben-Asher, Naomi, and Hayim Leaf. *The Junior Jewish Encyclopedia*. New York: Shengold Publishers, 1957.

Berger, Peter. *The Noise of Solemn Assemblies*. Garden City, NY: Doubleday, 1961.

Blake, Peter, ed. *An American Synagogue for Today and Tomorrow*. New York: Union of American Hebrew Congregations, 1954.

Brav, Stanley R. *Marriage and the Jewish Tradition*. New York: Philosophical Library, 1951.

Broner, E. M., and Naomi Nimrod. "A Women's Passover Haggadah and Other Revisionist Rituals." *Ms.* 5, no. 10 (April 1977): 53–56.

Cahan, Abraham. *The Rise of David Levinsky*. New York: Harper and Brothers, 1917.

"Charge that Jews 'Escape' Non-white City Neighbors Held Unwarranted." Jewish Telegraphic Agency, December 4, 1959. http://www.jta.org/1959/12/04/archive/charge-that-jews-escape-non-white-city-neighbors-held-unwarranted. Accessed June 20, 2016.

Charry, Elias. "Ben Torah: Bar Mitzvah at Sixteen." *Conservative Judaism* 16, no. 1 (Fall 1961): 52–55.

Chotzinoff, Samuel. "East Side Boyhood." *Holiday* 19, no. 155 (September 1954): 70–75.

———. *A Lost Paradise*. New York: Alfred Knopf, 1955.

"The Cost of Belonging to a Temple (continued)." *American Judaism* 7, no. 3 (May 1958): 6.

Cousens, Frances. "The Forward Look for Workmen's Circle." *The Call* 27, no. 1 (January 1958): 4.

Dawidowicz, Lucy. *From That Place and Time: A Memoir*. New York: W. W. Norton, 1989; repr., New Brunswick, NJ: Rutgers University Press, 2008.

———. "Middle-Class Judaism: A Case Study." *Commentary*, June 1960, 492–503.

Decter, Midge. "Belittling Sholom Aleichem's Jews: Folk Falsification of the Ghetto." *Commentary*, May 1954, 389–92.

———. "The Legacy of Henrietta Szold." *Commentary*, December 1960, 480–88.

———. *The Liberated Woman and Other Americans*. New York: Coward, McCann and Geoghegan, 1971.

———. *The New Chastity and Other Arguments against Women's Liberation*. New York: Coward, McCann and Geoghegan, 1972.

Dempsey, David. "Conformity, Inc." *New York Times*, June 23, 1957, 213.

"A Dreamer's Journey." *The Eternal Light*, broadcast January 25, 1953.

Duker, Abraham G. "Patterns That Preserve." Printed in the "Proceedings of the Second Conference on Jewish Values," *Congress Bi-Weekly* 28, no. 8 (April 17, 1961): 2–5.

Efron, Benjamin, and Alvan D. Rubin. "The Reality of Bar Mitzvah." *CCAR Journal* 8, no. 3 (October 1960) 31–33.

Eisendrath, Maurice N. "The Authority of the Rabbi." *CCAR Journal* 10, no. 39 (October 1962): 3–10.

———. "Paean of Praise, Wouk Style." *American Judaism* 9, no. 3 (Purim 1960): 6–7.

Fast, Howard. *Peekskill USA*. New York: Civil Rights Congress, 1951.

Folkman, Jerome. *Design for Jewish Living*. New York: Union of American Hebrew Congregations, 1955.

Forman, Molly. "Career Woman versus Housewife: A Happy Choice." *Women's League Outlook* 19, no. 3 (March 1949): 8–9.

Fortgang, Tal. "Why I'll Never Apologize for My White Male Privilege." *Time*, May 2, 2014. Originally printed in the *Princeton Tory*, April 2, 2014. http://time.com/85933/why-ill-never-apologize-for-my-white-male-privilege/. Accessed May 31, 2016.

Frazier, E. Franklin. *Black Bourgeoisie*. Glencoe, IL: Free Press, 1957.

Freedman, Morris. "The Jewish College Student, 1951 Model: Is the Old Idealism and Zeal for Learning Gone?" *Commentary*, October 1951, 305–13.

———. "New Jewish Community in Formation." *Commentary*, January 1955, 36–47.

Freeman, Jo. "On the Origins of the Women's Liberation Movement from a Strictly Personal Perspective." In *The Feminist Memoir Project: Voices from Women's Liberation*, edited by Rachel Blau DuPlessis and Ann Snitow, 172–208. New York: Three Rivers Press, 1998.

Friedan, Betty. *The Feminine Mystique*. New York: Norton, 1963.

Galbraith, John Kenneth. *The Affluent Society*. Boston: Houghton Mifflin, 1958.

Gamoran, Mamie G. *The New Jewish History, Book Three*. New York: Union of Hebrew Congregations, 1957.

Gans, Herbert. "Park Forest: Birth of a Jewish Community." *Commentary* April 1951, 330–39.

Gay, Ruth. "Nostalgia Is Not Enough." *Conservative Judaism* 14, no. 3 (Spring 1960): 32–39.

Geller, Victor B. "How Jewish Is Jewish Suburbia?" *Tradition: A Journal of Orthodox Jewish Thought* 2, no. 2 (Spring 1960): 318–30.

Gersh, Harry. "The New Suburbanites of the 50s: Jewish Division." *Commentary*, March, 1954, 209–21.

Gewirtz, Leonard B. *The Authentic Jew and His Judaism*. New York: Bloch Publishing, 1961.

Gittelsohn, Roland B. "Bar Mitzvah in Reform Judaism." *American Judaism* 6, no. 1 (September 1956): 14–16.

Glazer, Nathan. *American Judaism*. Chicago: University of Chicago Press, 1957.

———. "The Attainment of Middle-Class Rank." In *The Jews: Social Patterns of an American Group*, edited by Marshall Sklare, 138–46. New York: Free Press, 1958.

Glazer, Nathan, and Daniel Patrick Moynihan. *Beyond the Melting Pot*. Cambridge, MA: MIT Press, 1963.

Gold, Michael. "The East Side I Knew." *Jewish Life* (November 1954): 25–27.

Goldstein, Albert S. "Lets Bar Bar Mitzvah." *CCAR Journal* 3 (October 1953): 19.

Gordon, Albert. *Jews in Suburbia*. Boston: Beacon Press, 1959.

Greeley, Andrew M. *The Church and the Suburbs*. New York: Sheed and Ward, 1959.

Greenberg, Simon. "Dissatisfied but Not Unhappy." *Conservative Judaism* 17, nos. 3–4 (Spring–Summer 1963): 71–76.

Griefer, Julian L. "Suburbia and Jewish Conformity." *The Reconstructionist* 25, no. 2 (March 6, 1959): 12–15.

Grinstein, Hyman B. "Flight from the Slums." In *Essays on Jewish Life and Thought: Presented in Honor of Salo Wittmayer Baron*, edited by Joseph Blau, Philip Friedman, Arthur Hertzberg, and Isaac Mendelsohn, 285–97. New York: Columbia University Press, 1959.

Gruenwald [Gruenewald], Max. "Building Drive." *The Reconstructionist* 16, no. 5 (April 21, 1950): 27–29.

Gruber, Ruth. *Israel Today: Land of Many Nations*. New York: Hill and Wang, 1958.

———. *Israel without Tears*. New York: A. A. Wyn, 1950.

Harap, Louis. "Is American Jewry Prepared?" *Jewish Life* (January 1950): 112–16.

Harriton, Faye. "Twentieth Century Pioneers." *Women's League Outlook* 21, no. 1 (September 1950): 17.

Harris, Joel, and Jack Schuldenfrei. *Fourth World Haggadah*. London: World Union of Jewish Students, 1970.

Herberg, Will. *Protestant, Catholic, Jew: An Essay in American Religious Sociology*. Garden City, NY: Doubleday, 1955.

Herman, Erwin L. "Bar Mitzvah a la Carte." *American Judaism* 11, no. 4 (Summer 1962) 4–5.

Heschel, Abraham Joshua. *The Earth Is the Lord's: The Inner World of the Jew in Eastern Europe*. New York: Farrar, Straus, Giroux: 1949; repr., Woodstock, VT: Jewish Lights Publishing, 2008.

———. "Spirit of Jewish Prayer." *Proceedings of the 53rd Annual Convention of the Rabbinical Assembly of America* 17 (1953): 151.

Himmelfarb, Milton. "The Jewish Vote—Again." *Commentary*, June 1973, 81.

Hirsch, Shula. *An American Housewife in Israel*. New York: Citadel Press, 1962.

Howe, Irving, and Eliezer Greenberg. *A Treasury of Yiddish Stories*. New York: Viking Press, 1953.

"How Much Religious Education Do You Want for Your Children: Brotherhood Section." *American Judaism* 3, no. 1 (September 1953): 23–24.

Jacobson, Burt. "Blueprint for a Havurah." In *The Jewish Catalogue: A Do-It-Yourself Kit*, compiled and edited by Richard Siegel, Michael Strassfeld, and Sharon Strassfeld, 280–85. Philadelphia: Jewish Publication Society, 1973.

"Jewish Young Freedom Fighters and the Role of the Jewish Community: An Evaluation." *Jewish Currents* 19, no. 7 (July–August 1965): 4–23.

Joffe, Natalie F. "The Dynamics of Benefice among East European Jews." *Social Forces* 27, no. 3 (March 1949): 238–47.

Jones, Robert P., and Daniel Cox. *Chosen for What? Jewish Values in 2012: Findings from the 2012 Jewish Values Survey*. Washington, DC: Public Religion Research Institute, April 3, 2012.

"Judaism and Suburbia." *The Reconstructionist* 25, no. 9 (June 15, 1959): 2.

Kamins, Jeanette. *Everything but a Husband*. New York: St. Martins Press, 1962.

Klaperman, Gilbert, and Libby Klaperman. *The Story of the Jewish People*. Vol. 3. New York: Behrman House Publishing, 1958.

Klaperman, Gilbert, and Libby Klaperman. *The Story of the Jewish People*. Vol. 4. New York: Behrman House Publishing, 1961

Kling, Samuel G. "The Organization Woman." *Jewish Spectator* 27, no. 3 (March 1962): 22–23.

Kramer, Judith, and Seymour Leventman. *Children of the Gilded Ghetto*. New Haven: Yale University Press, 1961.

Lerner, Anne Lapidus. "'Who Hast Not Made Me a Man': The Movement for Equal Rights for Women in American Jewry." In *American Jewish Year Book* 77, 3–40. New York: American Jewish Committee and Jewish Publication Society, 1977.

"Letters from Readers." *Jewish Currents* 12, no. 5 (May 1958): 43.

"Letter to the Editor." *American Judaism* 7, no. 2 (November 1957): 2.

"*Life* Goes to a Bar Mitzvah." *Life* 33 (October 13, 1952): 170–72.

Lipman, Eugene J., and Myron Schoen. "A Reply to the Call for Help." *American Judaism* 7, no. 3 (January 1958): 8–9.

Kubie, Nora Benjamin. *The First Book of Israel*. New York: Franklin Watts, 1953.

Landes, Ruth, and Mark Zborowski. "Hypotheses concerning the Eastern European Jewish Family." *Psychiatry* 13, no. 4 (November 1950): 447–64.

Lazerwitz, Bernard. "Suburban Voting Trends, 1948–1956." *Social Forces* 39, no. 1 (October 1960): 29–36.

Learsi, Rufus. *The Jews in America: A History*. Cleveland: World Publishing, 1954.

Levi, Shoni B., and Sylvia Kaplan. *Across the Threshold: A Guide for the Jewish Homemaker*. New York: National Women's League of the United Synagogue of America and Farrar, Straus and Cudahy, 1959.

Levin, Meyer. "After All I Did for Israel." *Commentary*, July 1951, 57–62.

Levine, Hillel. "To Share a Vision." In *Jewish Radicalism*, edited by Jack Nusan Porter and Peter Drier, 183–94. New York: Grove Press, 1973.

Levinger, Elma Erlich. *Fighting Angel: The Story of Henrietta Szold*. New York: Behrman House, 1946.

Levinger, Lee J., Elma Ehrlich Levinger, and Harry Gersh. *The Story of the Jew*. New York: Behrman House Publishing, 1964.

Lipsky, Louis. *A Gallery of Zionist Profiles*. New York: Farrar, Straus and Cudahy, 1956.

Mandelkorn, Philip. "The Jewish Counterculture: From New Left to New Life." *Baltimore Jewish Times* 117, no. 2 (May 9, 1975): 16–20.

Marty, Martin E. *The New Shape of American Religion*. New York: Harper, 1959.

Meisler, Stanley. "Big Bar Mitzvah." *The Reconstructionist* 26, no. 2 (March 4, 1960): 21–24.

Mendelsohn, Eric. "In the Spirit of Our Age." *Commentary* June 1947: 541.

Menes, Abraham. "The East Side—Matrix of the Jewish Labor Movement." *Judaism* 3, no. 4 (Fall 1954): 366–80.

Milstone, Mark. "Bar Mitzvah—A New Approach." *The Call* 23, no. 6 (December 1954): 4.

Ornitz, Samuel Ornitz. *Haunch, Paunch, and Jowl*. New York: Boni and Liveright, 1923.

"Our Readers Respond." *The Call* 24, no. 4 (July 1960): 12.

"A Pattern for Jewish Boys Everywhere." *The Reconstructionist* 28, no. 19 (January 25, 1963): 4–5.

Pawel, Ernst. *From the Dark Tower*. New York: Macmillan, 1957.

Pekarsky, Nell Ziff. "Shopping, Swapping, *Shepping Nahas* in Israel." *Hadassah Newsletter*, March 1952, 6.

Perel, Abraham, and Rebecca Perel. "Jews in a Mill Town." *Jewish Life* (July 1952): 6–7.

Perl, Arnold. *The World of Sholom Aleichem*. New York: Dramatists Play Service, 1953.

Perlo, Victor. "Outlook for White Collar, Trade, and the Professions." *Jewish Life* (June 1954): 5–9.

Pessin, Deborah. *The Jewish People Book III*. New York: United Synagogue Commission on Jewish Education, 1953.

Pilch, Judah. "Old Values and New Purposes." In "Proceedings of the Second Conference on Jewish Values." *Congress Bi-Weekly* 28, no. 8 (April 17, 1961): 6–11.

Podhoretz, Norman. "My Negro Problem—And Ours." *Commentary* February 1963, 98–101.

Popkin, Jeremy. Introduction to *Quiet Street*, by Zelda Popkin, vii–xii. Lincoln: University of Nebraska Press, 2002.

Popkin, Zelda. *The Journey Home*. Philadelphia: Lippincott, 1945.

———. *Open Every Door*. New York: E. P. Dutton, 1956.

———. *Small Victory*. Philadelphia: Lippincott, 1947.

———. *Quiet Street*. Lippincott, 1951; repr., Lincoln: University of Nebraska Press, 2002.

Porter, Jack Nusan, and Peter Drier, eds. *Jewish Radicalism*. New York: Grove Press, 1973.

Postal, Bernard, and Lionel Koppman. *A Jewish Tourist's Guide to the United States*. Philadelphia: Jewish Publication Society of America, 1954.

"The Press: The Victim of Success." *Time*, December 28, 1962. http://www.time.com/time/magazine/article/0,9171,827975,00.html. Accessed July 19, 2010.

"Rabbi's Report." *Time Magazine*, July 13, 1959. http://content.time.com/time/magazine/article/0,9171,869180,00.html?iid=sr-link1. Accessed June 20, 2016.

"Report of Committee on Guide for Synagogue Decorum." 75th Annual Convention of the Central Conference of American Rabbis (1964). *CCAR Yearbook* 74 (1965): 60. Philadelphia: Press of Maurice Jacobs.

Ribalow, Harold. "From *Hungry Hearts* to *Marjorie Morningstar*: The Progress of an American Minority Told in Fiction." *Saturday Review* 40, no. 38 (September 14, 1957): 46–48.

Richler, Mordecai. "Land of Milk and Money." *Holiday* 38 (July 1965): 56–63.

Riesman, David, Nathan Glazer, and Reuel Denney. *The Lonely Crowd*. New Haven: Yale University Press, 1950.

Rosenberg, Bernard, and Gilbert Shapiro. "Marginality and Jewish Humor." *Midstream* 4, no. 2 (Spring 1958): 70–80.

Rosenberg, M. J. "To Uncle Tom and Other Jews." In *Jewish Radicalism*, edited by Jack Nusan Porter and Peter Drier, 5–10. New York: Grove Press, 1973.

Rosenthal, Erich. "Jewish Fertility in the United States." *American Jewish Yearbook* 57 (1961): 3–27.

———. "This Was North Lawndale: The Transplantation of a Jewish Community." *Jewish Social Studies* 23, no. 2 (April 1960): 67–82.

Rosenthal, Celia Stopnicka. "Deviation and Social Change in the Jewish Community of a Small Polish Town." *American Journal of Sociology* 60, no. 2 (September 1954): 177–81.

———. "How the Polish Jew Saw His World: A Study of a Small-Town Community before 1939." *Commentary*, January 1954, 70–75.

———. "Social Stratification of the Jewish Community in a Small Polish Town." *American Journal of Sociology* 59, no. 1 (July 1953): 1–10.

Roth, Philip. *Goodbye, Columbus*. New York: Houghton Mifflin, 1959.

———. "Writing about Jews." *Commentary*, December 1963, 446–52.

Rothchild, Sylvia. "My Mrs. Schnitzer." *Commentary*, May 1952, 463–68.

———. *Sunshine and Salt*. New York: Simon and Schuster, 1958.

Rothchild, Sylvia, writing as Evelyn Rossman. "The Community and I, Belonging: Its Satisfactions and Disatisfactions." *Commentary*, November 1954, 397–91.

———. "Judaism in Northrup, The Community and I: Part III." *Commentary*, November 1957, 383–91.

———. "A Fund-Raiser Comes to Northrup." *Commentary*, March 1962, 218–25.

Samuel, Maurice. "Why Israel Misunderstands American Jewry." *Commentary*, October 1953 300–310.

———. *The World of Sholom Aleichem*. New York: Knopf, 1943.

Sanders, Ronald. "Settling in Israel?" *Commentary*, August 1965 37–44.

Schafler, Samuel. "The Yom Kippur Service." In *Mas'at Rav: A Professional Supplement to Conservative Judaism*, 12. The Rabbinical Assembly, August 1965.

Schappes, Morris U. "Thirty Years of Jewish Life." *Jewish Life* (August 1952): 21–24.

Schlesinger, Arthur, Jr. "The Crisis of Masculinity." *Esquire: The Magazine for Men* 50, no. 5 (November 1958): 63–65.

Segal, Alfred. "Hot Rolls and Cream." *Jewish Exponent* 123, no. 51 (January 15, 1954): 42.

Sherman, Allan. "Harvey and Sheila." *My Son the Celebrity*. Warner Brothers Records, 1963.

Sherman, C. Bezalel. *The Jew within American Society*. Detroit: Wayne State University Press, 1960.

Shulman, Charles. "It's Hard to Be a Jew." *Congress Weekly*, May 13, 1957, 9–11.

Siegal, Danny. *Soulstoned*. New York: United Synagogue of America, 1969.

Siegal, Richard, Michael Strassfeld, and Sharon Strassfeld. *The Jewish Catalogue: A Do-It-Yourself Kit*. Philadelphia: Jewish Publication Society, 1973.

Silverman, Althea. *Habibi's Adventures in the Land of Israel*. New York: Bloch Publishing, 1951.

Simon, Kate. *New York: Places and Pleasures; An Uncommon Guidebook*. New York: Meridian Books, 1959.

Sklare, Marshall. *Jewish Identity on the Suburban Frontier*. Chicago: University of Chicago Press, 1967.

Spiro, Melford. *Kibbutz: Venture in Utopia*. New York: Schocken, 1956.

Stern, William. "Tipping the Scales." *The Call* 24, no. 1 (February 1955): 10.

———. "Tipping the Scales." *The Call* 26, no. 2 (March 1957): 7.

Stern, Sol. "My Jewish Problem—And Ours: Israel, the Left, and the Jewish Establishment." In *Jewish Radicalism*, edited by Jack Nusan Porter and Peter Drier, 351–75. New York: Grove Press, 1973.

Strassfeld, Sharon, and Michael Strassfeld. *The Second Jewish Catalogue: Sources and Resources*. Philadelphia: Jewish Publication Society, 1976.

———. *The Third Jewish Catalogue: Creating Community*. Philadelphia: Jewish Publication Society, 1980.

"Sweet Hemlock." *The Eternal Light*. Broadcast January 25, 1959.

Syrkin, Marie. *Blessed Is the Match*. Philadelphia: Jewish Publication Society of America, 1947.

———. *Golda Meir: Woman with a Cause*. New York: G. P. Putnam, 1963.

———. *Way of Valor: A Biography of Golda Myerson*. New York: Sharon Books, 1955.

Taylor, Sidney. *All-of-a-Kind Family*. New York: Follet Publishing, 1951.

Timberg, Bernard, director. *Thirteen Years*. 1971. Videocassette distributed by the National Jewish Film Archive.

Tumin, Melvin. "Conservative Trends in American Jewish Life." *Judaism* 13 (Spring 1964): 136–39.

"Two-Thirds of America's Jews Now Live in Suburbs, Expert Estimates." Jewish Telegraphic Agency, October 16, 1959. http://archive.jta.org. Accessed May 3, 2011.

"United Synagogue of America Standards for Synagogue Practice." *Conservative Judaism* 10, no. 4 (Summer 1956): 22–25.

Uris, Leon. *Exodus*. Garden City, NJ: Doubleday, 1958.

Vishniac, Roman. *Polish Jews: A Pictorial Record*. New York: Schocken, 1947.

Vorspan, Albert. "In St. Augustine." *Midstream* 10, no. 3 (September 1964): 20.

———. "The Negro Victory and the Jewish Failure." *American Judaism*, Fall 1963, 50–54.

Vorspan, Albert, and Eugene Lipman. *Justice and Judaism*. New York: Union of American Hebrew Congregations, 1956.

———. *A Tale of Ten Cities*. New York: Union of American Hebrew Congregations, 1962.

Wakefield, Dan. "New York's Lower East Side Today." *Commentary*, January, 1959, 461–71.

Waskow, Arthur. *The Freedom Seder: A New Haggadah for Passover*. Washington, DC: Micah Press/Holt, Rinehart and Winston Press, 1969.

Waxman, Meyer, Sulamith Ish-Kishor, and Jacob Sloan. *Blessed Is the Daughter*. New York: Shengold Publishers, 1959.

Weales, George. "Make Mine Manhattan: Guide to a Changing City." *Commentary*, January 1959, 344–45.

Weidman, Jerome. *I Can Get It for You Wholesale*. New York: Simon and Schuster, 1937.

Weingarten, Murray. *Life on a Kibbutz*. New York: Reconstructionist Press, 1955.

Weiss-Rosmarin, Trude. "The Three Days Season." *Jewish Spectator* 14, no. 8 (September 1951): 4–6.

Whyte, William. *The Organization Man*. New York: Simon and Schuster, 1956.

Winter, Gibson. *The Suburban Captivity of the Churches*. New York: Macmillan, 1962.

Wolf, Arnold Jacob. "Experimental Synagogue in Suburbia." *The Reconstructionist* 26, no. 7 (May 13, 1960): 15–19.

"Women of Valor." *Hadassah Newsletter*, December 1945, 46–47.

Wood, Robert C. *Suburbia: Its People and Their Politics*. Boston: Houghton Mifflin, 1958.

"The World of Sholom Aleichem." *The Eternal Light*, broadcast March 4, 1945.

Wouk, Herman. "For the Flavor of This Wonderful Land You Must Go There Yourself." *Hadassah Newsletter*, November 1955, 7.

———. *Marjorie Morningstar*. New York: Doubleday, 1955.

———. *This Is My God*, Garden City, NY: Doubleday, 1959.

Wylie, Philip. *Generation of Vipers*. New York: Holt, Rinehart and Winston, 1955.

Yezierska, Anzia. *Salome of the Tenements*. New York: Boni and Liveright, 1923.

Zborowski, Mark, and Elizabeth Herzog. *Life Is with People*. New York: Schocken, 1952.

Zuckoff, Aviva Cantor "The Oppression of America's Jews." In *Jewish Radicalism*, edited by Jack Nusan Porter and Peter Drier, 29–49. New York: Grove Press, 1973.

———. "Jewish Women's Haggadah." In *Sister Celebrations: Nine Worship Experiences*, edited by Arlene Swidler, 77–88. Philadelphia: Fortress Press, 1974.

Zuckoff, Aviva Cantor, Itzhak Epstein, and Jerry Kirschen. *Jewish Liberation Hagada*. New York: Jewish Liberation Project, 1970.

SECONDARY SOURCES

Alexander, Michael. *Jazz Age Jews*. Princeton: Princeton University Press, 2001.

Almog, Oz. *The Sabra: The Creation of the New Jew*. Berkeley: University of California Press, 2000.

Anderson, Benedict. *Imagined Communities*. London: Verso Press, 1983.

Antler, Joyce. "Between Culture and Politics: The Emma Lazarus Federation of Jewish Women's Clubs and the Promulgation of Women's History." In *U.S. History as Women's History: New Feminist Essays*, edited by Linda K. Kerber, Alice Kessler-Harris, and Kathryn Kish Sklar, 519–41. Chapel Hill: University of North Carolina Press, 1995.

———. "We Were Ready to Turn the World Upside Down." In *A Jewish Feminine Mystique? Jewish Women in the Postwar Era*, edited by Hasia Diner, Shira Kohn, and Rachel Kranson, 210–24. New Brunswick, NJ: Rutgers University Press, 2010.

Appiah, Kwame Anthony. *The Ethics of Identity*. Princeton: Princeton University Press, 2005.

Bauman, Mark, and Berkley Kalin. *The Quiet Voices: Southern Rabbis and Black Civil Rights*. Tuscaloosa: University of Alabama Press, 1997.

Baxandall, Rosalyn, and Elizabeth Ewen. *Picture Windows*. New York: Basic Books, 2000.

Beckerman, Gal. *When They Come for Us, We'll Be Gone: The Epic Struggle to Save Soviet Jewry*. New York: Mariner Books, 2010.

Benton, Maya. *Roman Vishniac Rediscovered*. New York: International Center of Photography/ Prestel Books, 2015.

Bercovitch, Sacvan. *The American Jeremiad*. Madison: University of Wisconsin Press, 1978.

Berman, Lila Corwin. "American Jews and the Ambivalence of Middle-Classness." *American Jewish History* 93, no. 4 (December 2007): 409–34.

———. "Gendered Journeys: Jewish Migrations and the City in Postwar America." In *Gender and Jewish History*, edited by Marion Kaplan and Deborah Dash Moore, 336–49. Bloomington: Indiana University Press, 2011.

————. *Metropolitan Jews*. Chicago: University of Chicago Press, 2016.

————. *Speaking of Jews: Rabbis, Intellectuals, and the Creation of an American Public Identity*. Berkeley: University of California Press, 2009.

Bernstein, Deborah S. "Daughters of the Nation: Between the Public and Private Spheres in Pre-state Israel." In *Israeli Women's Studies: A Reader*, edited by Esther Fuchs, 78–96. New Brunswick, NJ: Rutgers University Press, 2005.

Berrett, Jesse. "Feeding the Organization Man: Diet and Masculinity in Postwar America." *Journal of Social History* 30, no. 4 (1997): 805–25.

Biale, David. *Eros and the Jews*. Berkeley: University of California Press, 1997.

Biale, David, Michael Galchinsky, and Susannah Heschel, eds. *Insider/Outsider: American Jews and Multiculturalism*. Berkeley: University of California Press, 1998.

Bledstein, Burton, and Robert D. Johnston, eds. *The Middling Sorts: Explorations in the History of the American Middle Class*. New York: Routledge, 2001.

Bloom, Alexander. *Prodigal Sons: The New York Intellectuals and Their World*. Oxford: Oxford University Press, 1986.

Bogue, Donald J. *The Population of the United States*. Glencoe, IL: Free Press, 1959.

Boim-Wolf, Rebecca. "It's Good Americanism to Join Hadassah: Selling Hadassah in the Postwar Era." In *A Jewish Feminine Mystique? Jewish Women in the Postwar Era*, edited by Hasia Diner, Shira Kohn, and Rachel Kranson, 48–64. New Brunswick, NJ: Rutgers University Press, 2010.

Brautbar, Shirli. *From Fashion to Politics: Hadassah and Jewish American Women in the Post World War II Era*. Boston: American Studies Press, 2012.

Breines, Paul. *Tough Jews*. New York: Basic Books, 1990.

Brodkin, Karen. *How Jews Became White Folks and What That Says about Race in America*. New Brunswick, NJ: Rutgers University Press, 1998.

Chafe, William. *The American Woman: Her Changing Social, Economic, and Political Roles, 1920–1970*. New York: Oxford University Press, 1972.

Chiswick, Barry R. "The Postwar Economy of American Jews." In *A New Jewry? America since the Second World War*, edited by Peter Y. Medding, 92–98. New York: Oxford University Press, 1992.

Cohen, Jocelyn, and Daniel Soyer. *My Future Is in America: Autobiographies of Eastern-European Jewish Immigrants*. New York: New York University Press, 2006.

Dash, Joan. *Summoned to Jerusalem: The Life of Henrietta Szold*. New York: Harper and Row, 1979.

Dauber, Jeremy. *The Worlds of Sholem Aleichem*. New York: Nextbook/Schocken, 2013.

Diamond, Etan. *And I Will Dwell in Their Midst: Orthodox Jews in Suburbia*. Chapel Hill: University of North Carolina Press, 2000.

Diner, Hasia. *In an Almost Promised Land*. Westport, CT: Greenwood Press, 1977.

————. *The Jews of the United States*. Berkeley: University of California Press, 2004.

————. *Lower East Side Memories*. Princeton: Princeton University Press, 2002.

————. *A Time for Gathering: The Second Migration, 1820–1880*. Baltimore: Johns Hopkins University Press, 1992.

————. *We Remember with Reverence and Love*. New York: New York University Press, 2009.

Diner, Hasia, Shira Kohn, and Rachel Kranson, eds. *A Jewish Feminine Mystique? Jewish Women in Postwar America*. New Brunswick, NJ: Rutgers University Press, 2010.

Dinnerstein, Leonard. *Antisemitism in America*. New York: Oxford University Press, 1994.

Dollinger, Marc. *Quest for Inclusion: Jews and Liberalism in Modern America*. Princeton: Princeton University Press, 2000.

Ehrenreich, Barbara. *The Hearts of Men: American Dreams and the Flight from Commitment*. New York: Anchor Books, 1983.

"The Engel Case." In *Culture Wars: An Encyclopedia of Issues, Viewpoints and Voices*, edited by Roger Chapman and James Ciment, 580–81. NY: Routledge, 2014.

Epstein, Nadine. "The Other Rosenbergs." *Moment*, March–April 2011. http://momentmag.com/moment/issues/2011/04/rosenbergs.html. Accessed July 6, 2011.

Feingold, Henry. *Silent No More: Saving the Jews of Russia, the American Jewish Effort*. Syracuse: Syracuse University Press, 2007.

"The Feminist Revolution: Paula Hyman." *Jewish Women Archives*, http://jwa.org/feminism/_html/JWA039.htm. Accessed February 22, 2012.

Fermaglich, Kirstin. *American Dreams and Nazi Nightmares*. Waltham, MA: Brandeis University Press, 2006.

———. "Midge Decter." *Jewish Women: A Comprehensive Historical Encyclopedia*. http://jwa.org/encyclopedia/article/decter-midge. Accessed May 18, 2016.

Fishman, Aleisa R. "Keeping Up with the Goldbergs: Gender, Consumer Culture, and Jewish Identity in Suburban Nassau County." PhD dissertation, American University, 2004. UMI Dissertation Services, no. 3127795.

Fishman, Sylvia Barak. *A Breath of Life: Feminism in the American Jewish Community*. Waltham, MA: Brandeis University Press, 1993.

Forman, Seth. *Blacks in the Jewish Mind: A Crisis in Liberalism*. New York: New York University Press, 1998.

Fox, Margalit. "Arnold Jacob Wolf, a Leading Reform Rabbi, Is Dead at 84." *New York Times*, December 29, 2008, A-18.

Friedman, Murray. *The Neoconservative Revolution: Jewish Intellectuals and the Shaping of Public Policy*. Cambridge: Cambridge University Press, 2005.

———. *What Went Wrong? The Creation and Collapse of the Black-Jewish Alliance*. New York: Free Press, 1994.

Gamm, Gerald. *Urban Exodus: Why the Jews Left Boston and the Catholics Stayed*. Cambridge, MA: Harvard University Press, 1999.

Glenn, Susan. *Daughters of the Shtetl*. Ithaca, NY: Cornell University Press, 1990.

———. "The Vogue of Jewish Self-Hatred in Postwar World War II America." *Jewish Social Studies* 2, no. 3 (Spring–Summer 2006): 95–136.

Goldberg, J. J. "Seasons of Reinterpretation—Transforming Passover." *Jewish Journal of Los Angeles*, April 21, 2000. http://www.shalomctr.org/node/1259. Accessed September 16, 2009.

Goldman, Karla. "'Along with All Other Americans': The 1954 Tercentennial Celebration of American Jewish History and Life." Paper presented at the Biennial Scholars Conference on American Jewish History, 2004.

———. "The View from 1954: Celebrating 300 Years of American Jewish Life." Paper presented at the American Jewish Studies Conference, 2002.

Goldstein, Eric. *The Price of Whiteness: Jews, Race and American Identity*. Princeton: Princeton University Press, 2006.

Goren, Arthur. "Celebrating Zion in America." In *Encounters with the Holy Land*, edited by Jeffrey Shandler and Beth Wenger. Hanover, NH: University Press of New England for Brandeis University Press in association with the National Museum of American Jewish History and the Center for Judaic Studies at the University of Pennsylvania, 1997, 41–59.

———. *The Politics and Public Culture of American Jews*. Bloomington: Indiana University Press, 1999.

Grazian, David. *Blue Chicago: The Search for Authenticity in Urban Blues Clubs*. Chicago: University of Chicago Press, 2003.

Greenberg, Cheryl. "Liberal NIMBY: American Jews and Civil Rights." *Journal of Urban History* 38, no. 3 (May 2012): 452–66.

———. *Troubling the Waters*. Princeton: Princeton University Press, 2006.

Hale, Grace Elizabeth. *A Nation of Outsiders: How the White Middle Class Fell in Love with Rebellion in Postwar America*. Oxford: Oxford University Press, 2011.

Heinze, Andrew. *Adapting to Abundance: Jewish Immigrants, Mass Consumption, and the Search for American Identity*. New York: Columbia University Press, 1990.

Hertzberg, Arthur. *The Jews in America*. New York: Columbia University Press, 1997.

Hobsbawm, Eric, and Terence O. Ranger. *The Invention of Tradition*. Cambridge: Cambridge University Press, 1992.

Hochschild, Jennifer. *Facing Up to the American Dream: Race, Class and the Soul of the Nation*. Princeton: Princeton University Press, 1995.

Hollinger, David. "Communalist and Dispersionist Approaches to American Jewish History in an Increasingly Post-Jewish Era." *American Jewish History* 95, no. 1 (March 2009): 1–32.

———. "Rich, Powerful and Smart: Jewish Overrepresentation Should Be Explained Rather than Avoided or Mystified." *Jewish Quarterly Review* 94, no. 4 (Autumn 2004): 595–602.

Horowitz, Daniel. *The Anxieties of Affluence: Critiques of American Consumer Culture*. Amherst: University of Massachusetts Press, 2004.

———. "Jewish Women Remaking American Feminism/Women Remaking American Judaism: Reflections on the Life of Betty Friedan." In *A Jewish Feminine Mystique? Jewish Women in Postwar America*, edited by Hasia Diner, Shira Kohn, and Rachel Kranson, 235–56. New Brunswick, NJ: Rutgers University Press, 2010.

Hudnut-Beumler, James. *Looking for God in the Suburbs*. New Brunswick, NJ: Rutgers University Press, 1994.

Hunt, Andrew. "How New Was the New Left?" In *The New Left Revisited*, edited by John McMillian and Paul Buhle, 139–55. Philadelphia: Temple University Press, 2003.

Hyman, Paula. "Culture and Gender: Women in the Immigrant Jewish Community." In *The Legacy of Jewish Migration: 1881 and Its Impact*, edited by David Berger, 157-68. New York: Brooklyn College Press, 1983.

———. "Ezrat Nashim and the Emergence of a New Jewish Feminism." In *The Americanization of the Jews*, edited by Robert M. Seltzer and Norman S. Cohen, 284–95. New York: New York University Press, 1995.

———. "From City to Suburb: Temple Mishkan Tefila of Boston." In *The American Synagogue: A Sanctuary Transformed*, edited by Jack Wertheimer, 85–105. Cambridge: Cambridge University Press, 1987.

———. "Gender and the Immigrant Experience in the United States." In *Jewish Women in Historical Perspective*, edited by Judith Baskin, 224–25. Detroit: Wayne State Press, 1991.

Isserman, Maurice. *If I Had a Hammer*. Chicago: University of Illinois Press, 1993.

Ivers, Gregg. *To Build a Wall: American Jews and the Separation of Church and State*. Charlottesville: University Press of Virginia, 1995.

Jacobson, Matthew Frye. *Roots Too: White Ethnic Revival in Post–Civil Rights America*. Cambridge, MA: Harvard University Press, 2006.

Jamison, Andrew, and Ron Eyerman. *Seeds of the Sixties*. Berkeley and Los Angeles: University of California Press, 1994.

"Jewish Life/Jewish Currents." In *The Encyclopedia of the American Left*, edited by Mari Jo Buhle, Paul Buhle, and Dan Georgakas, 401–2. New York: Oxford University Press, 1998.

"Jewish Women in the United States." *Jewish Women: A Contemporary Encyclopedia*. http://jwa.org/encyclopedia/article/jewish-feminism-in-united-states. Accessed May 22, 2012.

Joselit, Jenna Weissman. *The Wonders of America: Reinventing Jewish Culture*. New York: Henry Holt, 1994.

Jumonville, Neil. *Critical Crossings: The New York Intellectuals in Postwar America*. Berkeley: University of California Press, 1991.

Kates, Judith. "Sylvia Rosner Rothchild." In *Jewish Women: A Contemporary Encyclopedia*. http://jwa.org/encyclopedia/article/rothchild-sylvia. Accessed March 22, 2012.

Katz, Emily. *Bringing Zion Home: Israel in American Jewish Culture, 1948–1967*. Albany: State University of New York Press, 2015.

Katznelson, Ira. *When Affirmative Action Was White*. New York: Norton, 2005.

Kaufman, Jonathan. *Broken Alliances: The Turbulent Times between Blacks and Jews in America*. New York: Scribner's, 1988.

Kessner, Carole. "Marie Syrkin." *Jewish Women: A Contemporary Encyclopedia*. http://jwa.org/encyclopedia/article/syrkin-marie. Accessed March 12, 2015.

Khoury, Peter. "William A. Stern, 90, Advocate for Jewish and Socialist Causes." *New York Times*, January 24, 2001. http://www.nytimes.com/2001/01/24/nyregion/william-a-stern-90-advocate-for-jewish-and-socialist-causes.html. Accessed May 23, 2016.

Kirshenblatt-Gimblett, Barbara. *Destination Culture: Tourism, Museums, and Heritage*. Oakland: University of California Press, 1998.

———. "Imagining Europe: The Popular Arts of American Jewish Ethnography." In *Divergent Jewish Cultures: Israel and America*, edited by Deborah Dash Moore and S. Ilan Troen, 155–91. New Haven: Yale University Press, 2001.

———. Introduction to *Life Is with People: The Culture of the Shtetl*, by Mark Zborowski and Elizabeth Herzog, ix–xlvii. New York: Schocken, 1995.

Laughlin, Kathleen. "'Our Defense against Despair': The Progressive Politics of the National Council of Jewish Women after World War II." In *A Jewish Feminine Mystique? Jewish Women in the Postwar Era*, edited by Hasia Diner, Shira Kohn, and Rachel Kranson, 65–86. New Brunswick, NJ: Rutgers University Press, 2010.

Lederhendler, Eli. *Jewish Immigrants and American Capitalism*. Cambridge: Cambridge University Press, 2009.

————. *New York Jews and the Decline of Urban Ethnicity*. Syracuse: Syracuse University Press, 2001.

Lehman, Marjorie. "Mamie Gamoran." *Jewish Women: A Contemporary Encyclopedia*. http://jwa.org/encyclopedia/article/gamoran-mamie. Accessed June 3, 2015.

Levine, Hillel, and Lawrence Harmon. *The Death of an American Jewish Community: A Tragedy of Good Intentions*. New York: Free Press, 1992.

Levine, Peter. *Ellis Island to Ebbet's Field: Sport and the American Jewish Experience*. New York: Oxford University Press, 1992.

Lindholm, Charles. *Culture and Authenticity*. Malden, MA: Blackwell, 2008.

Lipstadt, Deborah. "Feminism and American Judaism." In *Women and American Judaism*, edited by Pamela Nadell and Jonathan Sarna, 291–308. Hanover, NH: University Press of New England for Brandeis University Press, 2001.

MacCannell, Dean. *The Tourist: A New Theory of the Leisure Class*. New York: Schocken, 1976.

Marcus, Ivan G. *The Jewish Life Cycle: Rites of Passage from Biblical to Modern Times*. Seattle: University of Washington Press, 2004.

Markowitz, Ruth. *My Daughter the Teacher*. New Brunswick, NJ: Rutgers University Press, 1993.

Mart, Michelle. *Eye on Israel: How America Came to View Israel as an Ally*. Albany: State University of New York Press, 2006.

Mayer, Tamar. "From Zero to Hero: Masculinity in Jewish Nationalism." In *Israeli Women's Studies: A Reader*, edited by Esther Fuchs, 97–113. New Brunswick, NJ: Rutgers University Press, 2005.

Michels, Tony. *A Fire in Their Hearts: Yiddish Socialism in New York*. Cambridge, MA: Harvard University Press, 2005.

Miller, James. *Democracy is in the Streets: From Port Huron to the Siege of Chicago*. Cambridge, MA: Harvard University Press, 1987

Moore, Deborah Dash. *At Home in America*. New York: Columbia University Press, 1981.

————. *East European Jews in Two Worlds*. Chicago: Northwestern University Press, 1989.

————. *GI Jews: How World War II Changed a Generation*. Cambridge, MA: Harvard University Press, 2004.

————. "Reconsidering the Rosenbergs: Symbol and Substance in Second-Generation American Jewish Consciousness." *Journal of American Ethnic History* 8 (Fall 1988): 21–37.

————. *To the Golden Cities*. Cambridge, MA: Harvard University Press, 1994.

Mosse, George. *Confronting the Nation: Jewish and Western Nationalism*. Hanover, NH: University Press of New England for Brandeis University Press, 1993.

Murray, Sylvie. *The Progressive Housewife: Community Activism in Suburban Queens*. Philadelphia: University of Pennsylvania Press, 2003.

Nadell, Pamela. "Women and American Judaism." In *Women and Judaism: New Insights and Scholarship*, edited by Frederick Greenspahn, 155–81. New York: New York University Press, 2009.

"National Jewish Book Award Winners." http://www.jewishbookcouncil.org/awards/njba-list. Accessed November 24, 2014.

Newhouse, Alana. "A Closer Reading of Roman Vishniac." *New York Times Sunday Magazine*, April 1, 2010, 36.

Nicolaides, Becky, and Andrew Wiese. *The Suburb Reader*. New York: Routledge, 2006.

Oppenheimer, Mark. *Knocking on Heaven's Door: American Religion in the Age of Counterculture*. New Haven: Yale University Press, 2003.

Ortner, Sherry B. *New Jersey Dreaming: Capital, Culture, and the Class of 1958*. Durham, NC: Duke University Press, 2006.

———. "Reading America: Preliminary Notes on Class and Culture." In *Anthropology and Social Theory: Culture, Power and the Acting Subject*, 19–41. Durham, NC: Duke University Press, 2006.

Penslar, Derek. *Shylock's Children: Economics and Jewish Identity in Modern Europe*. Berkeley: University of California Press, 2001.

Peterson, Richard. *Creating Country Music: Fabricating Authenticity*. Chicago: University of Chicago Press, 1997.

Petigny, Alan. *The Permissive Society*. New York: Cambridge University Press, 2009.

Pollack, Jonathan Z. S. "Where Have all the Cohens Gone? Jewish Radicals, Restrictions, and Renewal at the University of Wisconsin." *Journal of Jewish Identities: Special Issue on Jewish Youth in the Global 1960s* 8, no. 2 (2015): 159–78. Edited by Adriana Brodsky, Bea Gurwitz, and Rachel Kranson.

Popkin, Jeremy D. Introduction to *Quiet Street*, by Zelda Popkin, vii–xii. Lincoln: University of Nebraska Press, 2002.

Prell, Riv-Ellen. "America, Mordecai Kaplan, and the Postwar Jewish Youth Revolt." *Jewish Social Studies* 12, no. 2 (Winter 2006): 158–71.

———. "Community and the Discourse of Elegy: The Postwar Suburban Debate." In *Imagining the Jewish Community*, edited by Jack Wertheimer, 67–90. Waltham, MA: Brandeis University Press, 2007.

———. *Fighting to Become Americans: Assimilation and the Trouble between Jewish Women and Jewish Men*. Boston: Beacon Press, 1999.

———. *Prayer and Community: The Havurah in American Judaism*. Detroit: Wayne State University Press, 1989.

———. "Triumph, Accommodation, and Resistance: American Jewish Life from the End of World War II to the Six Day War." In *The Columbia History of Jews and Judaism in America*, edited by Marc Lee Raphael, 114–41. New York: Columbia University Press, 2008.

———, ed. *Women Remaking American Judaism*. Detroit: Wayne State University Press, 2007.

Presner, Todd Samuel. *Muscular Judaism*. London: Routledge, 2007.

Price, Jay M. *Temples for a Modern God: Religious Architecture in Postwar America*. Oxford: Oxford University Press, 2012.

Raphael, Marc Lee. "d. a. levy and the Cleveland Jewish Counterculture of the 1960s." *American Jewish History* 99, no. 4 (October 2015): 353–65.

Rieder, Jonathan. *Canarsie: The Jews and Italians of Brooklyn against Liberalism*. Cambridge, MA: Harvard University Press, 1985.

Rosenthal, Steven T. "Long-Distance Nationalism: American Jews, Zionism, and Israel." In *American Judaism*, edited by Dana Evan Kaplan, 209–13. New York: Cambridge University Press, 2005.

Rossinow, Doug. *The Politics of Authenticity: Liberalism, Christianity and the New Left in America*. New York: Columbia University Press, 1998.

Rottenberg, Catherine. *Performing Americanness: Race, Class and Gender in Modern African-American and Jewish-American Literature*. Hanover, NH: Dartmouth University Press, 2008.

Rubin-Schwartz, Shuly. "Henrietta Szold: The Making of an Icon." In *New Essays in American Jewish History*, edited by Pamela Nadell, Jonathan Sarna, and Lance Sussman, 455–66. Cincinnati: American Jewish Archives of Hebrew Union College-Jewish Institute of Religion, distributed by Ktav Publishing House, 2010.

Sarna, Jonathan. *American Judaism*. New Haven: Yale University Press, 2004.

———. "The Crucial Decade in Jewish Camping." In *A Place of Our Own: The Rise of Reform Jewish Camping*, edited by Michael Lorge and Gary Zola, 27–51. Tuscaloosa: University of Alabama Press, 2006.

———. "The Cult of Synthesis in American Jewish Culture." *Jewish Social Studies* 5, no. 1 (Fall 1998): 52–79.

Schultz, Debra. *Going South: Jewish Women in the Civil Rights Movement*. New York: New York University Press, 2001.

Seaman, Barbara. "Ruth Gruber." *Jewish Women: A Contemporary Encyclopedia*. http://jwa.org/encyclopedia/article/gruber-ruth. Accessed July 29, 2015.

Shandler, Jeffrey. "Heschel and Yiddish: A Struggle with Signification." *Journal of Jewish Thought and Philosophy* 2 (1993): 268–84.

———. "Religion, Democracy, and the Radio Waves: The Eternal Light." In *Entertaining America: Jews, Movies, and Broadcasting*, edited by J. Hoberman and Jeffrey Shandler. Princeton: Princeton University Press, 2003, 130–32

———. *Shtetl: A Vernacular Intellectual History*. New Brunswick, NJ: Rutgers University Press, 2014.

Shapiro, Edward S. *A Time for Healing*. Baltimore: Johns Hopkins University Press, 1992.

Shechner, Mark. *After the Revolution*. Bloomington: Indiana University Press, 1987.

Sicherman, Barbara. "Reading *Marjorie Morningstar* in the Age of the Feminine Mystique." In *A Jewish Feminine Mystique? Jewish Women in the Postwar Era*, edited by Hasia Diner, Shira Kohn, and Rachel Kranson, 194–209. New Brunswick, NJ: Rutgers University Press, 2010.

Silver, M. M. *Our Exodus: Leon Uris and the Americanization of Israel's Founding Story*. Detroit: Wayne State University Press, 2010.

Simmons, Erica B. *Hadassah and the Zionist Project*. Lanham, MD: Rowman and Littlefield, 2006.

Sinkoff, Nancy. "The Polishness of Lucy S. Dawidowicz's Jewish Cold War." In *A Jewish Feminine Mystique? Jewish Women in the Postwar Era*, edited by Hasia Diner, Shira Kohn, and Rachel Kranson, 31–47. New Brunswick, NJ: Rutgers University Press, 2010.

Siry, Joseph. *Beth Sholom Synagogue: Frank Lloyd Wright and Modern Religious Architecture*. Chicago: University of Chicago Press, 2011.

Solomon, Alisa. *Wonder of Wonders: A Cultural History of Fiddler on the Roof*. New York: Holt, Henry, 2013.

Sorin, Gerald. *The Prophetic Minority: American Jewish Immigrant Radicals, 1880–1920*. Bloomington: Indiana University Press, 1985.

Stanger-Ross, Jordan. "Neither Fight nor Flight: Urban Synagogues in Postwar Philadelphia." *Journal of Urban History* 32, no. 6 (September 2006): 791–812.

Staub, Michael. *The Jewish 1960s: An American Sourcebook*. Waltham, MA: Brandeis University Press, 2004.

———. *Torn at the Roots: The Crisis of Jewish Liberalism in Postwar America*. New York: Columbia University Press, 2004.

Stein, Regina. "The Road to Bat Mitzvah in America." In *Women and American Judaism*, edited by Pamela Nadell and Jonathan Sarna. Hanover, NH: University Press of New England for Brandeis University Press, 223–34.

"Suburban Trend Blasted." *Jewish Currents* 14, no. 1 (January 1960): 20.

Sussman, Lance Jonathan. "The Suburbanization of American Judaism." *American Jewish History* 75 (1985): 31–47.

Svonkin, Stuart. *Jews against Prejudice: American Jews and the Fight for Civil Liberties*. New York: Columbia University Press, 1999.

Taylor, Charles. *The Ethics of Authenticity*. Cambridge, MA: Harvard University Press, 1992.

Wald, Alan. *The New York Intellectuals: The Rise and Decline of the Anti-Stalinist Left from the 1930s to the 1980s*. Chapel Hill: University of North Carolina Press, 1987.

Walkowitz, Daniel. *Working with Class: Social Workers and the Politics of Middle-Class Identity*. Chapel Hill: University of North Carolina Press, 1999.

Wasserman, Suzanne. "Re-creating Recreations on the Lower East Side: Restaurants, Cabarets, Cafes, and Coffeehouses in the 1930s." In *Remembering the Lower East Side*, edited by Hasia Diner, Jeffrey Shandler, and Beth Wenger, 155–75. Bloomington: Indiana University Press, 2000.

Webb, Clive. *Fight against Fear: Southern Jews and Black Civil Rights*. Athens: University of Georgia Press, 2001.

Wechsler, Harold. "The Rationale for Restriction: Ethnicity and College Admission in America, 1910–1980." *American Quarterly* 36, no. 5 (Winter 1984): 643–67.

Weinberg, Sydney Stahl. *World of Our Mothers: The Lives of Jewish Immigrant Women*. Chapel Hill: University of North Carolina Press, 1988.

Wenger, Beth. "Constructing Manhood in American Jewish Culture." In *Gender and Jewish History*, edited by Marion Kaplan and Deborah Dash Moore, 350–66. Bloomington: Indiana University Press, 2011.

———. *History Lessons: The Creation of American Jewish Heritage*. Princeton: Princeton University Press, 2010.

———. *Uncertain Promise: New York Jews and the Great Depression*. Syracuse: Syracuse University Press, 1999.

Whitfield, Stephen. *The Culture of the Cold War*. Baltimore: Johns Hopkins University Press, 1991.

———. "Fiddling with Sholem Aleichem: A History of *Fiddler on the Roof*." In *Key Texts in American Jewish Culture*, edited by Jack Kugelmass, 105–28. New Brunswick, NJ: Rutgers University Press, 2003.

Zeitz, Joshua M. *White Ethnic New York: Jews, Catholics, and the Shaping of Postwar Politics*. Chapel Hill: University of North Carolina Press, 2007.

Zipperstein, Steven. *Imagining Russian Jewry*. Seattle: University of Washington Press, 1999.

Index

130–31, 139, 155. *See also* Genocide of
European Jews
Homemakers, 42, 114, 116–23, 128–29,
131–36, 147
Housewives. *See* Homemakers
Howe, Irving, 19, 46
Hungary, 14, 125–26
Hyman, Paula, 145–46, 190n65

Inauthenticity of middle-class Jewish
culture (imagined), 15–16, 49–50, 57–59,
70–80, 85, 91–96, 137–38, 140, 154–55, 165
Individualism, 10, 98
Integration, Jewish, 14, 17–18, 21, 24, 32,
43, 46, 76; racial, 48, 54–59. *See also*
Assimilation
International Women's Day, 149–50
Irgun, 107–9
Israel: American Jews' support of, 36–37,
92, 109, 121–23; austerity in, 17, 35, 38–43,
110, 124–25, 128–32, 152; authentic Jewish
life in, 17–18, 36, 42–43, 110, 140, 152–53;
emigration to, 36, 41, 109–10, 122–23, 125,
143, 152–53; independence of, 37, 110, 123,
131; policy toward Palestinians, 141; role
of women in, 122–32; romanticizing of,
4, 35–43; soldiers in, 98, 106–13

Jerusalem, 41–42, 128–29, 131–32, 146
Jewish Agency for Israel, 93, 152–53
Jewish Book Council, 35, 100
Jewish Catalogue, The, 156–59
Jewish community centers, 12, 32, 157
Jewish Currents. See Jewish Life
Jewish holidays, 19, 23; alternative
celebrations, 157–61; Chanukah, 117, 161;
high holidays, 37, 48, 72, 75–77, 79, 92,
104, 142; Passover, 117, 159–60; Purim, 35
Jewish humor, 24, 38–39, 42, 97, 112, 168–69
Jewish Labor Committee, 33, 143
Jewish Liberation Project, 139, 148, 160
Jewish Life (magazine), 33, 60, 63–65,
178n48
Jewish newspapers, 12–13, 25, 32, 59–60, 63,
82, 124–25, 142–43, 153–56

Jewish organizations, 52–54, 61–62, 117,
121, 143, 151, 158, 168. *See also names of
organizations*
Jewish People's Fraternal Order, 60
Jewish Publication Society, 125, 127
"Jewish research group," 22–23
Jewish Spectator, 75–76, 119–20
Jewish studies, xii–xiii, 19, 76
Jewish Theological Seminary
(Conservative), 20, 24, 102–3, 105, 127
Jewish Women's Conference, 147, 150–51
Jews for Urban Justice, 142, 145, 157, 159–60
Joffe, Natalie, 22–23
Jokes, 38–39, 97, 112, 168–69
Journalists, 10, 25, 27, 30, 32, 38, 41, 74–76,
86, 98, 124–25, 160
Junior Hadassah, 41, 122–23

Kamins, Jeanette, 136
Kaplan, Sylvia R., 118, 121
Kazin, Alfred, 102
Kehilath Anshei Maarav (KAM), Chicago,
Ill., 80–81
Khrushchev, Nikita, 61, 143
Kibbutzim, 40, 42–43, 110, 123, 125–26
Kiev, Ukraine, 126, 144
King, Martin Luther, Jr., 54, 81
Klaperman, Gilbert, 26–27, 32, 39
Klaperman, Libby, 26–27, 32, 39
Kling, Samuel, 119–20
Kramer, Judith R., 72, 100
Kreitman, Benjamin, 56, 74
Kubie, Nora Benjamin, 40–41

Labor: movement, 7–9, 30, 33, 59–60,
65–66, 99, 149; unions, 7–8, 30, 49,
63–64; unpaid, 82, 84, 116, 120–22
Law, Jews in, 52, 64, 97, 99–100, 112, 135, 153
Leadership of Jewish community, 4–8,
165–66; and bar mitzvah celebration,
87–95; and civil rights, 53–59;
countercultural, 139, 155, 162–63; and
critique of affluence, 7, 11–15, 69–73,
95–96, 137, 140, 162–64; and gender norms,
97–100, 106, 114, 117–18, 121, 136–37, 151;

and Jewish authenticity, 18, 26, 28–29, 95–96, 137; lay, 12–13, 51, 79, 82–85, 93–95, 117–18; and politics, 44–48, 52–66; and separation of church and state, 51–53; by women, 114–18, 120–23, 139, 145–48

Leaf, Hayim, 32, 128

Leftist politics, 26, 33, 44–50, 59–67, 95, 138, 140–44, 149, 154, 159–60, 162, 167–68

Lesbians, 139, 150–52, 161

Leventman, Seymour, 72, 100

Levi, Shonie B., 118, 121

Levin, Meyer, 109–11

Levinger, Elma Ehrlich, 27–28, 37, 128

Levinger, Lee J., 27–28, 37

Levinthal, Israel H., 56–57, 76

Levittown, Long Island, N.Y., 117

Levittown, Pa., 58

levy, d. a., 154–55

Liberalism (political), 26, 44–67, 145, 167–68

Lilith (magazine), xii, 151–52

Lipis, Philip, 72

Lipman, Eugene, 79–80, 118–19

Long Island, N.Y., 4, 31–32, 44, 47–49, 51–52, 56, 80, 91–92, 117

Los Angeles, Calif., 13, 42

Lower East Side, 17–18, 29–36, 43

Lynbrook, N.Y., 4, 44

Lyons Bar-David, Molly, 128–32

Mandate Palestine, 37, 107, 125–28

Marginalization of Jews, 3, 30–31, 34, 43, 54, 64, 69–70, 139, 163, 169

Marjorie Morningstar (Wouk), 36, 87–88, 135–36

Marx, Karl, 9, 172n17

Masculinity, 5, 97–113, 124, 151

McCarthy, Joseph, 34, 45, 60–62

Mead, Margaret, 22

Medicine, Jews in, 64, 99–100, 112

Meir, Golda, 126–27, 185n29

Meisler, Stanley, 86–87

Menes, Abraham, 33

Men's clubs, 50, 68, 79. *See also* Brotherhoods, synagogue

Middle-class Jews: ambivalence of, 1, 3–4, 68–71, 80, 112, 121–24, 136–37, 140, 163; conventionality of, 31–35, 50, 132, critique of, 4–7, 10–12, 15–16, 21, 50, 76–77, 95, 116, 138–64, 165–69; economic security of, 12, 30, 45, 66, 98–100, 111, 116, 139–40, 165; and gender norms, 5, 10, 97–137, 147–51; and political identity, 44–67; professions of, 8, 9, 64–65, 99–102, 111–12, 116, 151

Middle East, 14, 38, 93, 110, 127, 141

Millstone, Mark, 92–93

Mintz, Alan, 142, 190n65

Minyan (prayer quorum), 85–86, 146

Mishkan Tefila, Newton, Mass., 55

Mississippi, 53–54, 59, 61

Modern Orthodox Judaism, 26–27, 71, 90

Moment (magazine), 1

Moynihan, Daniel Patrick, 30, 47

"Muscle Jews," 106–7

Myers, William and Daisy, 58

NAACP (National Association for the Advancement of Colored People), 54

National Broadcasting Company (NBC), 24, 34

National Women's League of Conservative Judaism, 118–19

Nazi Germany, 14, 20, 38, 54, 61, 73, 76, 125–27, 169

Negros. *See* African Americans

Neoconservatism, 26, 63

New Jersey, 54, 78, 89, 100, 119

"New Jews," 138–64

New Left, 140–43, 159–60, 162, 167

Newsletters, congregational, 12–13, 56, 58, 68, 85, 89

Newton, Mass., 48, 55, 89, 117–18

New York, N.Y., 7, 12, 17, 29–36, 38, 146, 157; Bronx, 42, 86; Greenwich Village, 49; Queens, 48, 74–76

New York Havurah, 146, 157, 190n65

"New York intellectuals," 46, 63

New York Times, 25, 50, 142

Nonconformist congregations, 68–69, 72, 81, 94, 166

Nordau, Max, 106
North Shore (Chicago), 41, 72, 80, 96
Nostalgia, 4, 19, 24, 29–30, 34, 49

Orthodox Judaism, 26–27, 36, 64, 90, 101, 120

Pawel, Ernst, 50
Perel, Abraham and Rebecca, 63–64
Peretz, Isaac Leib, 18, 25
Perl, Arnold, 24–26
Pessin, Deborah, 26–29, 32
Philadelphia, Pa., 13, 25, 55–56, 58, 74, 87
Philanthropy, 19–20, 28, 37, 134, 155, 186n5.
    See also Fundraising
Pilch, Judah, 17–18
Pioneer settlers in Israel, 17, 105, 122–23, 129
Plainview, N.Y., 51
Plaques, 83, 156, 158. See also Donor
    recognition
Poland, 14, 19–22, 29
Popkin, Zelda Feinberg, 130–32
Porter, Jack Nusan, 144, 154
Poverty, 3–6, 10–11, 16–43, 45, 47, 66, 99, 121,
    137–40, 155, 161, 165–69, 186n5; of Israelis,
    4, 35–43; of shtetl Jews, 4, 17–29, 43,
    147–49, 186n7; of urban Jews, 1, 4, 7–8,
    17–18, 29–35, 43, 133
Prayer quorum (minyan), 85–86, 146
Princeton University, 44, 169
Privilege: middle-class, 4, 7, 16, 18, 37, 43,
    45, 112, 128, 137–40, 163–65, 169; white-
    skin, 3, 8–9, 15, 53–54, 99, 139–40, 160,
    165, 186n7
Prophets, biblical, 45, 85, 105, 168
Protestants, 3, 9, 11, 45, 61, 71, 120, 142, 152
Public schools: racial segregation in, 45–46,
    53; religion in, 48–49, 51–52
Puerto Ricans, 31, 168, 176n1, 190n6

Queens, N.Y., 48, 74–77

Rabbinical Assembly (Conservative), 77, 146
Rabbis: ambivalence of, 70, 77–78, 92,
    95, 105; and counterculture, 142, 144,

157–59; and critique of affluence, 12, 20,
    43, 69, 76–78, 85, 88–92, 137, 154, 162–65;
    and fundraising, 80, 83, 92; and gender
    norms, 117–18; and politics, 44, 48–52,
    55–59; and "religious revival," 70–72;
    salaries of, 12, 70, 97; status of, 12, 97–98,
    104–6, 112–13; women, 13, 146
Race, 3, 8–11, 15, 45–46, 53–59, 139–42,
    159–60, 165, 168–69, 186n3, 186n7
Reconstructionist, The (Journal), 73, 76, 78,
    86, 93
Reconstructionist Judaism, 73, 76, 78,
    86–87, 93, 146, 157
Red Cross, 130–31
Reform Judaism, 64, 73–74, 79, 89–90, 101,
    118–19, 146; congregations, 1, 41, 55–56,
    58, 68–69, 71, 80; leaders, 20, 37, 44, 72,
    80–81, 89–90, 118; organizations, 26, 32,
    54, 57, 79–80, 105, 162–63
Religious schools, 1, 3, 26, 75, 79, 81, 83,
    91–92, 94, 117, 119–20, 159, 162, 190n65
Republican Party (GOP), 44–45, 47–48
Response (journal), 142, 147
Richler, Mordecai, 165
Riesman, David, 10–12, 98
Ritual, 3, 5–6, 19, 36, 72, 85, 117–18, 134,
    146–47, 156, 161; bar mitzvah, 85–86,
    89–96; bat mitzvah, 86, 89, 93–96, 121,
    124; confirmation, 89–90
Romanticizing: of Israel, 35–43, 106–11,
    123–25, 152; of Jewish histories of
    poverty, 4–6, 18–35, 43, 132–34, 140
Rose, Sharon, 142, 145
Rosenberg, Julius and Ethel, 46, 61
Rosenberg, Michael, 152
Rosenthal, Celia Stopnicka, 22–23
Rosenthal, Erich, 120
Rossman, Evelyn. See Rothchild, Sylvia
Roth, Philip, 12, 100–102
Rothchild, Sylvia, 1–3, 7, 12, 48–50, 78–79,
    132–34

Sabbath, 23–24, 35, 40, 76, 118, 134
Samuel, Maurice, 24–25, 121

Sanders, Ronald, 41–42

Saperstein, Harold, 4, 44, 48–50, 91

Schafler, Samuel, 76–78

Schoen, Myron, 79–80

Schools: Jewish, 55, 63; public, 48–49, 51–52; racial segregation in, 45–46, 53; religious, 1, 3, 26, 75, 79, 81, 83, 91–92, 94, 117, 119–20, 159, 162, 190n65; Yiddish, 60, 92, 95

Segregation, racial, 45–46, 54, 57–58, 99, 142

Senesh, Hannah, 125–27

Separation of church and state, 45, 48–49, 51–53

Sephardic Jews, 14, 86, 151

Sermons, 12–13, 37, 41, 48, 72, 74, 80, 92, 104, 119

Serrota, Gerald, 144–45

Services: experimental, 68, 138, 142, 146, 157; prayer, 68, 71; synagogue, 1, 55–56, 70, 73, 75–76, 80–81, 85–87, 89, 94, 101, 146, 155. See also Worship

Sexual Identity. See Gays; Lesbians

Sharon, Mass., 1, 48

Shtetl life, 17–29, 35–36, 43, 147–49, 173n3

Shulman, Charles, 37, 72

Simon, Kate, 31–32

Siskin, Edgar, 41, 92, 104

Sisterhoods, 68, 75, 79, 117, 119–20

Skeist, Robbie, 151

Sklare, Marshall, 57–58, 111–12, 117, 178n34, 180n23

Sleeper, James, 142, 190n65

Slums, 7–8, 17–18, 29–30, 33–35, 43

Smolar, Boris, 51

Social Forces (journal), 22–23

Socialists, 42, 59–60, 63, 65–66, 92, 110, 124–25

Social justice, 23, 43, 45, 58, 66, 118, 138, 168–69

Social status: class, 9–10; high, 5; insider, 140; of men, 98–99, 102–3, 112–13; of middle-class Jews, 14, 18, 44, 47–48, 57, 59, 64, 68, 70–72, 91, 95, 165–67; outsider, 4; of rabbis, 12, 104–5, 113; in the shtetls, 23; of women, 116–18, 121, 128, 136, 145–48

Sociologists, 10–11, 22–23, 30, 47, 57–58, 63, 71–73, 75, 100, 111, 117, 120, 168

Solel. *See* Congregation Solel, Highland Park, Ill.

Soviet Jewry, 139, 143–45, 154, 161

Soviet Union, 46, 60–62, 70, 143–44

Spirituality: of countercultural Jews, 142, 153–55, 160–61; of Eastern European Jews, 4, 17, 20–26; of Israeli Jews, 41–43, 153; of middle-class Jews, 3, 66, 68, 70, 73–76, 80, 82, 90–91, 94, 104–5, 117

Stalin, Joseph, 61, 143

Stern, William, 65

Stevenson, Adlai, 48

Students for a Democratic Society (SDS), 141–42

Summer camps, 3, 60, 63, 162–63, 190n65

Synagogues: affiliation, 55, 70–73, 95, 119, 134; amenities in, 76–78, 92; boards of directors, 59, 72–73, 79–85, 93–95; Conservative, 1, 55–56, 71, 76, 90; construction of, 3, 12, 68–70, 73, 78–85, 92, 95, 117, 155; in Europe, 75; leadership, 105, 117–18, 145–46; memorials in, 19; modernist, 73–74; Reform, 1, 32, 41, 44, 55–56, 58, 68–69, 71, 73–74, 80–85, 89–90; as social centers, 74–76, 78; standards of decorum, 90; as status symbols, 4–5, 72, 142, 154–55; suburban, 1, 3, 50–51, 55–59, 68–85, 91–96, 154–60, 165–66, 177n29; support for Israel, 36; urban, 1, 55–57, 73–74, 177n29

Syrkin, Marie, 124–26

Szold, Henrietta, 121, 127–28

Taxation, 28–29, 39, 46, 158, 167

Taylor, Sydney, 35

Temple Gates of Prayer, Flushing, N.Y., 77

Tercentennial of Jewish settlement in America, 14, 34

Textbooks, 26–28, 36–37, 39

Time (magazine), 32, 89–90

Torah, 20–21, 23, 27–28, 74, 85–87, 94, 159

Trilling, Lionel, 102